Yarg! and other stories
33305233624851
0jgn            8/6/15

D0925049

KIT
EM SERIES

A COMB

VOL 2

YARG!
AND
OTHER STORIES

by **Ray Friesen**

 **Don't Eat Any Bugs Productions · California**

# TABLE *of* CONTENTS

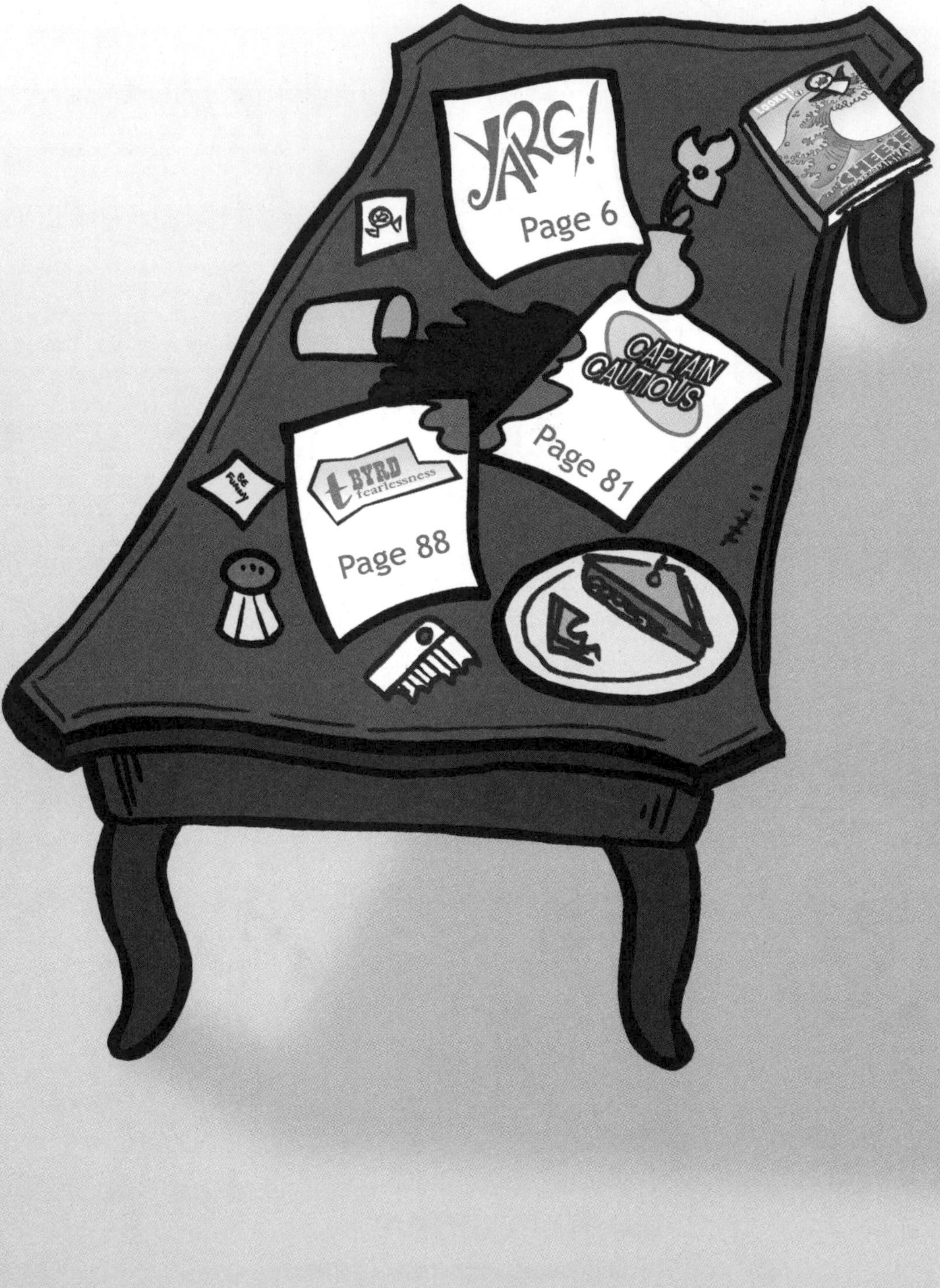
YARG!
Page 6
CAPTAIN CAUTIOUS
Page 81
t BYRD fearlessness
Page 88
BE Funny

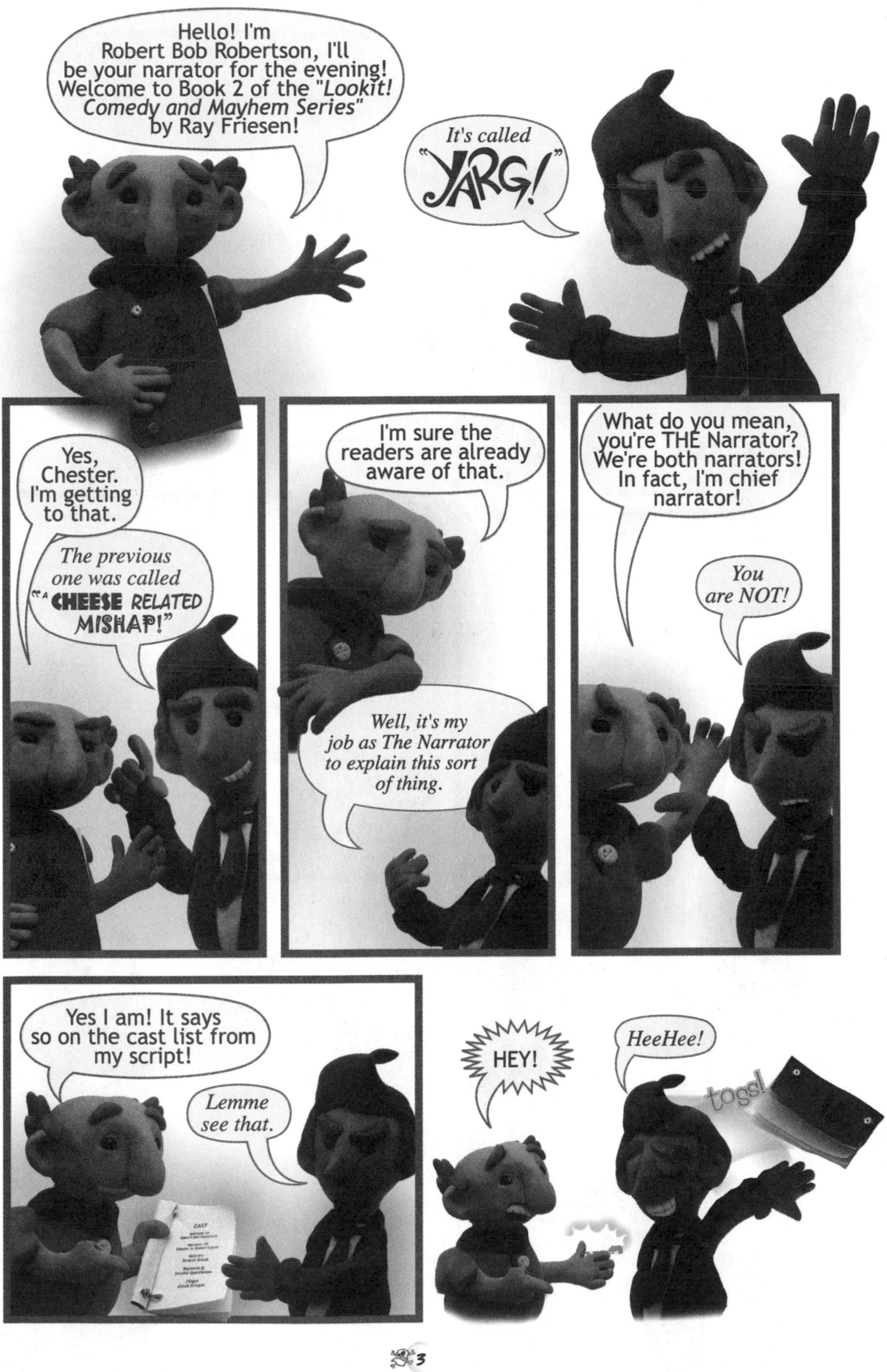
Hello! I'm Robert Bob Robertson, I'll be your narrator for the evening! Welcome to Book 2 of the "*Lookit! Comedy and Mayhem Series*" by Ray Friesen!
It's called "YARG!"
Yes, Chester. I'm getting to that.
The previous one was called "A CHEESE RELATED MISHAP!"
I'm sure the readers are already aware of that.
Well, it's my job as The Narrator to explain this sort of thing.
What do you mean, you're THE Narrator? We're both narrators! In fact, I'm chief narrator!
You are NOT!
Yes I am! It says so on the cast list from my script!
Lemme see that.
CAST
HEY!
HeeHee!
togs!

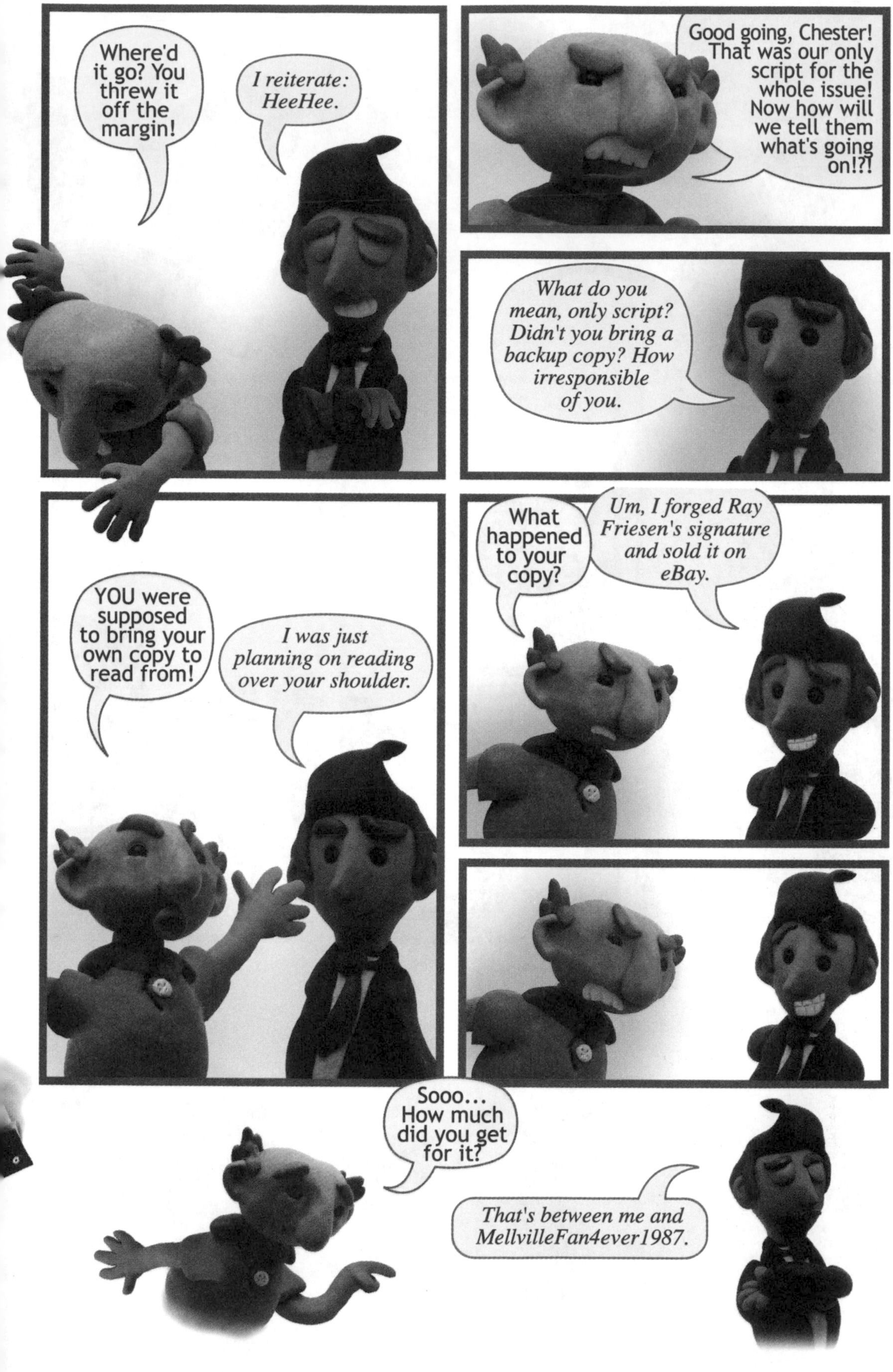
Where'd it go? You threw it off the margin!
I reiterate: HeeHee.
Good going, Chester! That was our only script for the whole issue! Now how will we tell them what's going on!?!
What do you mean, only script? Didn't you bring a backup copy? How irresponsible of you.
YOU were supposed to bring your own copy to read from!
I was just planning on reading over your shoulder.
What happened to your copy?
Um, I forged Ray Friesen's signature and sold it on eBay.
Sooo... How much did you get for it?
That's between me and MellvilleFan4ever1987.

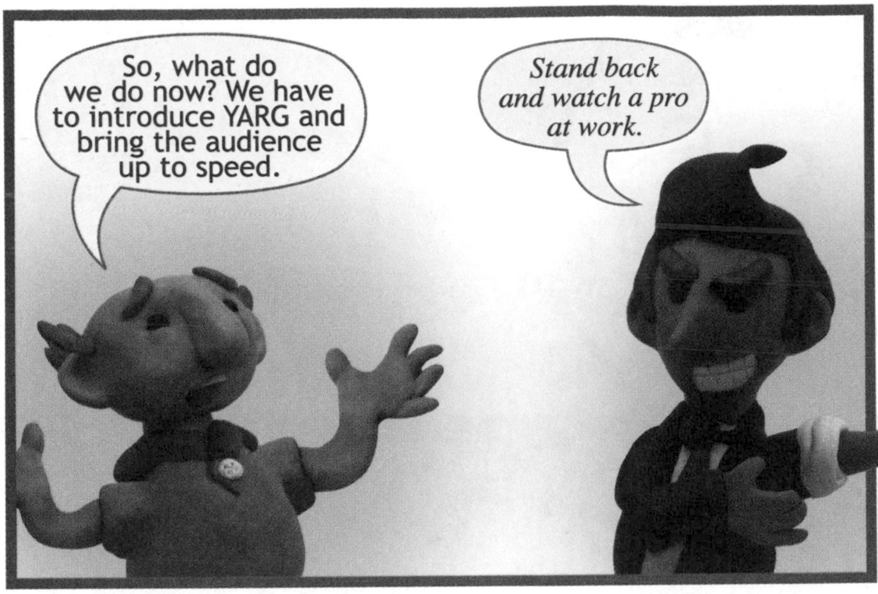
So, what do we do now? We have to introduce YARG and bring the audience up to speed.
*Stand back and watch a pro at work.*

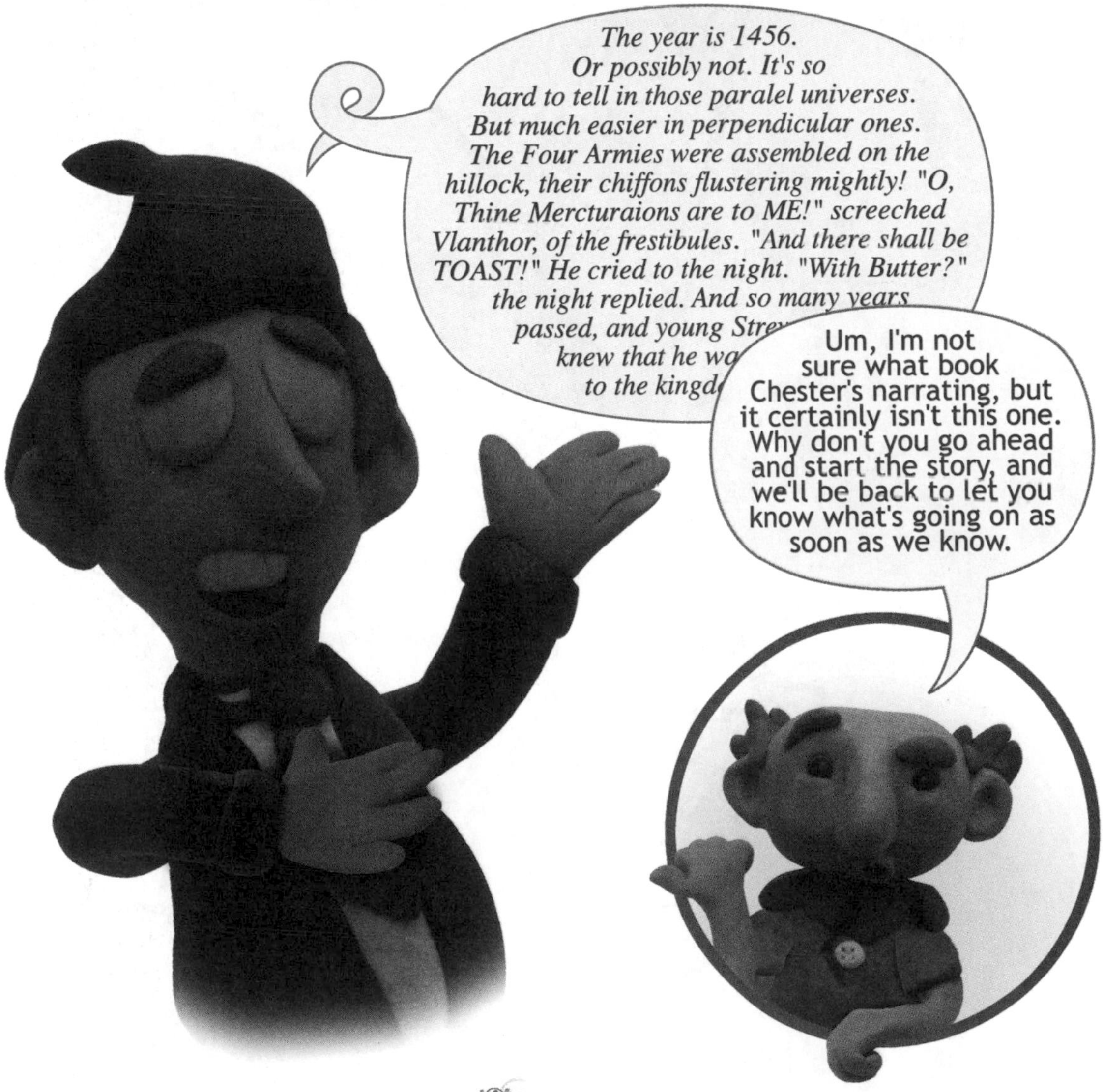
*The year is 1456. Or possibly not. It's so hard to tell in those paralel universes. But much easier in perpendicular ones. The Four Armies were assembled on the hillock, their chiffons flustering mightly! "O, Thine Mercturaions are to ME!" screeched Vlanthor, of the frestibules. "And there shall be TOAST!" He cried to the night. "With Butter?" the night replied. And so many years passed, and young Strey*
*knew that he wa*
*to the kingd*
Um, I'm not sure what book Chester's narrating, but it certainly isn't this one. Why don't you go ahead and start the story, and we'll be back to let you know what's going on as soon as we know.

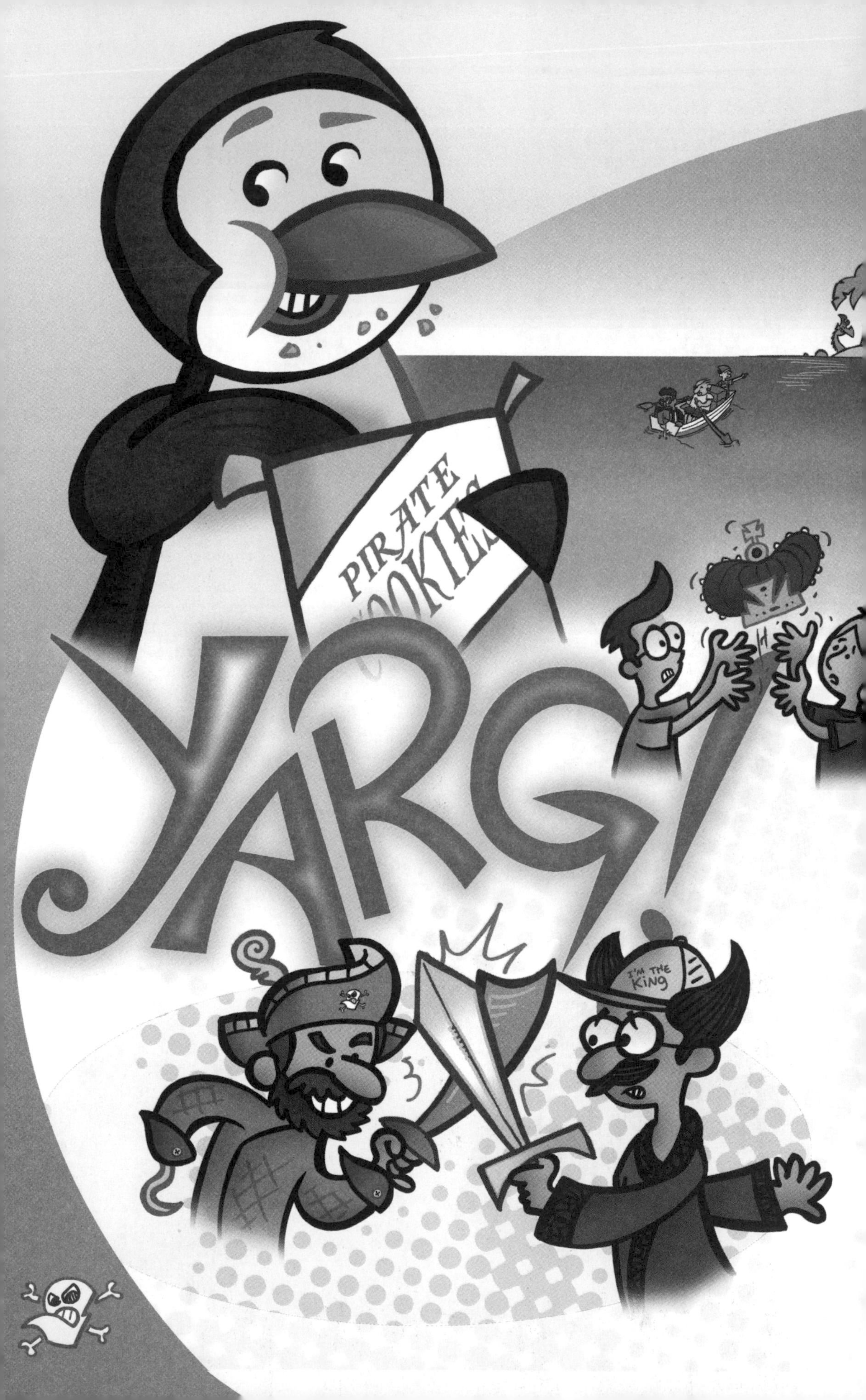
PIRATE COOKIES
YARG!
I'M THE KING

# CAST OF CHARACTERS

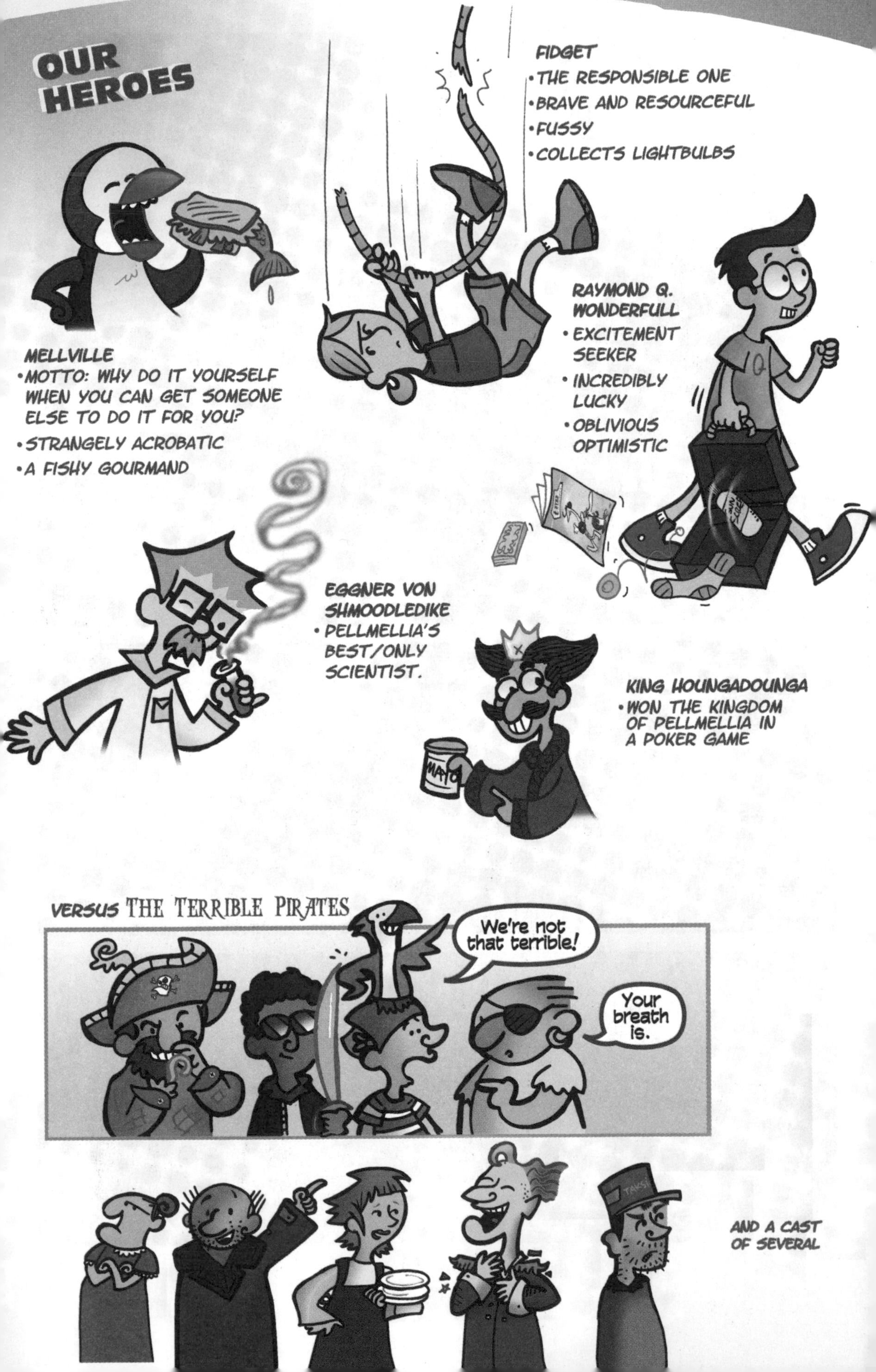
OUR HEROES
FIDGET
•THE RESPONSIBLE ONE
•BRAVE AND RESOURCEFUL
•FUSSY
•COLLECTS LIGHTBULBS
MELLVILLE
•MOTTO: WHY DO IT YOURSELF WHEN YOU CAN GET SOMEONE ELSE TO DO IT FOR YOU?
•STRANGELY ACROBATIC
•A FISHY GOURMAND
RAYMOND Q. WONDERFULL
•EXCITEMENT SEEKER
•INCREDIBLY LUCKY
•OBLIVIOUS OPTIMISTIC
Q
EGGNER VON SHMOODLEDIKE
•PELLMELLIA'S BEST/ONLY SCIENTIST.
KING HOUNGADOUNGA
•WON THE KINGDOM OF PELLMELLIA IN A POKER GAME
MAYO
VERSUS THE TERRIBLE PIRATES
We're not that terrible!
Your breath is.
TAKSI
AND A CAST OF SEVERAL

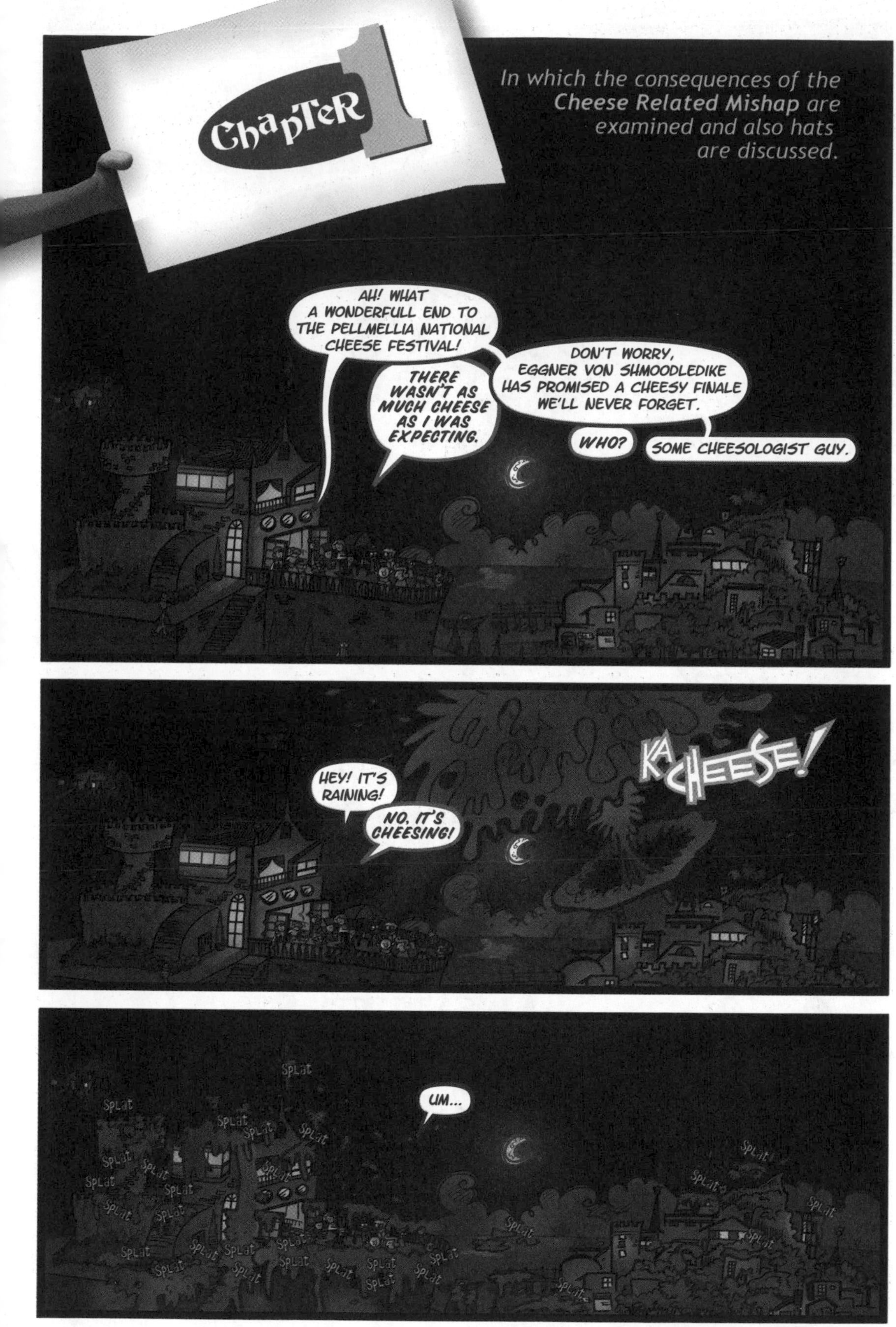
ChapTeR 1
In which the consequences of the Cheese Related Mishap are examined and also hats are discussed.
AH! WHAT A WONDERFULL END TO THE PELLMELLIA NATIONAL CHEESE FESTIVAL!
THERE WASN'T AS MUCH CHEESE AS I WAS EXPECTING.
DON'T WORRY, EGGNER VON SHMOODLEDIKE HAS PROMISED A CHEESY FINALE WE'LL NEVER FORGET.
WHO?
SOME CHEESOLOGIST GUY.
KA CHEESE!
HEY! IT'S RAINING!
NO, IT'S CHEESING!
UM...
SpLat

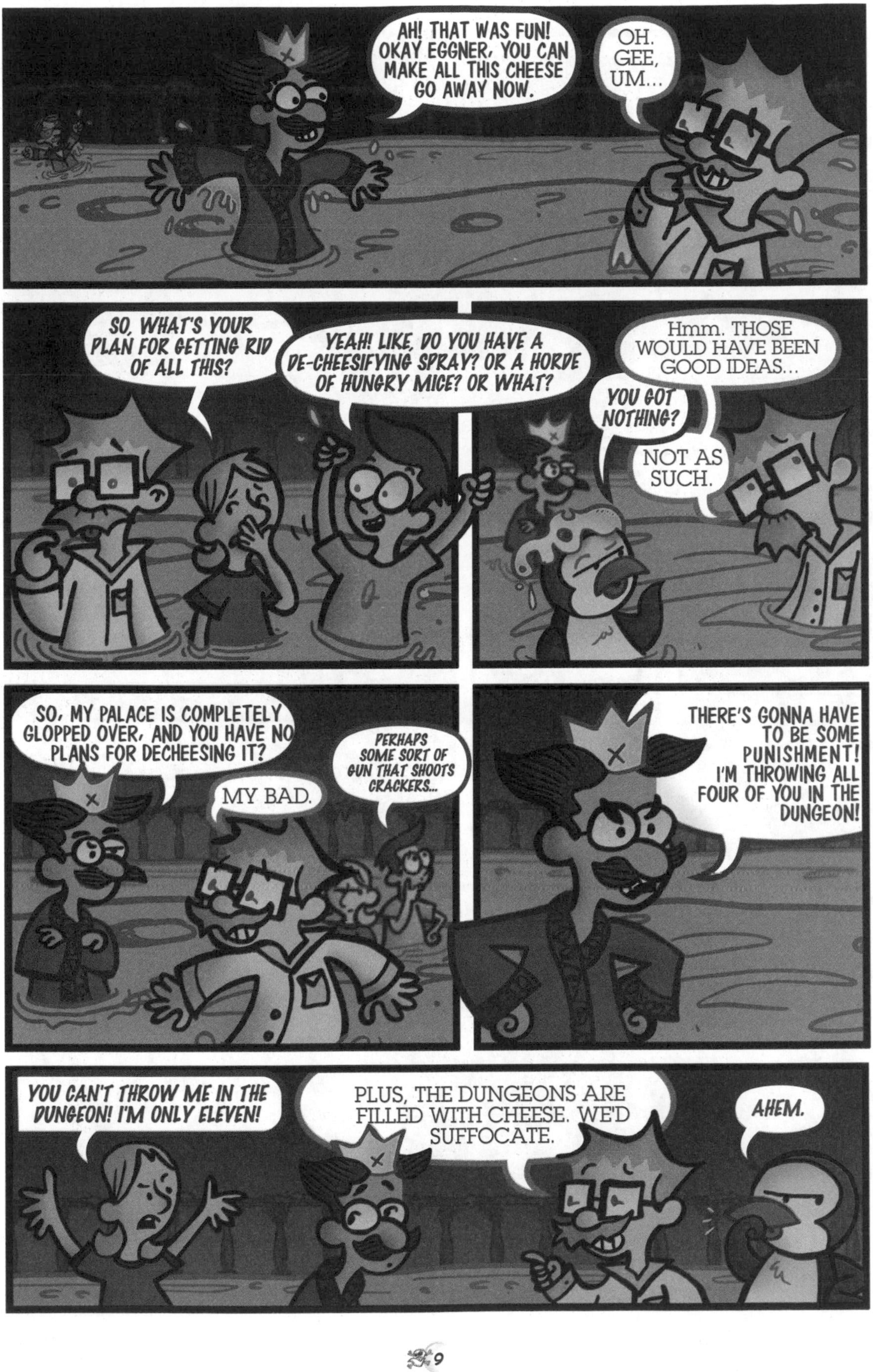
AH! THAT WAS FUN! OKAY EGGNER, YOU CAN MAKE ALL THIS CHEESE GO AWAY NOW.
OH. GEE, UM...
SO, WHAT'S YOUR PLAN FOR GETTING RID OF ALL THIS?
YEAH! LIKE, DO YOU HAVE A DE-CHEESIFYING SPRAY? OR A HORDE OF HUNGRY MICE? OR WHAT?
Hmm. THOSE WOULD HAVE BEEN GOOD IDEAS...
YOU GOT NOTHING?
NOT AS SUCH.
SO, MY PALACE IS COMPLETELY GLOPPED OVER, AND YOU HAVE NO PLANS FOR DECHEESING IT?
MY BAD.
PERHAPS SOME SORT OF GUN THAT SHOOTS CRACKERS...
THERE'S GONNA HAVE TO BE SOME PUNISHMENT! I'M THROWING ALL FOUR OF YOU IN THE DUNGEON!
YOU CAN'T THROW ME IN THE DUNGEON! I'M ONLY ELEVEN!
PLUS, THE DUNGEONS ARE FILLED WITH CHEESE. WE'D SUFFOCATE.
AHEM.

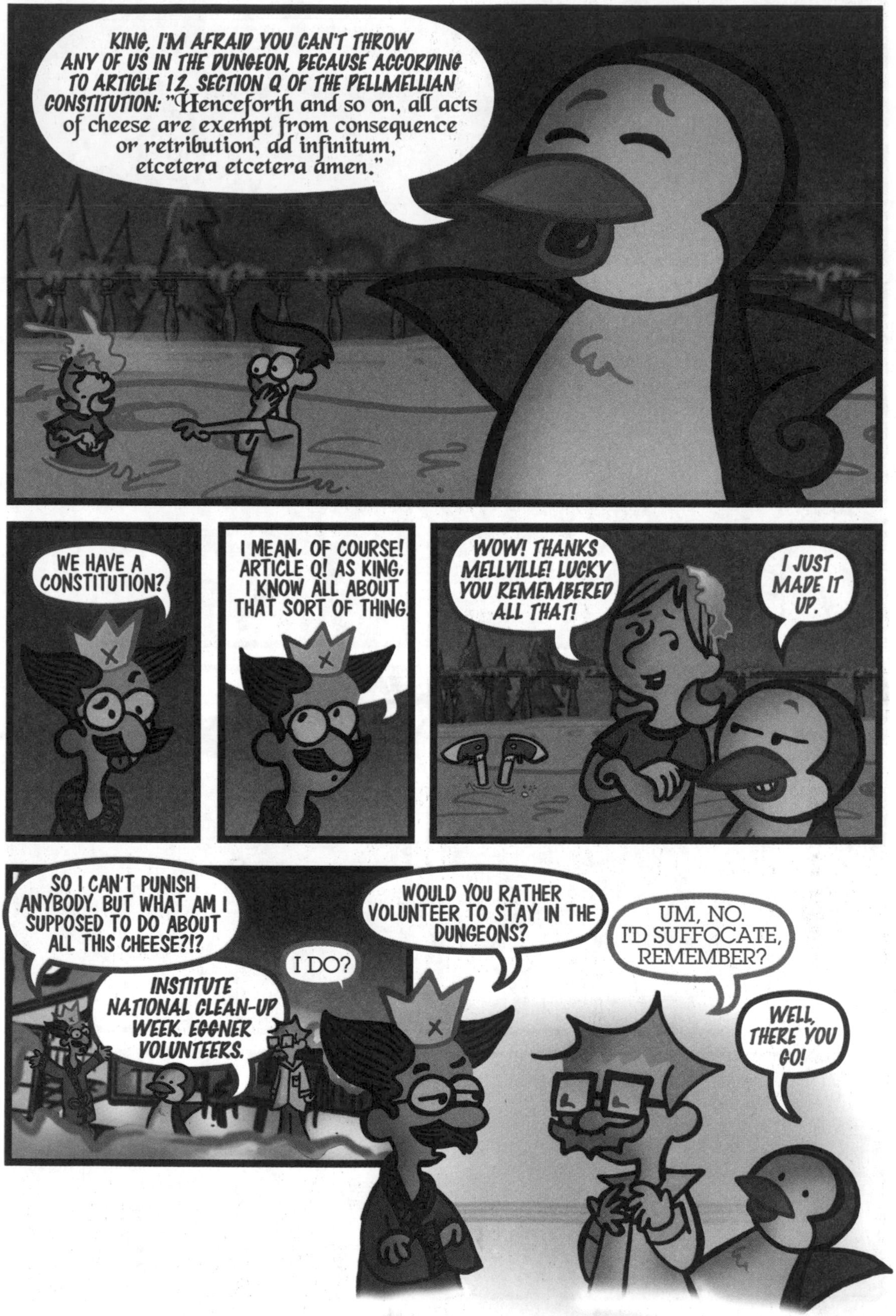

KING, I'M AFRAID YOU CAN'T THROW ANY OF US IN THE DUNGEON, BECAUSE ACCORDING TO ARTICLE 12, SECTION Q OF THE PELLMELLIAN CONSTITUTION: "Henceforth and so on, all acts of cheese are exempt from consequence or retribution, ad infinitum, etcetera etcetera amen."
WE HAVE A CONSTITUTION?
I MEAN, OF COURSE! ARTICLE Q! AS KING, I KNOW ALL ABOUT THAT SORT OF THING.
WOW! THANKS MELLVILLE! LUCKY YOU REMEMBERED ALL THAT!
I JUST MADE IT UP.
SO I CAN'T PUNISH ANYBODY. BUT WHAT AM I SUPPOSED TO DO ABOUT ALL THIS CHEESE?!?
INSTITUTE NATIONAL CLEAN-UP WEEK. EGGNER VOLUNTEERS.
I DO?
WOULD YOU RATHER VOLUNTEER TO STAY IN THE DUNGEONS?
UM, NO. I'D SUFFOCATE, REMEMBER?
WELL, THERE YOU GO!

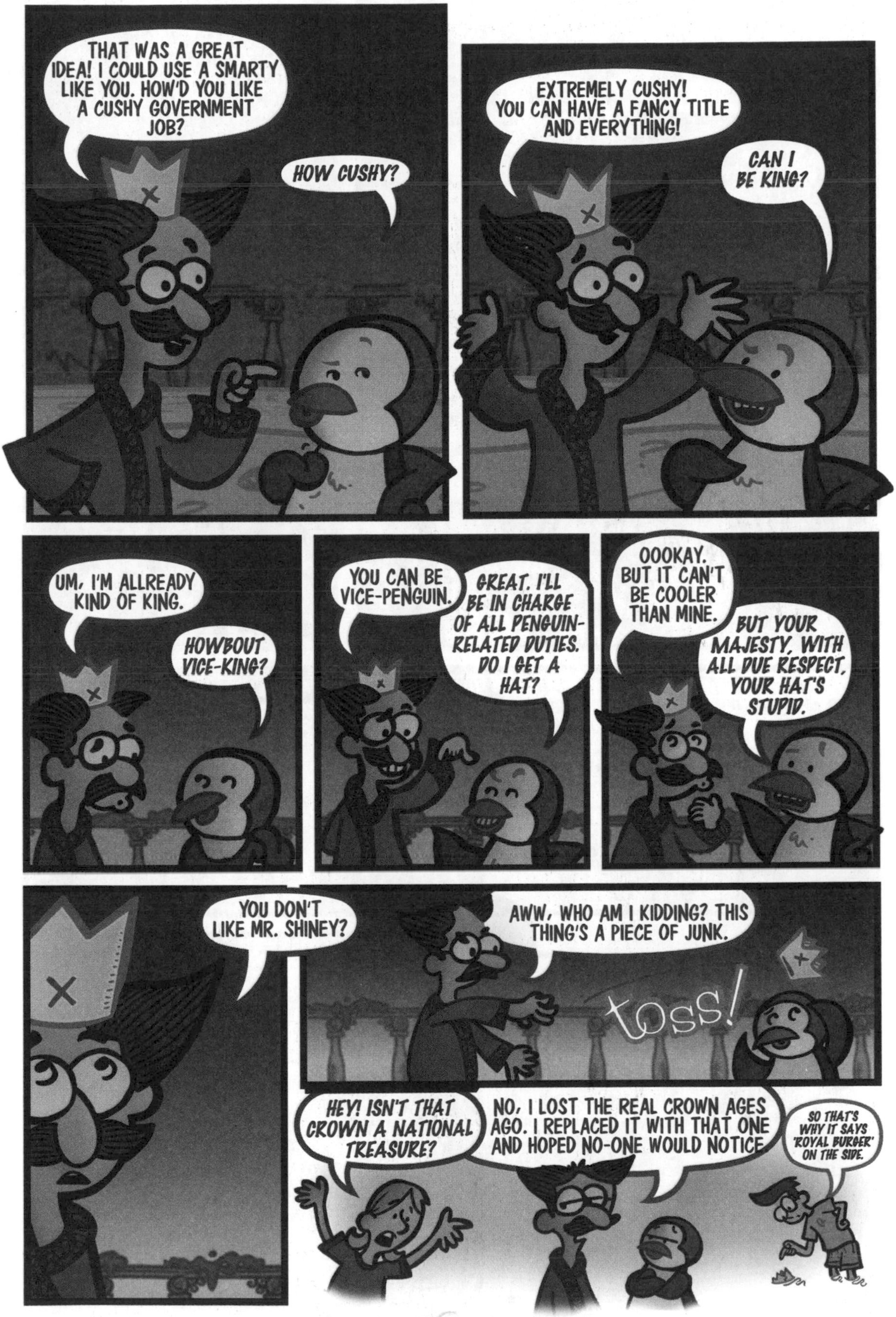
THAT WAS A GREAT IDEA! I COULD USE A SMARTY LIKE YOU. HOW'D YOU LIKE A CUSHY GOVERNMENT JOB?
HOW CUSHY?
EXTREMELY CUSHY! YOU CAN HAVE A FANCY TITLE AND EVERYTHING!
CAN I BE KING?
UM, I'M ALLREADY KIND OF KING.
HOWBOUT VICE-KING?
YOU CAN BE VICE-PENGUIN.
GREAT. I'LL BE IN CHARGE OF ALL PENGUIN-RELATED DUTIES. DO I GET A HAT?
OOOKAY. BUT IT CAN'T BE COOLER THAN MINE.
BUT YOUR MAJESTY, WITH ALL DUE RESPECT, YOUR HAT'S STUPID.
YOU DON'T LIKE MR. SHINEY?
AWW, WHO AM I KIDDING? THIS THING'S A PIECE OF JUNK.
toss!
HEY! ISN'T THAT CROWN A NATIONAL TREASURE?
NO, I LOST THE REAL CROWN AGES AGO. I REPLACED IT WITH THAT ONE AND HOPED NO-ONE WOULD NOTICE.
SO THAT'S WHY IT SAYS 'ROYAL BURGER' ON THE SIDE.

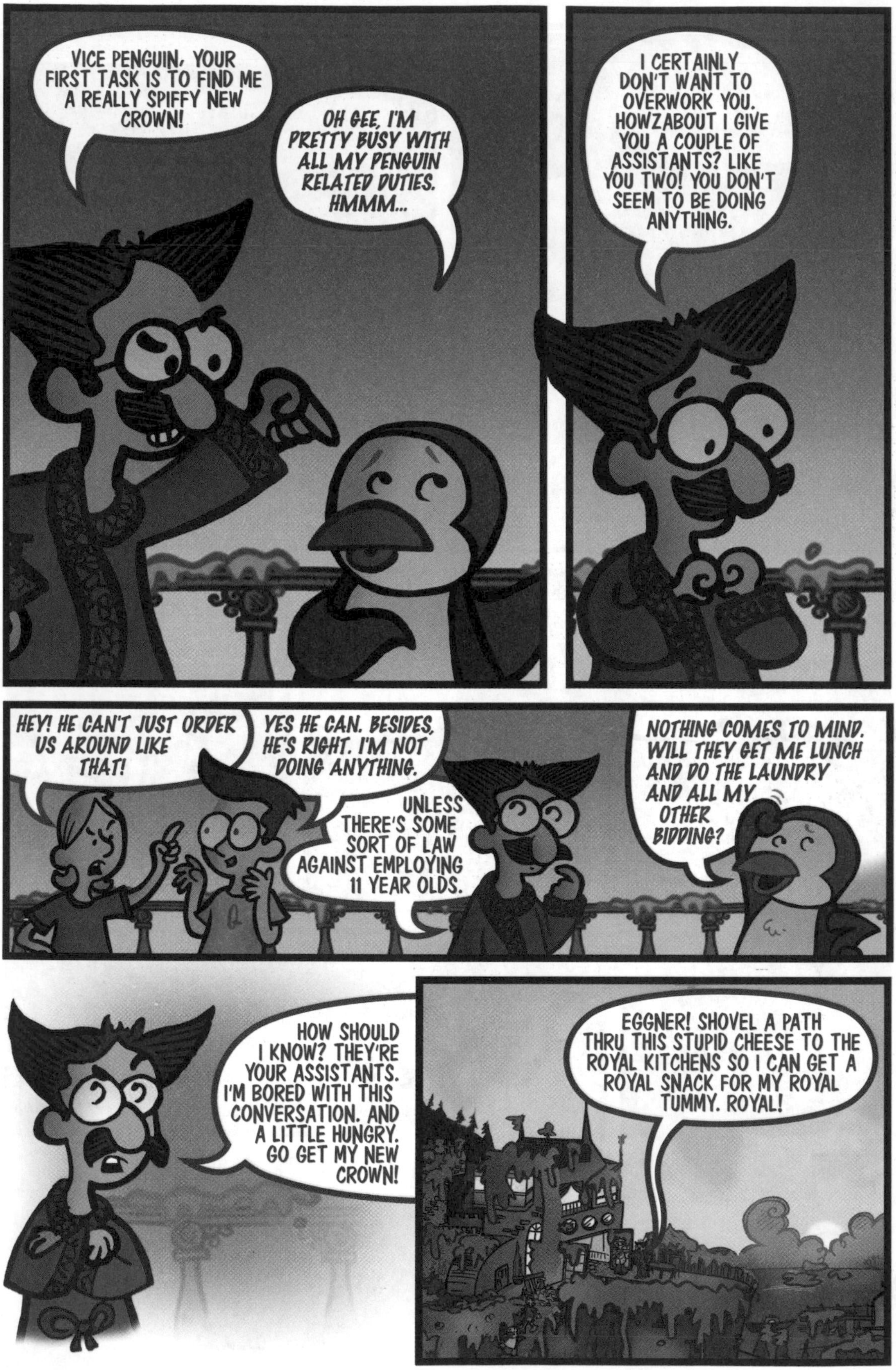
VICE PENGUIN, YOUR FIRST TASK IS TO FIND ME A REALLY SPIFFY NEW CROWN!
OH GEE, I'M PRETTY BUSY WITH ALL MY PENGUIN RELATED DUTIES. HMMM...
I CERTAINLY DON'T WANT TO OVERWORK YOU. HOWZABOUT I GIVE YOU A COUPLE OF ASSISTANTS? LIKE YOU TWO! YOU DON'T SEEM TO BE DOING ANYTHING.
HEY! HE CAN'T JUST ORDER US AROUND LIKE THAT!
YES HE CAN. BESIDES, HE'S RIGHT. I'M NOT DOING ANYTHING.
UNLESS THERE'S SOME SORT OF LAW AGAINST EMPLOYING 11 YEAR OLDS.
NOTHING COMES TO MIND. WILL THEY GET ME LUNCH AND DO THE LAUNDRY AND ALL MY OTHER BIDDING?
HOW SHOULD I KNOW? THEY'RE YOUR ASSISTANTS. I'M BORED WITH THIS CONVERSATION. AND A LITTLE HUNGRY. GO GET MY NEW CROWN!
EGGNER! SHOVEL A PATH THRU THIS STUPID CHEESE TO THE ROYAL KITCHENS SO I CAN GET A ROYAL SNACK FOR MY ROYAL TUMMY. ROYAL!

# Chapter 2

*In which some pirates get cranky.*

The Union of Pirates, Buccaneers and Swashbucklers local 42 will come to order!

YARG!

YARG!

YARG!

YARG!

When yer name be called, answer 'Here I Be' or the such like. Peg-Leg Pete?

Here I be!

No-Eyes Johnson?

The such like.

Yo-Ho Joe?

Yo.

Lester?

Are we doing the accents then?

YARG! I mean, um, we don't have to. It's just us.

Good. That always gives me such a throat ache.

Here, try one of these lozenges!

Ooh, how soothing!

First order of business: Have ye, I mean YOU all seen this?

Yeah! Who does King Houngadounga think he is?

I'm Outraged!

I'm angry!

I'm Lester!

Let's storm the Palace!

Yes, lets!

We'll take the minivan!

PiratesWeBe.com

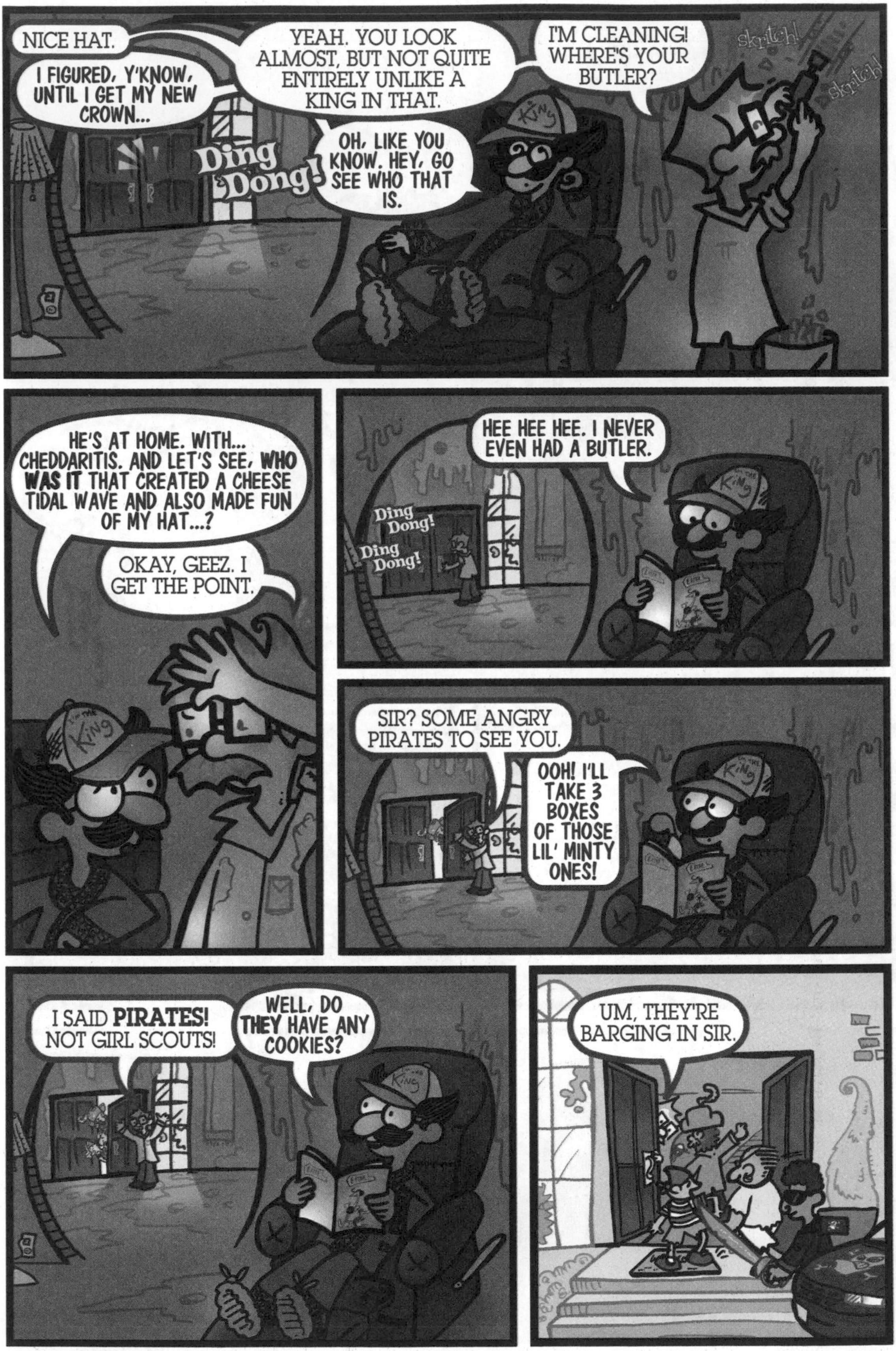
NICE HAT.
I FIGURED, Y'KNOW, UNTIL I GET MY NEW CROWN...
YEAH. YOU LOOK ALMOST, BUT NOT QUITE ENTIRELY UNLIKE A KING IN THAT.
I'M CLEANING! WHERE'S YOUR BUTLER?
skritch! skritch!
Ding Dong!
OH, LIKE YOU KNOW. HEY, GO SEE WHO THAT IS.
HE'S AT HOME. WITH... CHEDDARITIS. AND LET'S SEE, WHO WAS IT THAT CREATED A CHEESE TIDAL WAVE AND ALSO MADE FUN OF MY HAT...?
OKAY, GEEZ. I GET THE POINT.
HEE HEE HEE. I NEVER EVEN HAD A BUTLER.
Ding Dong! Ding Dong!
SIR? SOME ANGRY PIRATES TO SEE YOU.
OOH! I'LL TAKE 3 BOXES OF THOSE LIL' MINTY ONES!
I SAID PIRATES! NOT GIRL SCOUTS!
WELL, DO THEY HAVE ANY COOKIES?
UM, THEY'RE BARGING IN SIR.

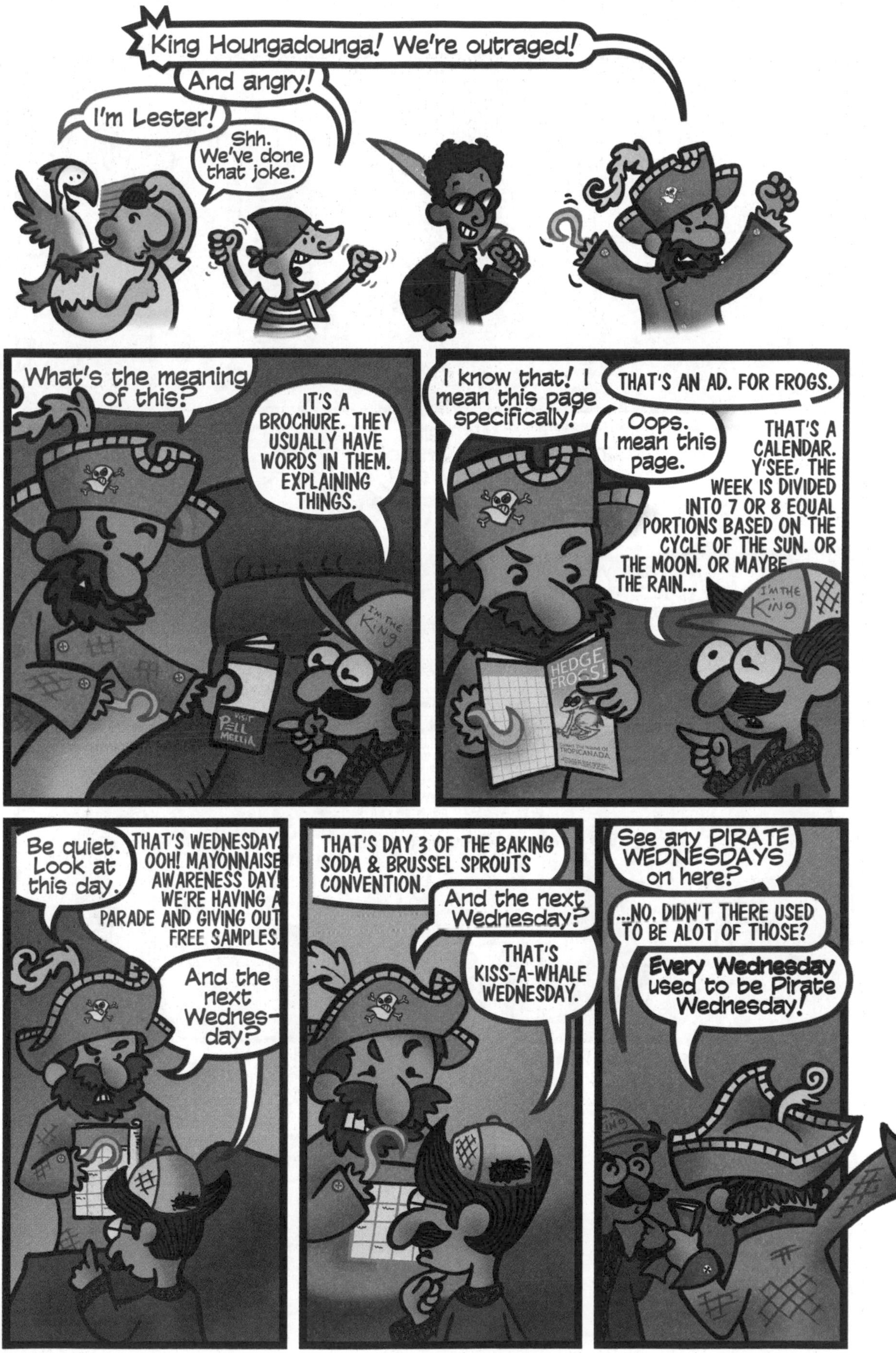
King Houngadounga! We're outraged!
And angry!
I'm Lester!
Shh. We've done that joke.
What's the meaning of this?
IT'S A BROCHURE. THEY USUALLY HAVE WORDS IN THEM. EXPLAINING THINGS.
VISIT PELL MELLIA
I'M THE King
I know that! I mean this page specifically!
THAT'S AN AD. FOR FROGS.
Oops. I mean this page.
THAT'S A CALENDAR. Y'SEE, THE WEEK IS DIVIDED INTO 7 OR 8 EQUAL PORTIONS BASED ON THE CYCLE OF THE SUN. OR THE MOON. OR MAYBE THE RAIN...
I'M THE King
HEDGE FROGS!
TROPICANADA
Be quiet. Look at this day.
THAT'S WEDNESDAY. OOH! MAYONNAISE AWARENESS DAY! WE'RE HAVING A PARADE AND GIVING OUT FREE SAMPLES.
And the next Wednes-day?
THAT'S DAY 3 OF THE BAKING SODA & BRUSSEL SPROUTS CONVENTION.
And the next Wednesday?
THAT'S KISS-A-WHALE WEDNESDAY.
See any PIRATE WEDNESDAYS on here?
...NO. DIDN'T THERE USED TO BE ALOT OF THOSE?
Every Wednesday used to be Pirate Wednesday!

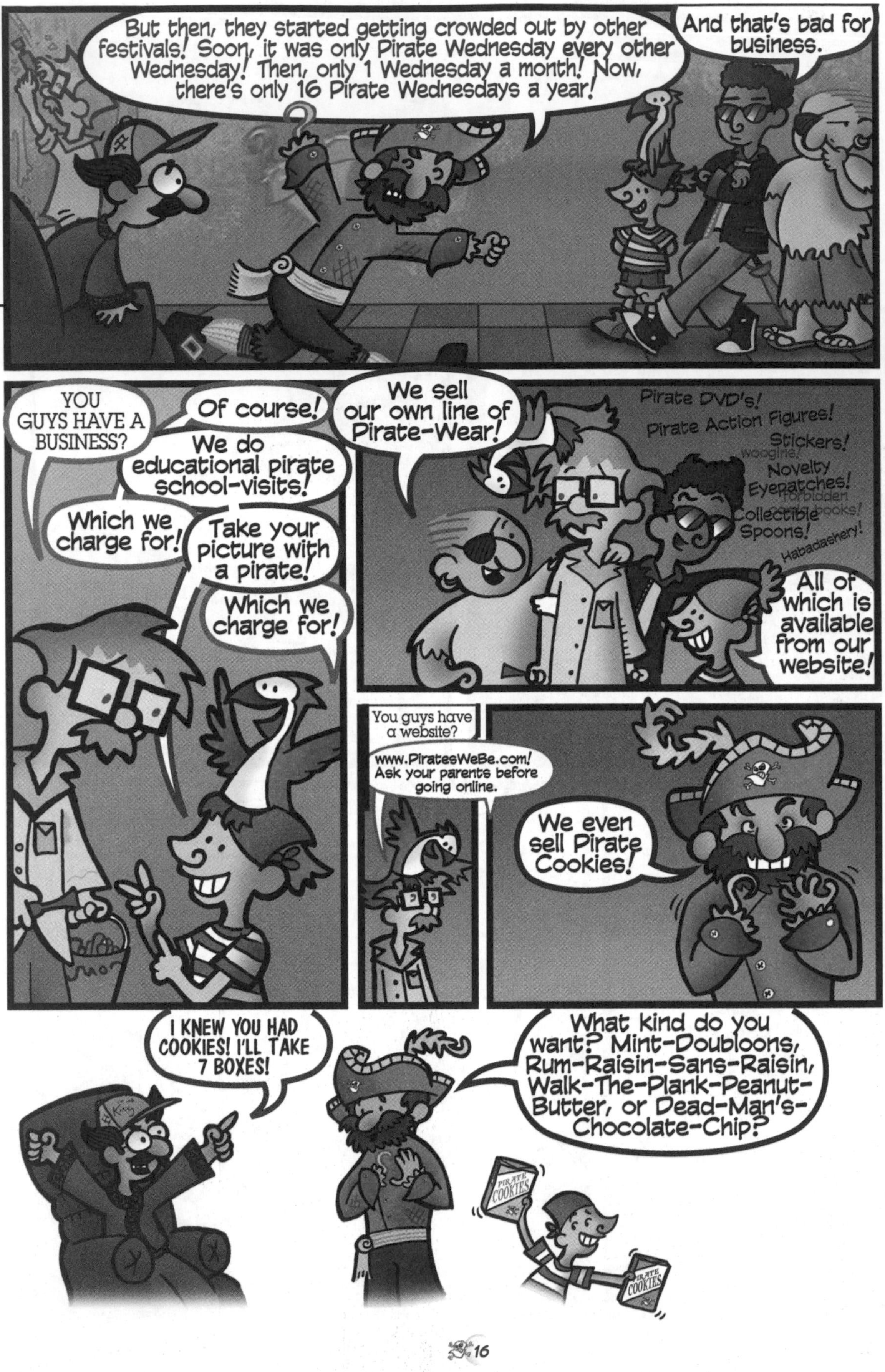

But then, they started getting crowded out by other festivals! Soon, it was only Pirate Wednesday every other Wednesday! Then, only 1 Wednesday a month! Now, there's only 16 Pirate Wednesdays a year!
And that's bad for business.
YOU GUYS HAVE A BUSINESS?
Of course!
We do educational pirate school-visits!
Which we charge for!
Take your picture with a pirate!
Which we charge for!
We sell our own line of Pirate-Wear!
Pirate DVD's!
Pirate Action Figures!
Stickers!
Woogine!
Novelty Eyepatches!
Forbidden
books!
Collectible Spoons!
Habadashery!
All of which is available from our website!
You guys have a website?
www.PiratesWeBe.com! Ask your parents before going online.
We even sell Pirate Cookies!
I KNEW YOU HAD COOKIES! I'LL TAKE 7 BOXES!
What kind do you want? Mint-Doubloons, Rum-Raisin-Sans-Raisin, Walk-The-Plank-Peanut-Butter, or Dead-Man's-Chocolate-Chip?
PIRATE COOKIES
PIRATE COOKIES

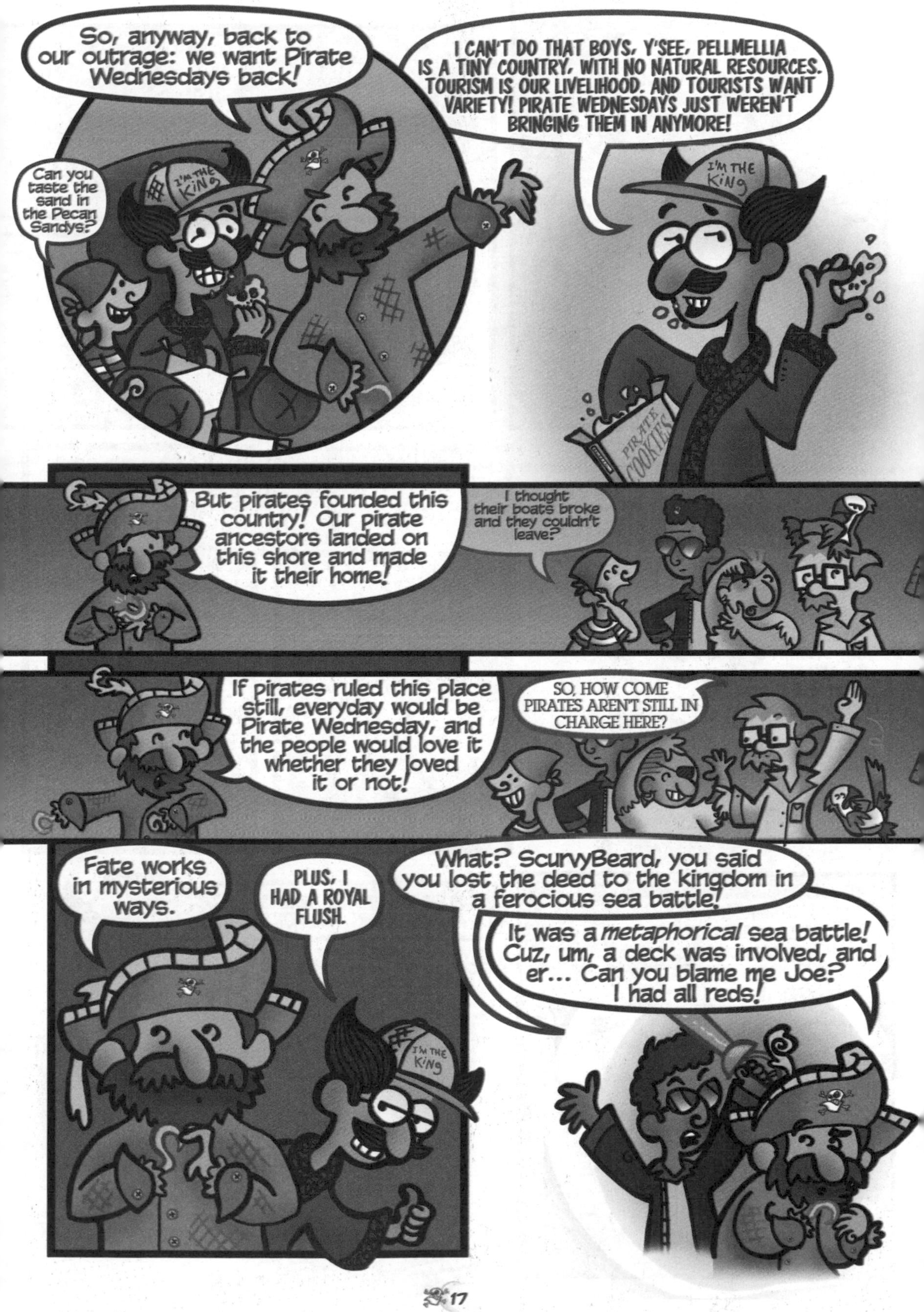
So, anyway, back to our outrage: we want Pirate Wednesdays back!
Can you taste the sand in the Pecan Sandys?
I'M THE KING
I CAN'T DO THAT BOYS, Y'SEE, PELLMELLIA IS A TINY COUNTRY, WITH NO NATURAL RESOURCES. TOURISM IS OUR LIVELIHOOD. AND TOURISTS WANT VARIETY! PIRATE WEDNESDAYS JUST WEREN'T BRINGING THEM IN ANYMORE!
I'M THE KING
PIRATE COOKIES
But pirates founded this country! Our pirate ancestors landed on this shore and made it their home!
I thought their boats broke and they couldn't leave?
If pirates ruled this place still, everyday would be Pirate Wednesday, and the people would love it whether they loved it or not!
SO, HOW COME PIRATES AREN'T STILL IN CHARGE HERE?
Fate works in mysterious ways.
PLUS, I HAD A ROYAL FLUSH.
I'M THE KING
What? ScurvyBeard, you said you lost the deed to the kingdom in a ferocious sea battle!
It was a *metaphorical* sea battle! Cuz, um, a deck was involved, and er... Can you blame me Joe? I had all reds!

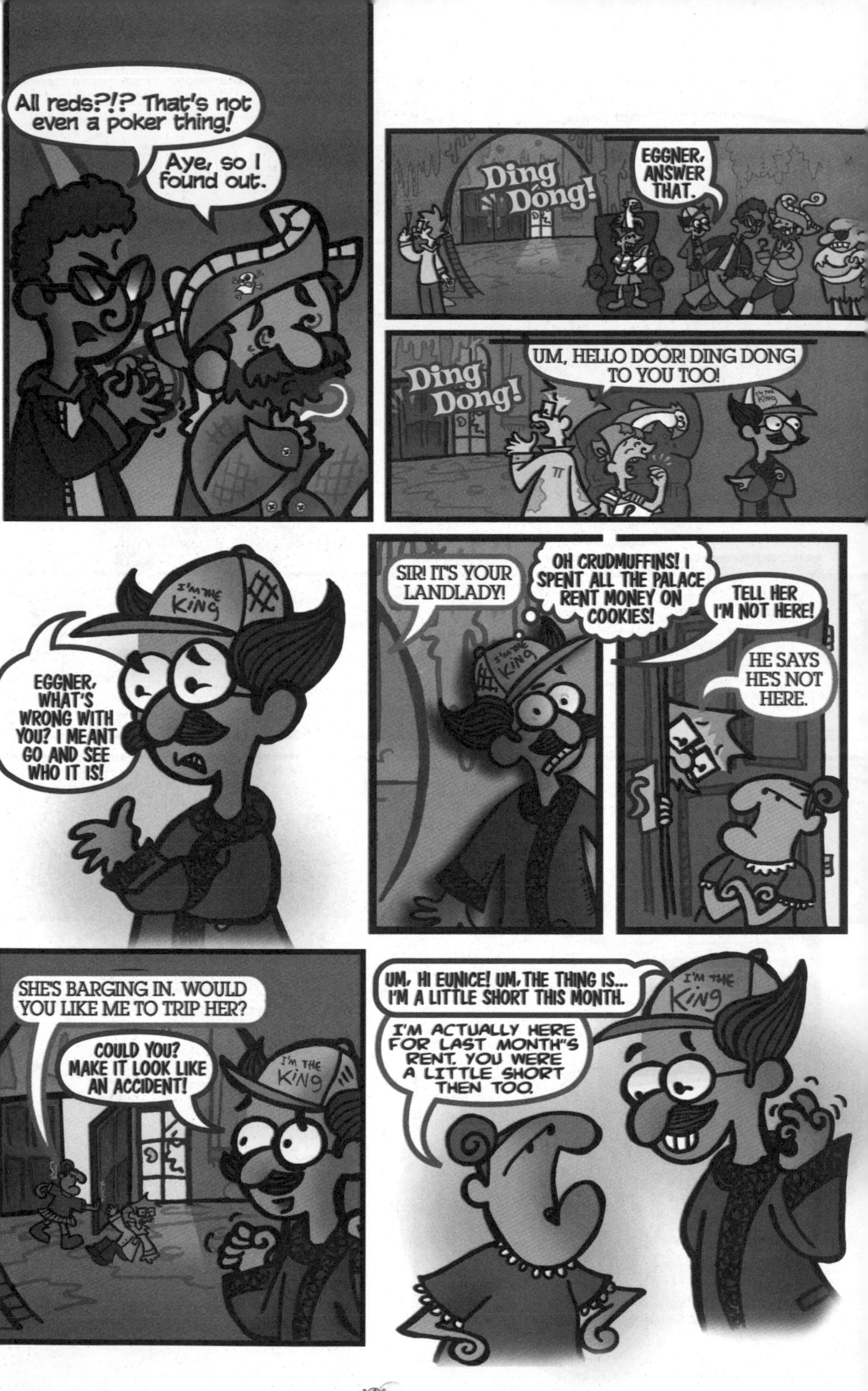

All reds?!? That's not even a poker thing!
Aye, so I found out.
Ding Dong!
EGGNER, ANSWER THAT.
Ding Dong!
UM, HELLO DOOR! DING DONG TO YOU TOO!
EGGNER, WHAT'S WRONG WITH YOU? I MEANT GO AND SEE WHO IT IS!
SIR! IT'S YOUR LANDLADY!
OH CRUDMUFFINS! I SPENT ALL THE PALACE RENT MONEY ON COOKIES!
TELL HER I'M NOT HERE!
HE SAYS HE'S NOT HERE.
SHE'S BARGING IN. WOULD YOU LIKE ME TO TRIP HER?
COULD YOU? MAKE IT LOOK LIKE AN ACCIDENT!
UM, HI EUNICE! UM, THE THING IS... I'M A LITTLE SHORT THIS MONTH.
I'M ACTUALLY HERE FOR LAST MONTH"S RENT. YOU WERE A LITTLE SHORT THEN TOO.

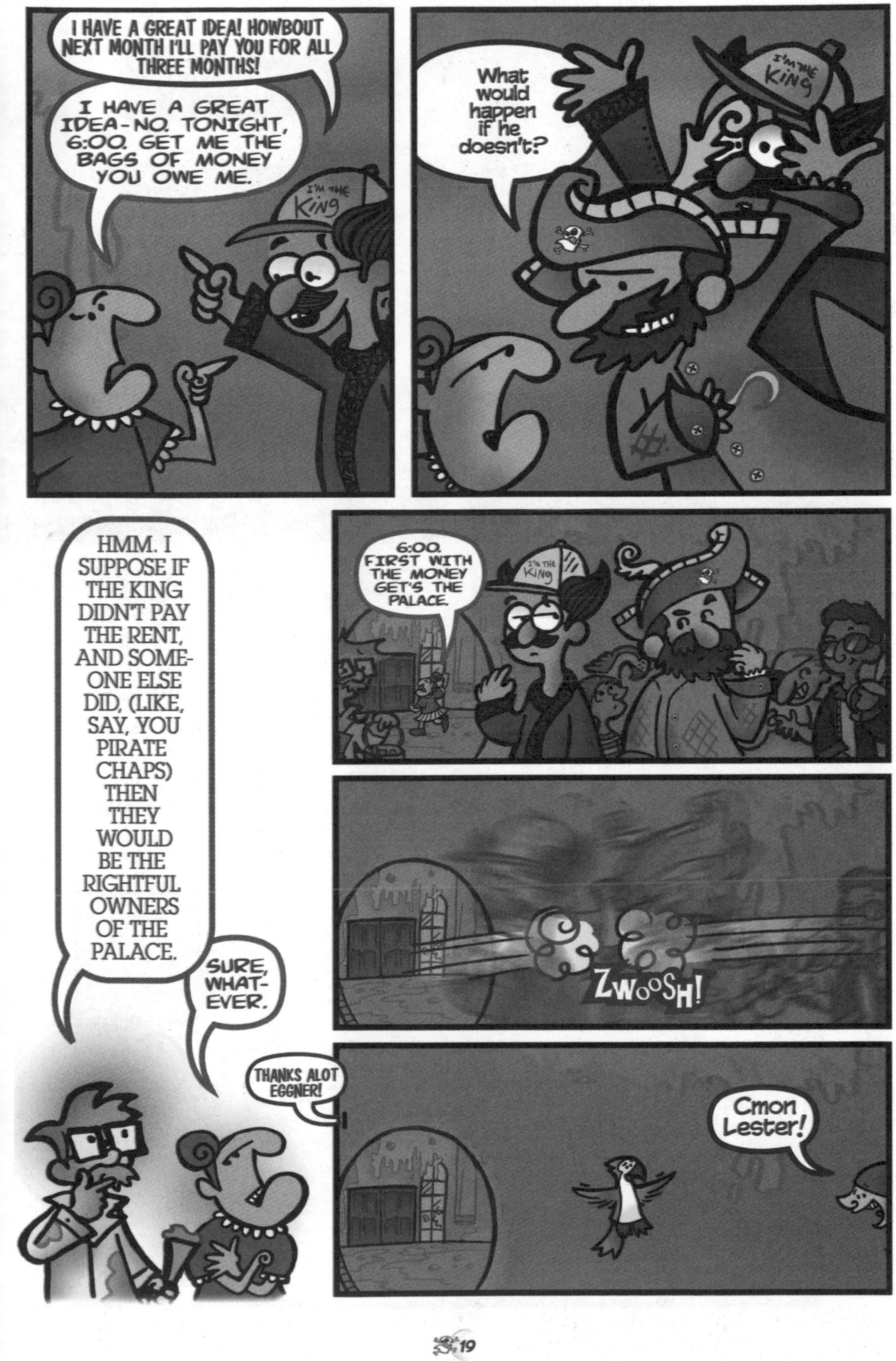
I HAVE A GREAT IDEA! HOWBOUT NEXT MONTH I'LL PAY YOU FOR ALL THREE MONTHS!
I HAVE A GREAT IDEA-NO. TONIGHT, 6:00. GET ME THE BAGS OF MONEY YOU OWE ME.
I'M THE KING
What would happen if he doesn't?
I'M THE KING
HMM. I SUPPOSE IF THE KING DIDN'T PAY THE RENT, AND SOME-ONE ELSE DID, (LIKE, SAY, YOU PIRATE CHAPS) THEN THEY WOULD BE THE RIGHTFUL OWNERS OF THE PALACE.
SURE, WHAT-EVER.
6:00. FIRST WITH THE MONEY GET'S THE PALACE.
I'M THE KING
ZWOOSH!
THANKS ALOT EGGNER!
Cmon Lester!

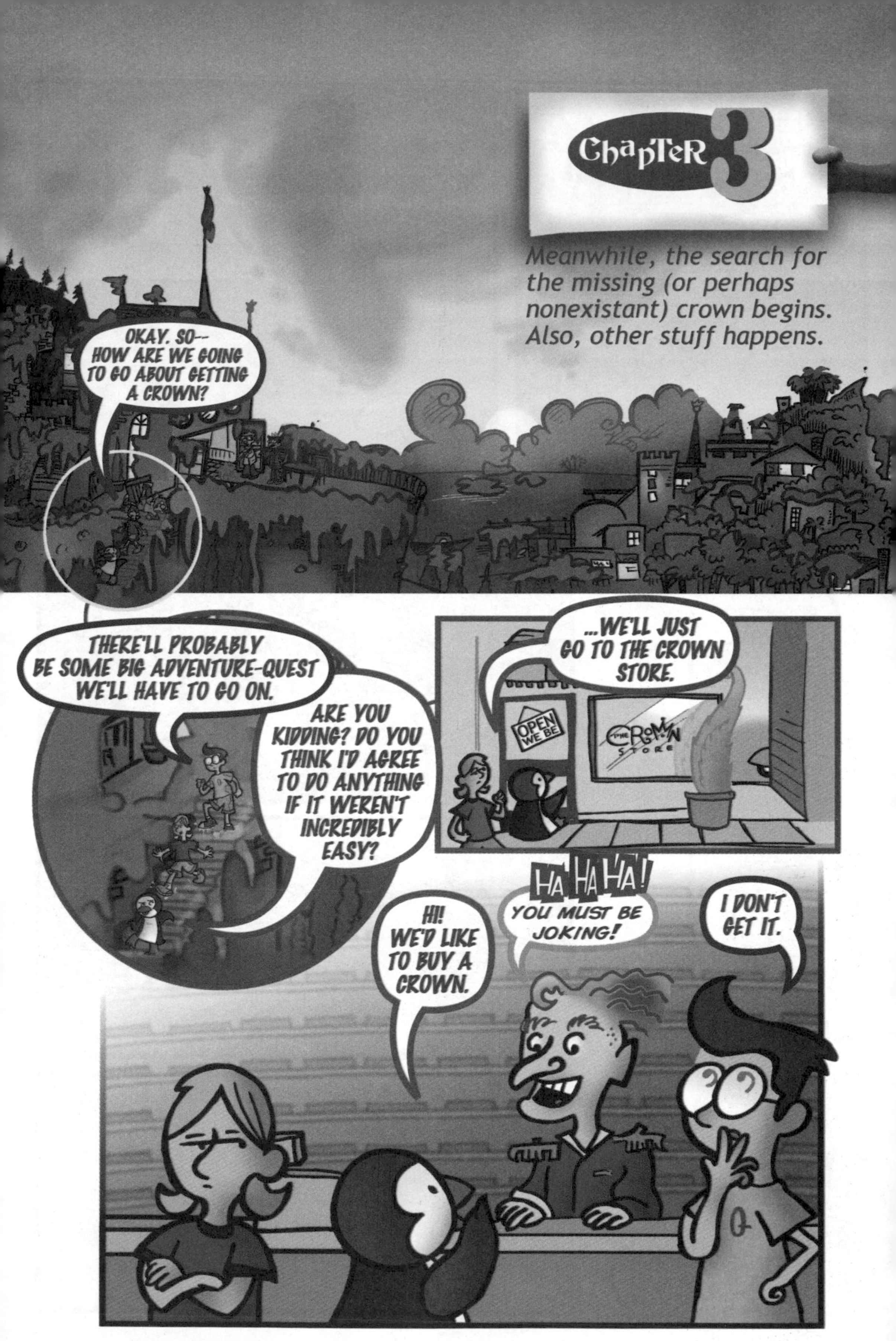

ChapTeR 3
Meanwhile, the search for the missing (or perhaps nonexistant) crown begins. Also, other stuff happens.
OKAY. SO-- HOW ARE WE GOING TO GO ABOUT GETTING A CROWN?
THERE'LL PROBABLY BE SOME BIG ADVENTURE-QUEST WE'LL HAVE TO GO ON.
ARE YOU KIDDING? DO YOU THINK I'D AGREE TO DO ANYTHING IF IT WEREN'T INCREDIBLY EASY?
...WE'LL JUST GO TO THE CROWN STORE.
OPEN WE BE
THE CROWN STORE
HI! WE'D LIKE TO BUY A CROWN.
HA HA HA!
YOU MUST BE JOKING!
I DON'T GET IT.

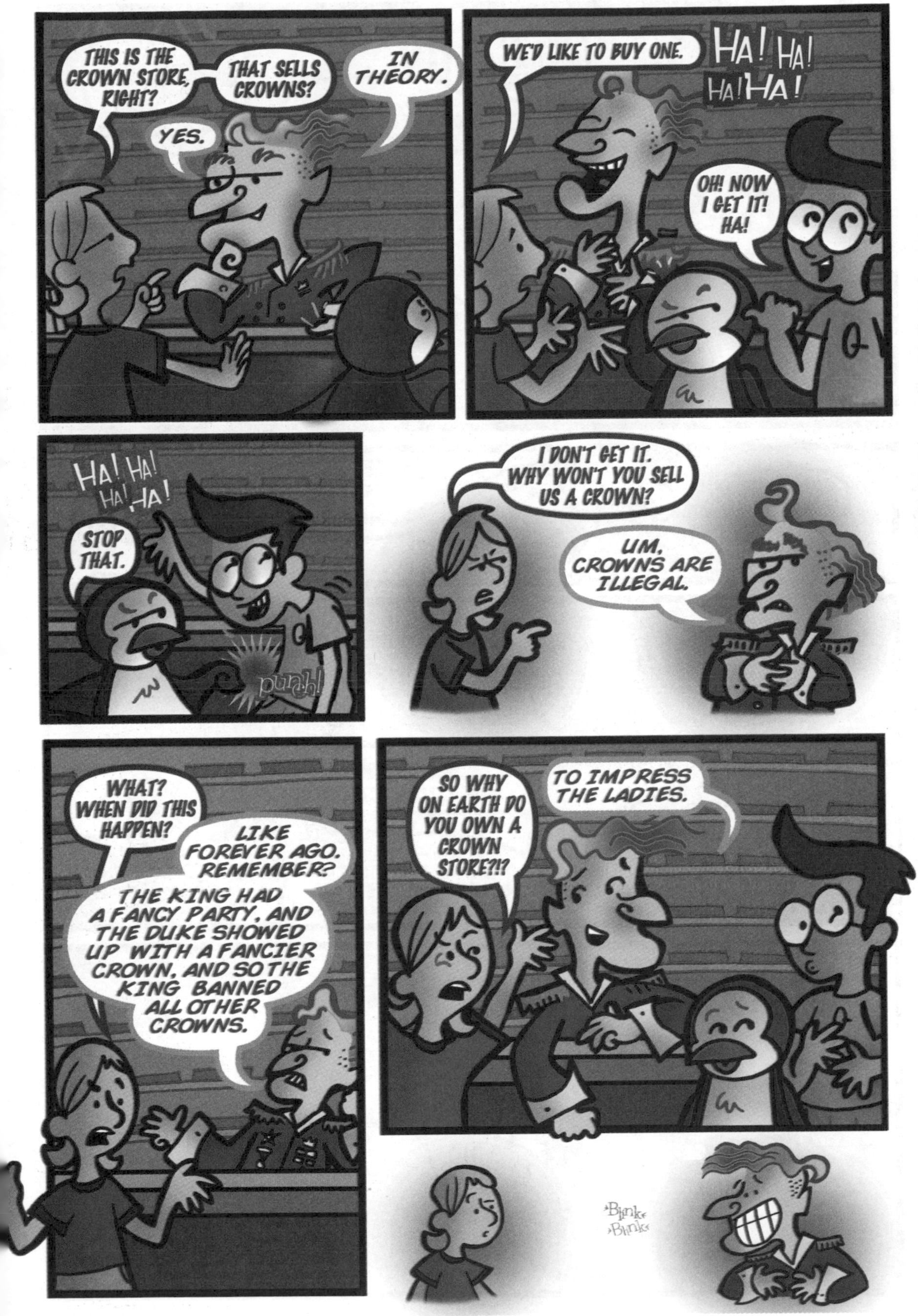
THIS IS THE CROWN STORE, RIGHT?
THAT SELLS CROWNS?
YES.
IN THEORY.
WE'D LIKE TO BUY ONE.
HA! HA! HA! HA!
OH! NOW I GET IT! HA!
HA! HA! HA! HA!
STOP THAT.
punch!
I DON'T GET IT. WHY WON'T YOU SELL US A CROWN?
UM, CROWNS ARE ILLEGAL.
WHAT? WHEN DID THIS HAPPEN?
LIKE FOREVER AGO. REMEMBER?
THE KING HAD A FANCY PARTY, AND THE DUKE SHOWED UP WITH A FANCIER CROWN, AND SO THE KING BANNED ALL OTHER CROWNS.
SO WHY ON EARTH DO YOU OWN A CROWN STORE?!?
TO IMPRESS THE LADIES.
Blink Blink

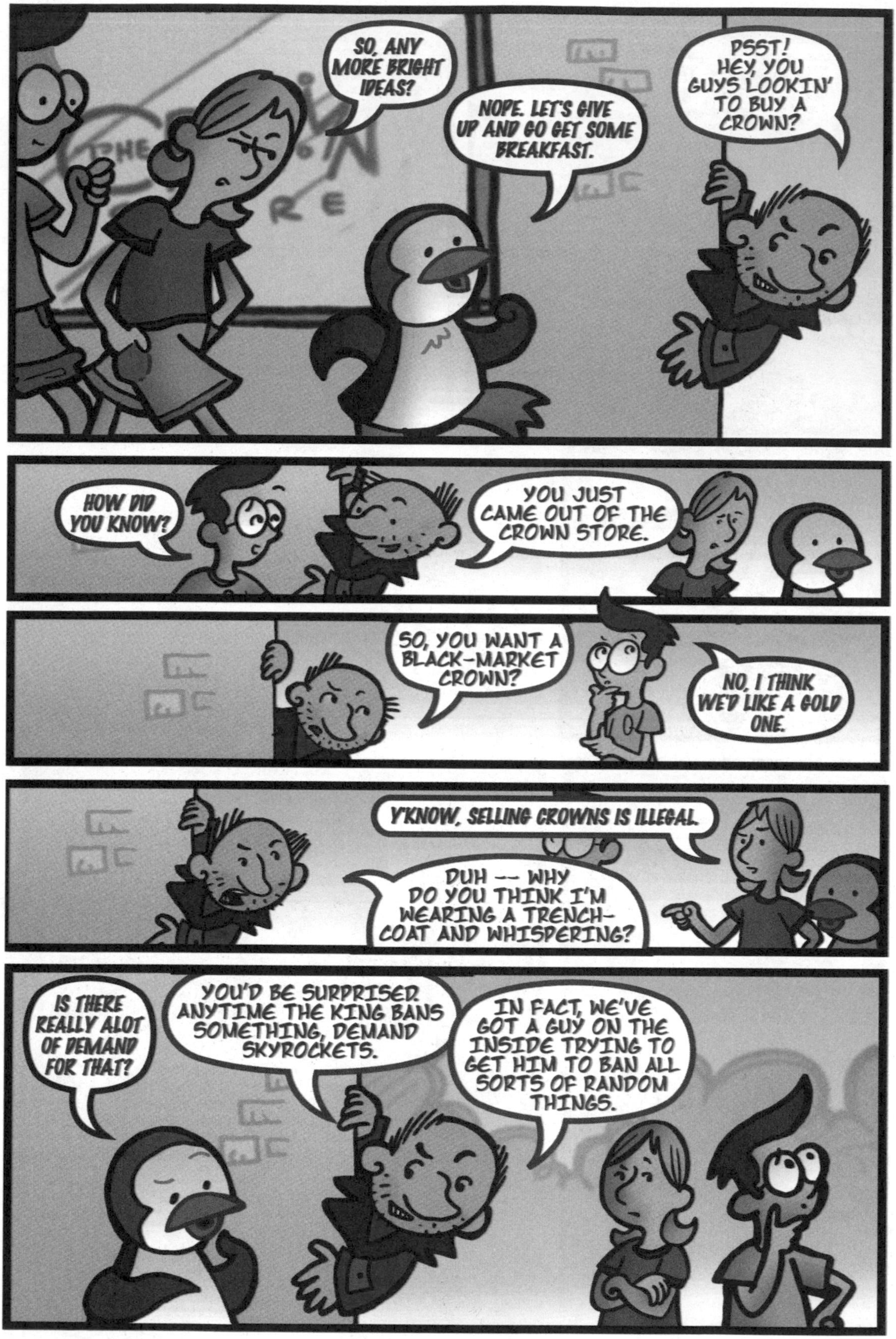
SO, ANY MORE BRIGHT IDEAS?
NOPE. LET'S GIVE UP AND GO GET SOME BREAKFAST.
PSST! HEY, YOU GUYS LOOKIN' TO BUY A CROWN?
HOW DID YOU KNOW?
YOU JUST CAME OUT OF THE CROWN STORE.
SO, YOU WANT A BLACK-MARKET CROWN?
NO, I THINK WE'D LIKE A GOLD ONE.
Y'KNOW, SELLING CROWNS IS ILLEGAL.
DUH -- WHY DO YOU THINK I'M WEARING A TRENCH-COAT AND WHISPERING?
IS THERE REALLY ALOT OF DEMAND FOR THAT?
YOU'D BE SURPRISED. ANYTIME THE KING BANS SOMETHING, DEMAND SKYROCKETS.
IN FACT, WE'VE GOT A GUY ON THE INSIDE TRYING TO GET HIM TO BAN ALL SORTS OF RANDOM THINGS.

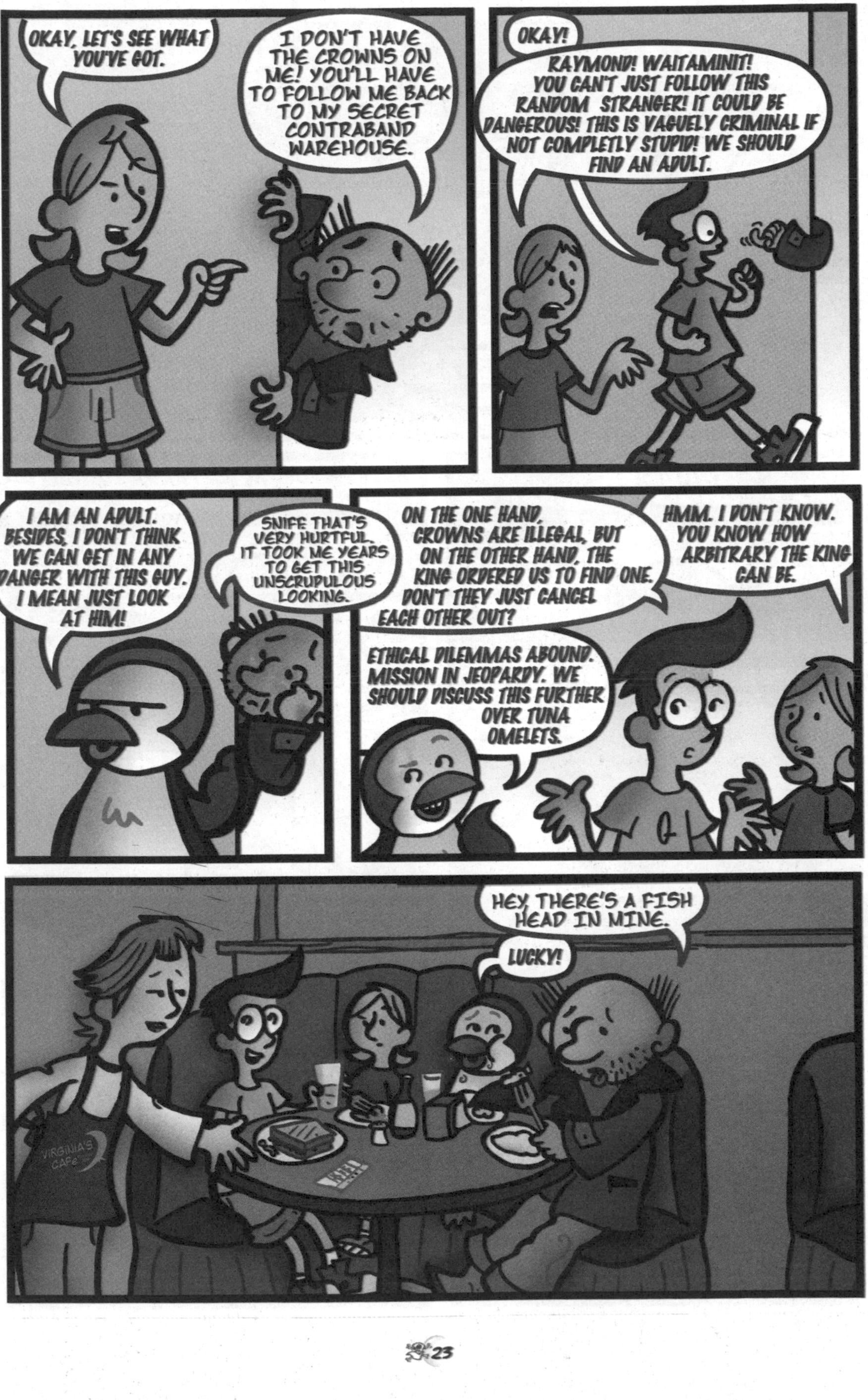
OKAY, LET'S SEE WHAT YOU'VE GOT.
I DON'T HAVE THE CROWNS ON ME! YOU'LL HAVE TO FOLLOW ME BACK TO MY SECRET CONTRABAND WAREHOUSE.
OKAY!
RAYMOND! WAITAMINIT! YOU CAN'T JUST FOLLOW THIS RANDOM STRANGER! IT COULD BE DANGEROUS! THIS IS VAGUELY CRIMINAL IF NOT COMPLETLY STUPID! WE SHOULD FIND AN ADULT.
I AM AN ADULT. BESIDES, I DON'T THINK WE CAN GET IN ANY DANGER WITH THIS GUY. I MEAN JUST LOOK AT HIM!
SNIFF. THAT'S VERY HURTFUL. IT TOOK ME YEARS TO GET THIS UNSCRUPULOUS LOOKING.
ON THE ONE HAND, CROWNS ARE ILLEGAL, BUT ON THE OTHER HAND, THE KING ORDERED US TO FIND ONE. DON'T THEY JUST CANCEL EACH OTHER OUT?
HMM. I DON'T KNOW. YOU KNOW HOW ARBITRARY THE KING CAN BE.
ETHICAL DILEMMAS ABOUND. MISSION IN JEOPARDY. WE SHOULD DISCUSS THIS FURTHER OVER TUNA OMELETS.
HEY, THERE'S A FISH HEAD IN MINE.
LUCKY!
VIRGINIA'S CAFE

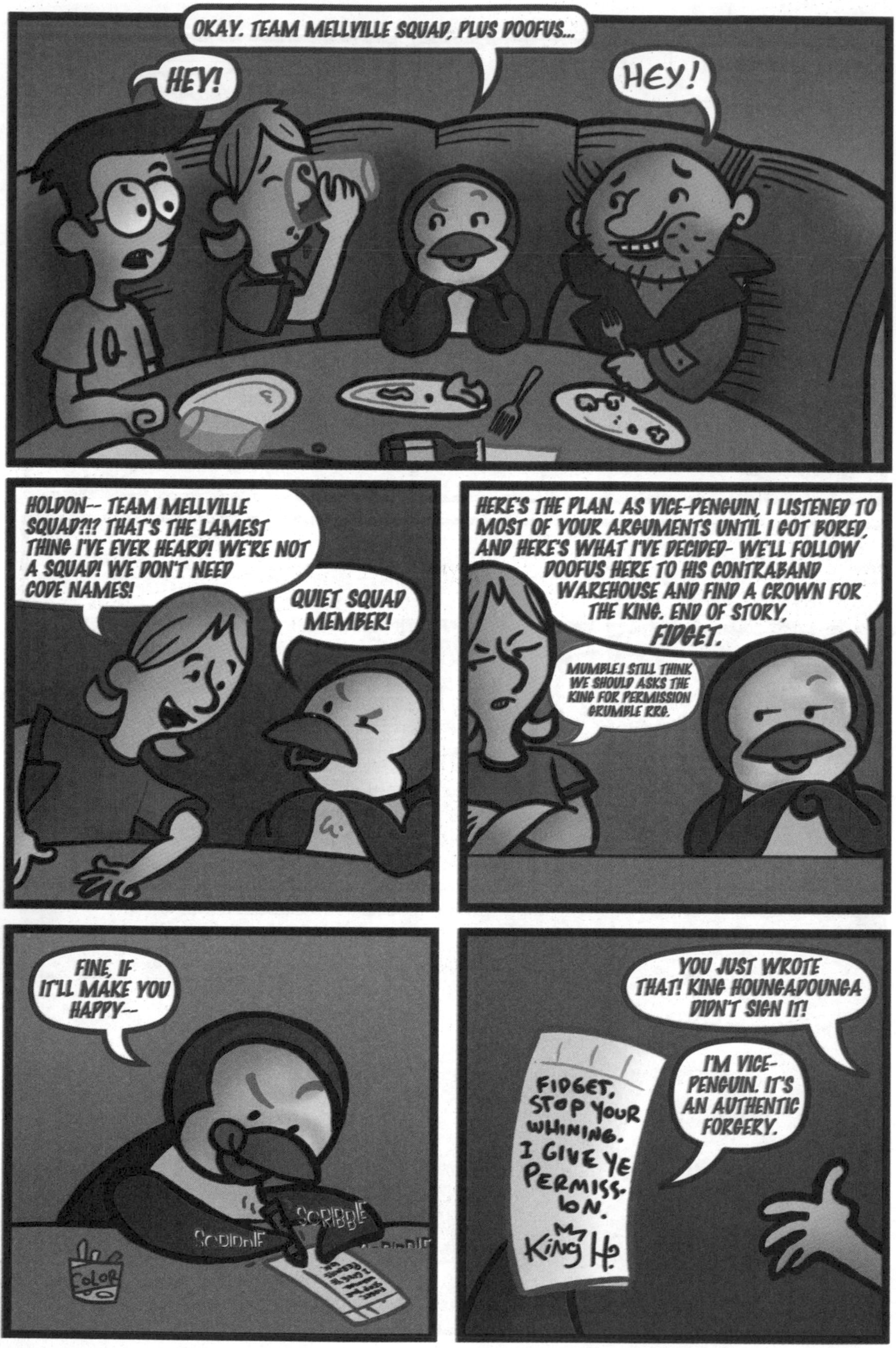
OKAY. TEAM MELLVILLE SQUAD, PLUS DOOFUS...
HEY!
HEY!
HOLDON-- TEAM MELLVILLE SQUAD?!? THAT'S THE LAMEST THING I'VE EVER HEARD! WE'RE NOT A SQUAD! WE DON'T NEED CODE NAMES!
QUIET SQUAD MEMBER!
HERE'S THE PLAN. AS VICE-PENGUIN, I LISTENED TO MOST OF YOUR ARGUMENTS UNTIL I GOT BORED, AND HERE'S WHAT I'VE DECIDED- WE'LL FOLLOW DOOFUS HERE TO HIS CONTRABAND WAREHOUSE AND FIND A CROWN FOR THE KING. END OF STORY, FIDGET.
MUMBLE.I STILL THINK WE SHOULD ASKS THE KING FOR PERMISSION GRUMBLE RRG.
FINE, IF IT'LL MAKE YOU HAPPY--
SCRIBBLE
SCRIBBLE
COLOR
YOU JUST WROTE THAT! KING HOUNGADOUNGA DIDN'T SIGN IT!
FIDGET, STOP YOUR WHINING. I GIVE YE PERMISSION. King H.
I'M VICE-PENGUIN. IT'S AN AUTHENTIC FORGERY.

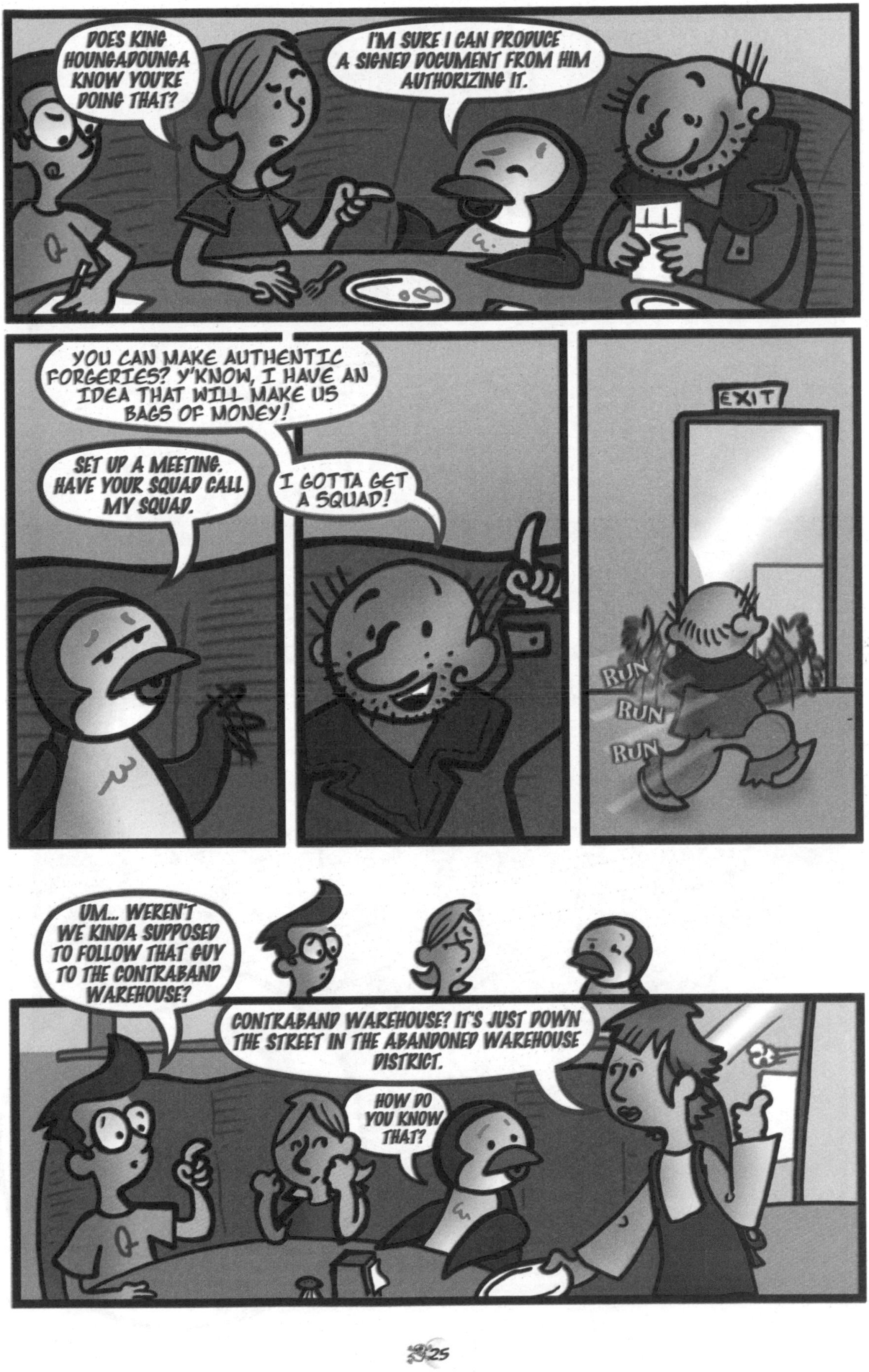
DOES KING HOUNGADOUNGA KNOW YOU'RE DOING THAT?
I'M SURE I CAN PRODUCE A SIGNED DOCUMENT FROM HIM AUTHORIZING IT.
YOU CAN MAKE AUTHENTIC FORGERIES? Y'KNOW, I HAVE AN IDEA THAT WILL MAKE US BAGS OF MONEY!
SET UP A MEETING. HAVE YOUR SQUAD CALL MY SQUAD.
I GOTTA GET A SQUAD!
EXIT
RUN
RUN
RUN
UM... WEREN'T WE KINDA SUPPOSED TO FOLLOW THAT GUY TO THE CONTRABAND WAREHOUSE?
CONTRABAND WAREHOUSE? IT'S JUST DOWN THE STREET IN THE ABANDONED WAREHOUSE DISTRICT.
HOW DO YOU KNOW THAT?

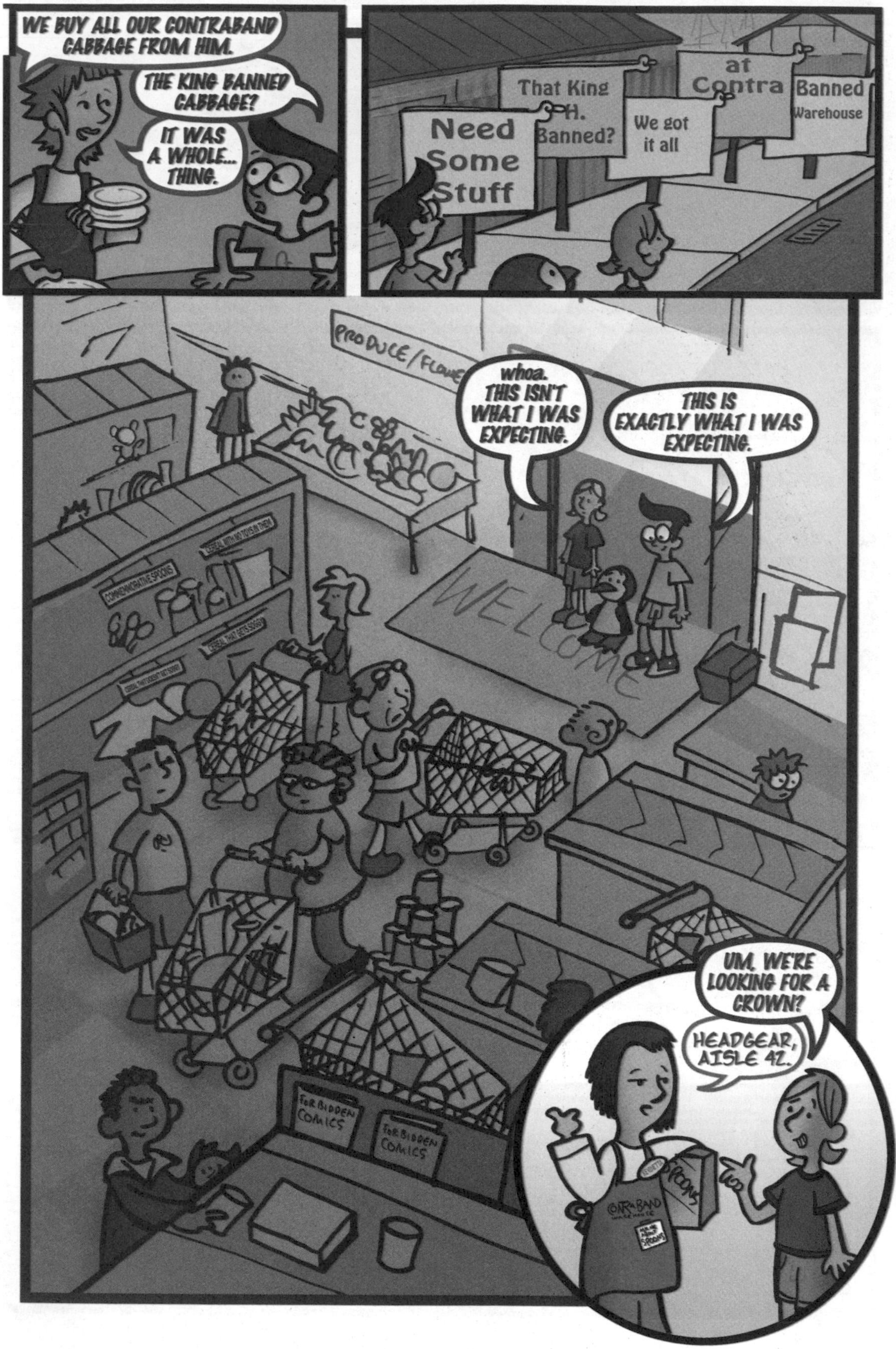
WE BUY ALL OUR CONTRABAND CABBAGE FROM HIM.
THE KING BANNED CABBAGE?
IT WAS A WHOLE... THING.
Need Some Stuff
That King H. Banned?
We got it all
at Contra
Banned Warehouse
PRODUCE/FLOWE
COMMEMORATIVE SPOONS
CEREAL WITH NO TOYS IN THEM
CEREAL THAT GETS SOGGY
CEREAL THAT DOESN'T GET SOGGY
whoa. THIS ISN'T WHAT I WAS EXPECTING.
THIS IS EXACTLY WHAT I WAS EXPECTING.
WELCOME
FORBIDDEN COMICS
FORBIDDEN COMICS
UM, WE'RE LOOKING FOR A CROWN?
HEADGEAR, AISLE 42.
SPOONS
CONTRABAND WAREHOUSE

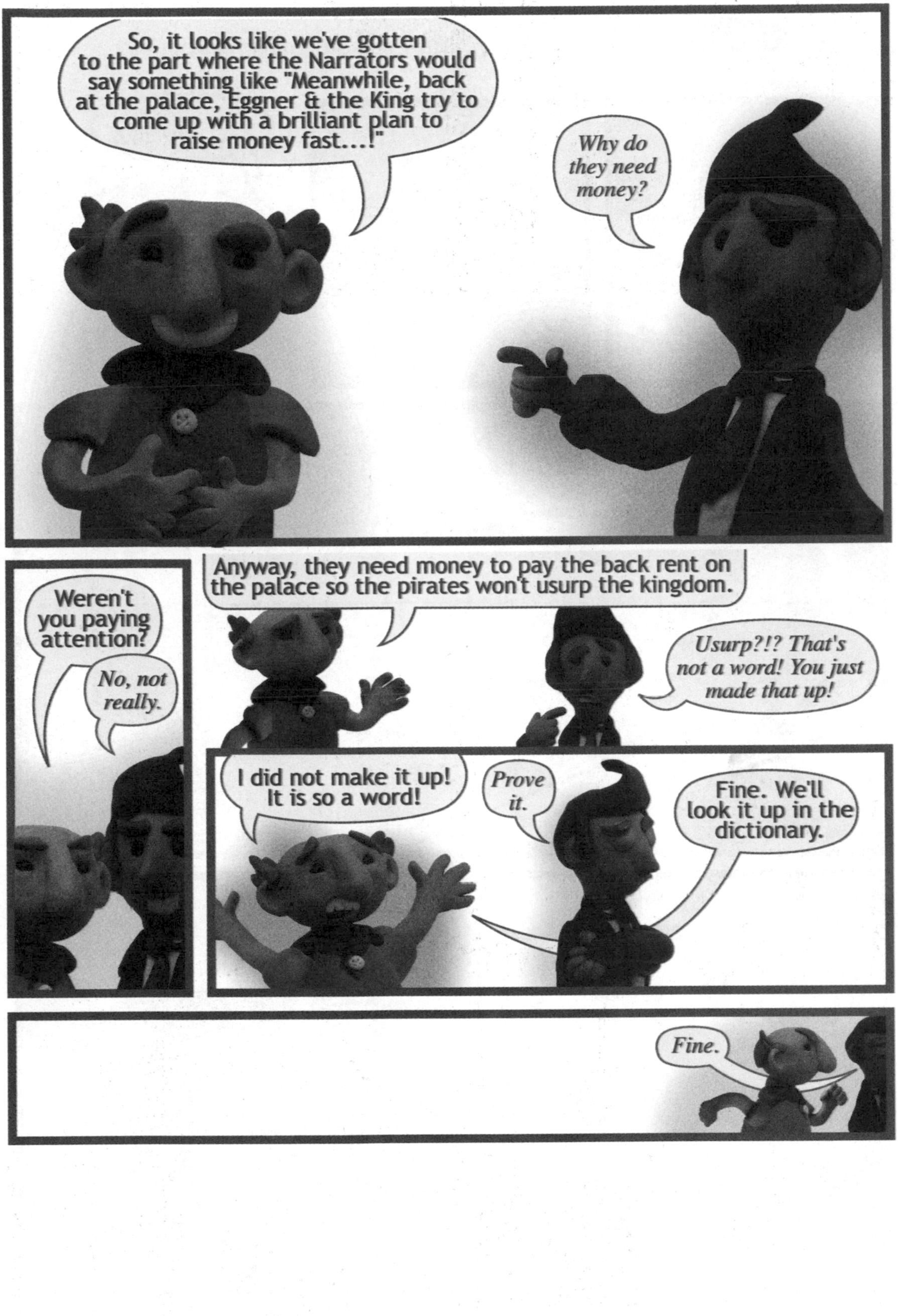
So, it looks like we've gotten to the part where the Narrators would say something like "Meanwhile, back at the palace, Eggner & the King try to come up with a brilliant plan to raise money fast...!"
Why do they need money?
Weren't you paying attention?
No, not really.
Anyway, they need money to pay the back rent on the palace so the pirates won't usurp the kingdom.
Usurp?!? That's not a word! You just made that up!
I did not make it up! It is so a word!
Prove it.
Fine. We'll look it up in the dictionary.
Fine.

# Chapter 4

*In which... um... just read it. You'll figure it out.*

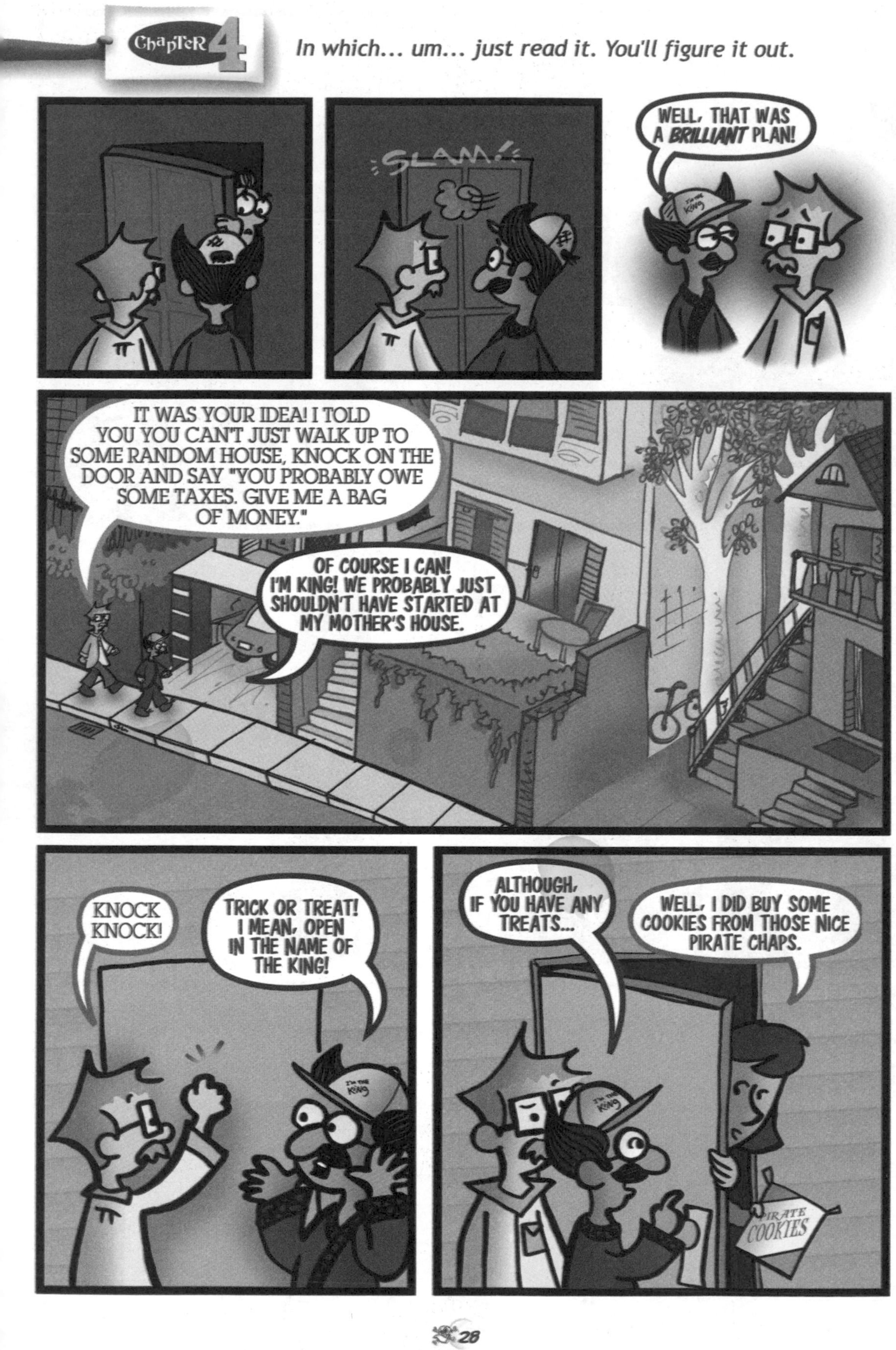

SLAM!
WELL, THAT WAS A *BRILLIANT* PLAN!
IT WAS YOUR IDEA! I TOLD YOU YOU CAN'T JUST WALK UP TO SOME RANDOM HOUSE, KNOCK ON THE DOOR AND SAY "YOU PROBABLY OWE SOME TAXES. GIVE ME A BAG OF MONEY."
OF COURSE I CAN! I'M KING! WE PROBABLY JUST SHOULDN'T HAVE STARTED AT MY MOTHER'S HOUSE.
KNOCK KNOCK!
TRICK OR TREAT! I MEAN, OPEN IN THE NAME OF THE KING!
ALTHOUGH, IF YOU HAVE ANY TREATS...
WELL, I DID BUY SOME COOKIES FROM THOSE NICE PIRATE CHAPS.
PIRATE COOKIES

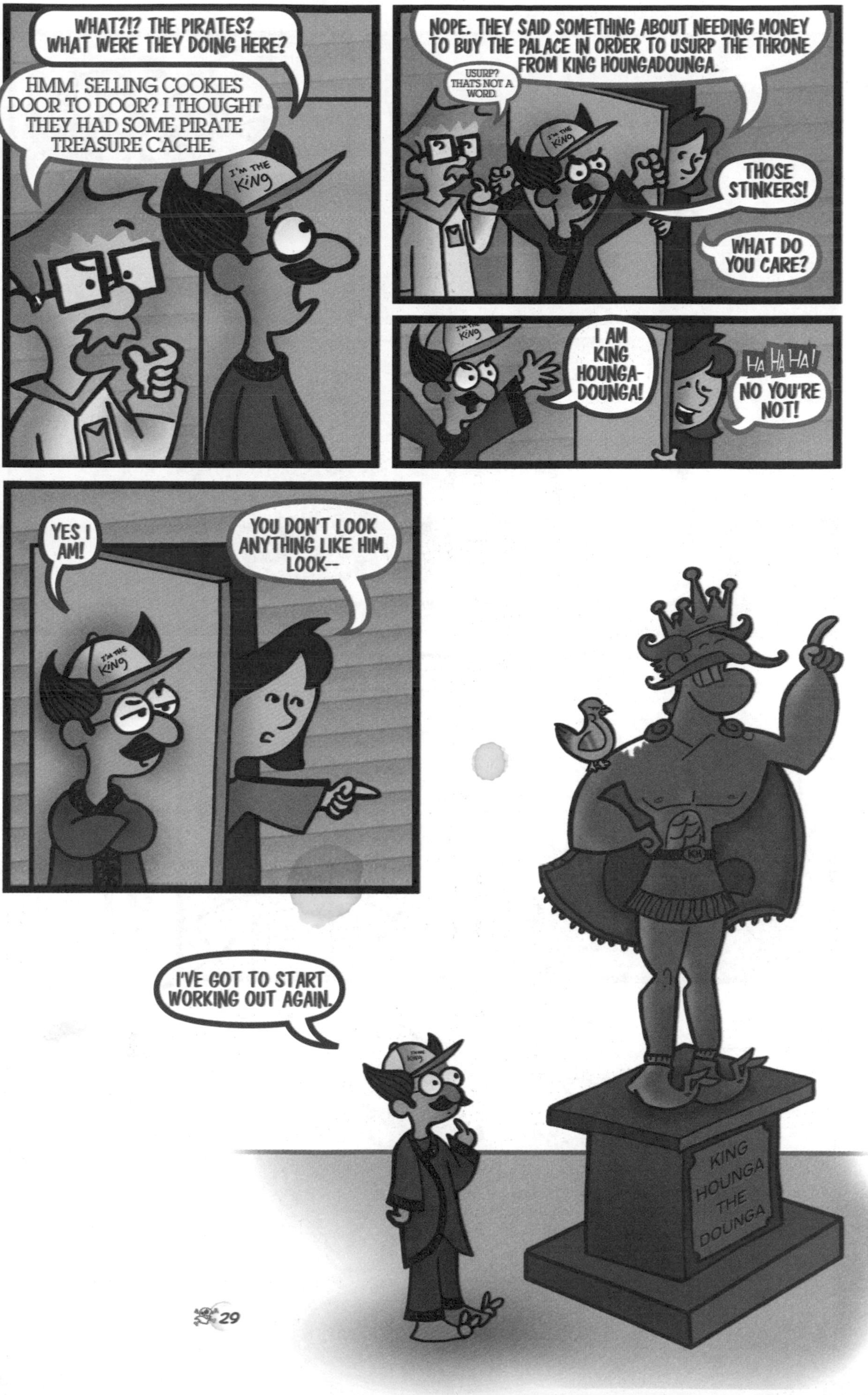

WHAT?!? THE PIRATES? WHAT WERE THEY DOING HERE?
HMM. SELLING COOKIES DOOR TO DOOR? I THOUGHT THEY HAD SOME PIRATE TREASURE CACHE.
I'M THE KING
NOPE. THEY SAID SOMETHING ABOUT NEEDING MONEY TO BUY THE PALACE IN ORDER TO USURP THE THRONE FROM KING HOUNGADOUNGA.
USURP? THAT'S NOT A WORD.
I'M THE KING
THOSE STINKERS!
WHAT DO YOU CARE?
I'M THE KING
I AM KING HOUNGA-DOUNGA!
HA HA HA!
NO YOU'RE NOT!
YES I AM!
YOU DON'T LOOK ANYTHING LIKE HIM. LOOK--
I'M THE KING
KH
I'VE GOT TO START WORKING OUT AGAIN.
KING HOUNGA THE DOUNGA

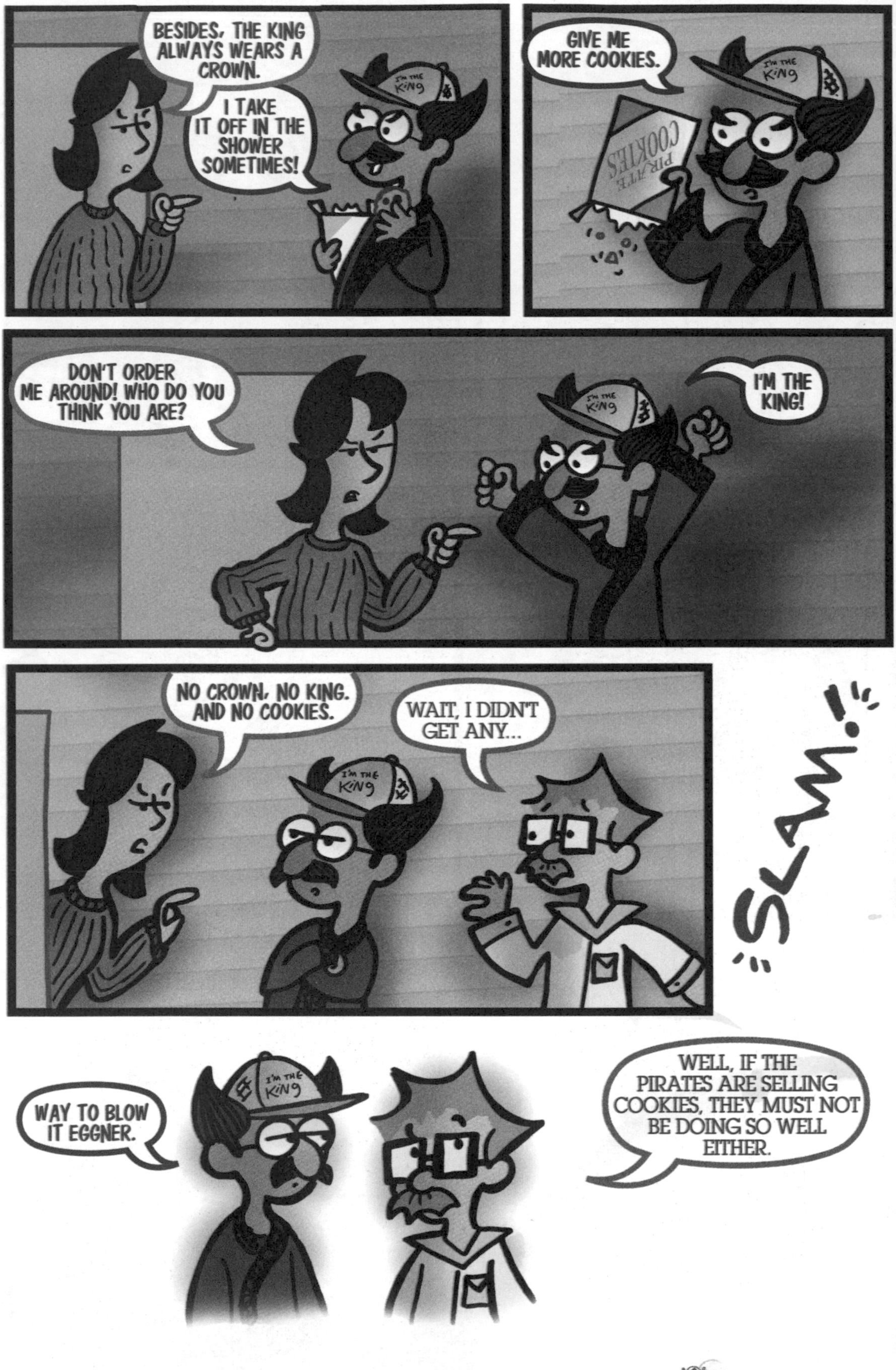
BESIDES, THE KING ALWAYS WEARS A CROWN.
I TAKE IT OFF IN THE SHOWER SOMETIMES!
I'M THE KING
GIVE ME MORE COOKIES.
PIRATE COOKIES
I'M THE KING
DON'T ORDER ME AROUND! WHO DO YOU THINK YOU ARE?
I'M THE KING!
I'M THE KING
NO CROWN, NO KING. AND NO COOKIES.
WAIT, I DIDN'T GET ANY...
I'M THE KING
SLAM!
WAY TO BLOW IT EGGNER.
I'M THE KING
WELL, IF THE PIRATES ARE SELLING COOKIES, THEY MUST NOT BE DOING SO WELL EITHER.

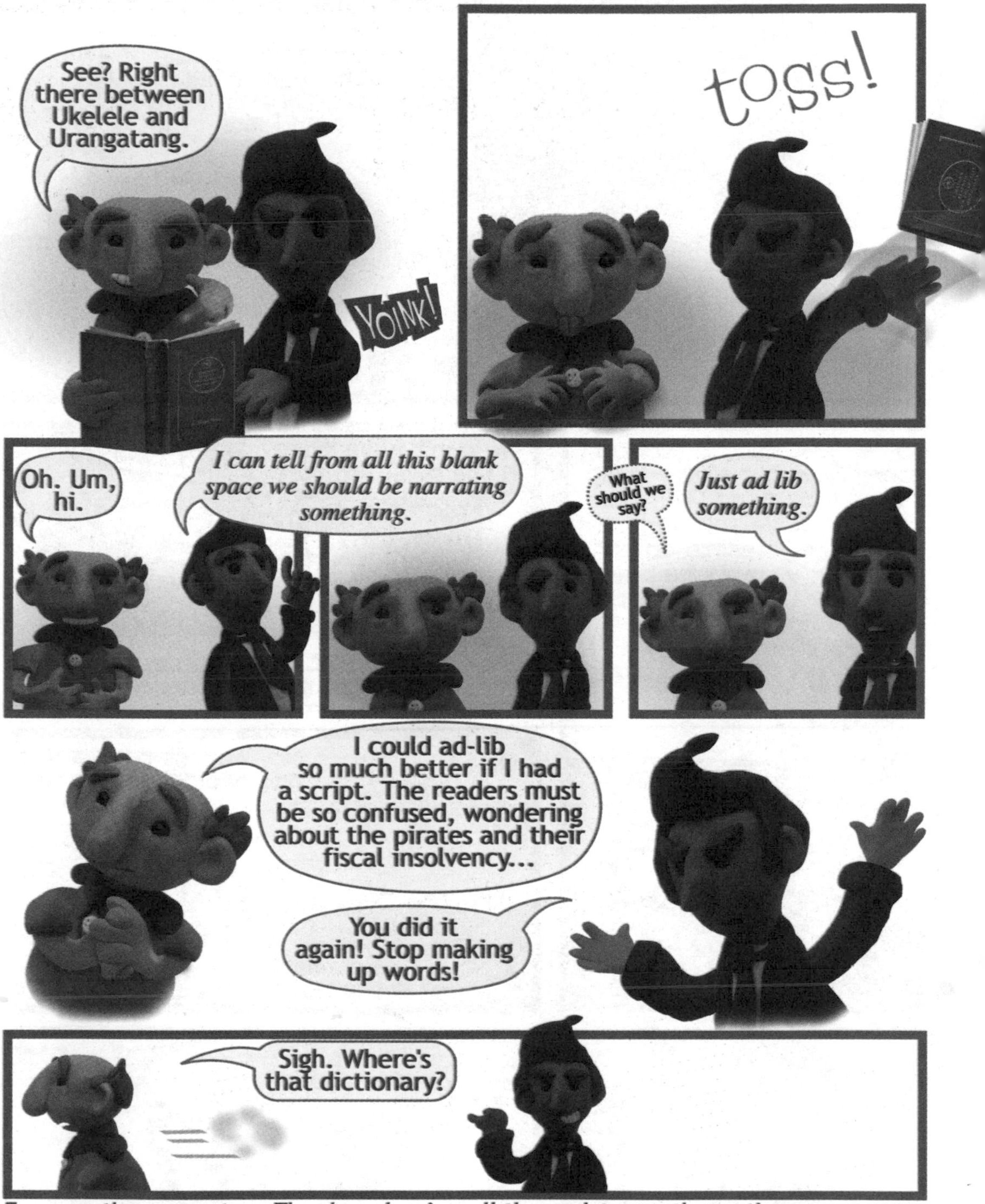
See? Right there between Ukelele and Urangatang.
YOINK!
toss!
Oh. Um, hi.
I can tell from all this blank space we should be narrating something.
What should we say?
Just ad lib something.
I could ad-lib so much better if I had a script. The readers must be so confused, wondering about the pirates and their fiscal insolvency...
You did it again! Stop making up words!
Sigh. Where's that dictionary?

*Fooey on those narrators. They keep leaving all the work to me, the caption guy.*

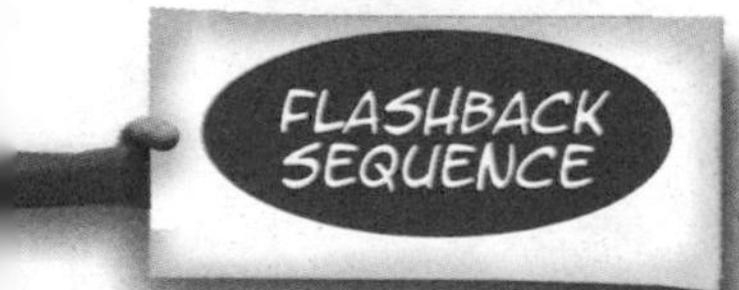
FLASHBACK SEQUENCE

*in which we discover the reasons for the pirate's fiscal insolvency and also what happened to all their treasure.*

*As you'll recall, back at the palace -->*

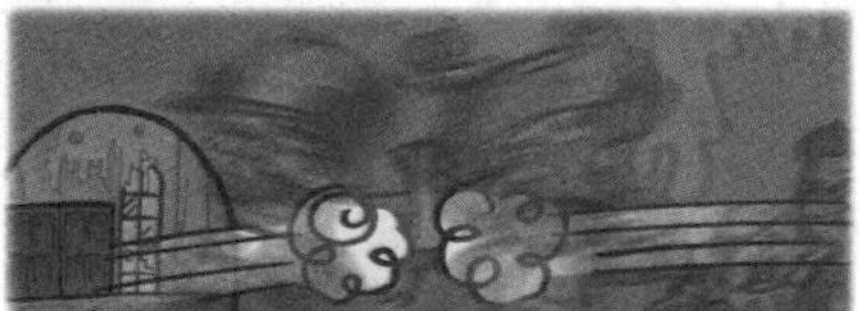

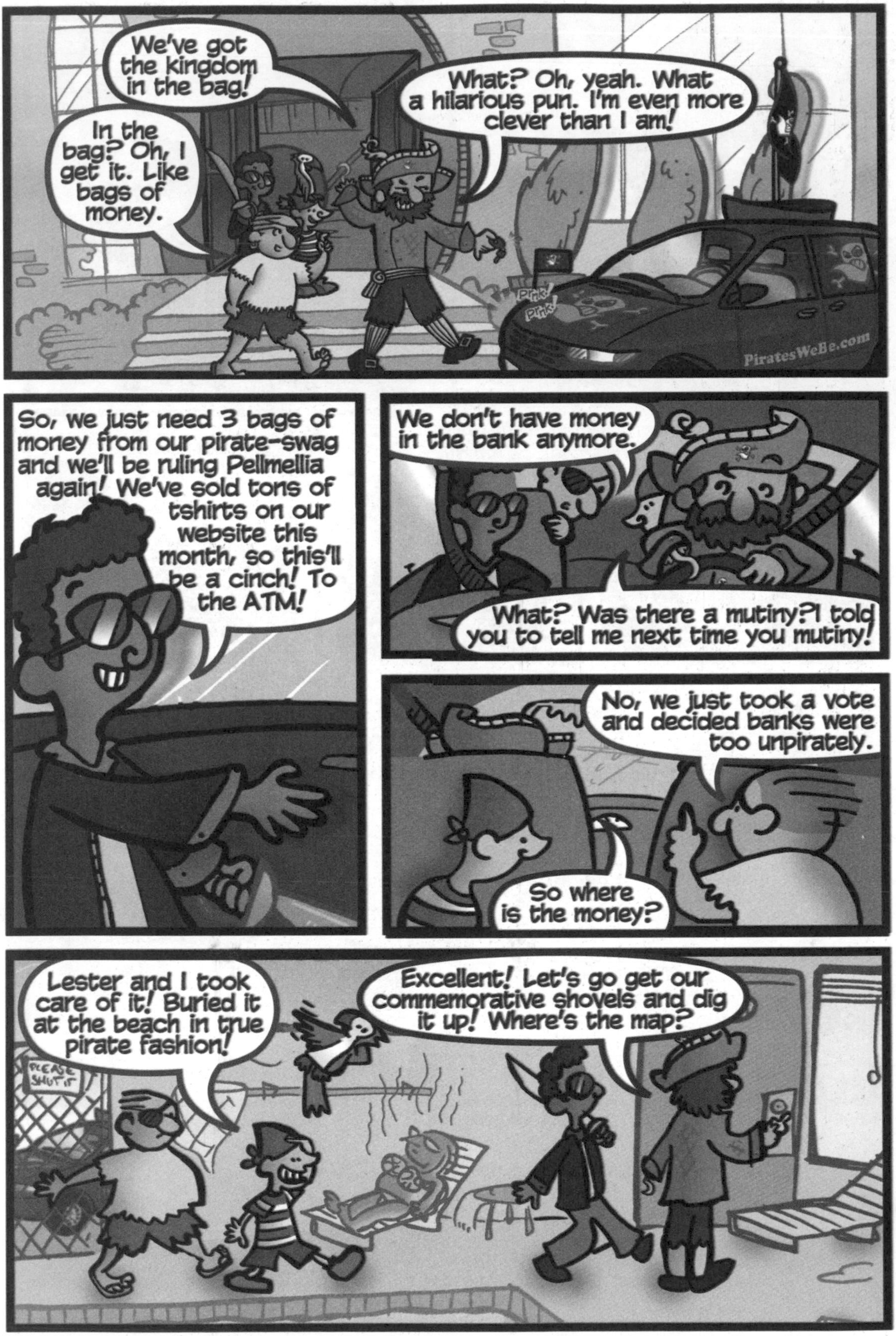
We've got the kingdom in the bag!
In the bag? Oh, I get it. Like bags of money.
What? Oh, yeah. What a hilarious pun. I'm even more clever than I am!
Pink! Pink!
PiratesWeBe.com
So, we just need 3 bags of money from our pirate-swag and we'll be ruling Pellmellia again! We've sold tons of tshirts on our website this month, so this'll be a cinch! To the ATM!
We don't have money in the bank anymore.
What? Was there a mutiny?I told you to tell me next time you mutiny!
No, we just took a vote and decided banks were too unpirately.
So where is the money?
Lester and I took care of it! Buried it at the beach in true pirate fashion!
Excellent! Let's go get our commemorative shovels and dig it up! Where's the map?
PLEASE SHUT IT

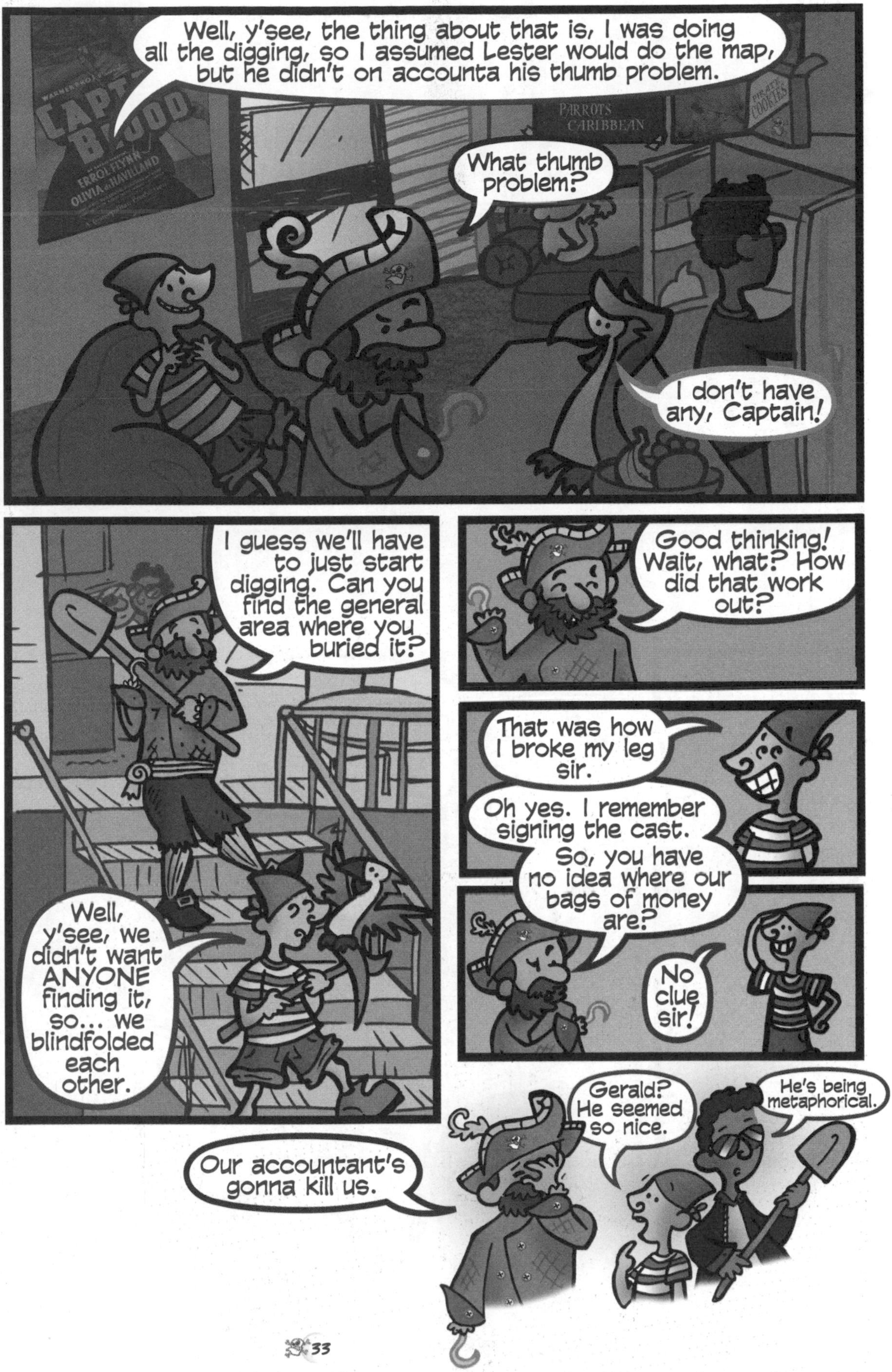
Well, y'see, the thing about that is, I was doing all the digging, so I assumed Lester would do the map, but he didn't on accounta his thumb problem.
CAPTAIN BLOOD
ERROL FLYNN
OLIVIA de HAVILLAND
PARROTS CARIBBEAN
PIRATE COOKIES
What thumb problem?
I don't have any, Captain!
I guess we'll have to just start digging. Can you find the general area where you buried it?
Well, y'see, we didn't want ANYONE finding it, so... we blindfolded each other.
Good thinking! Wait, what? How did that work out?
That was how I broke my leg sir.
Oh yes. I remember signing the cast.
So, you have no idea where our bags of money are?
No clue sir!
Our accountant's gonna kill us.
Gerald? He seemed so nice.
He's being metaphorical.

Several Digging-Related Hours Later--

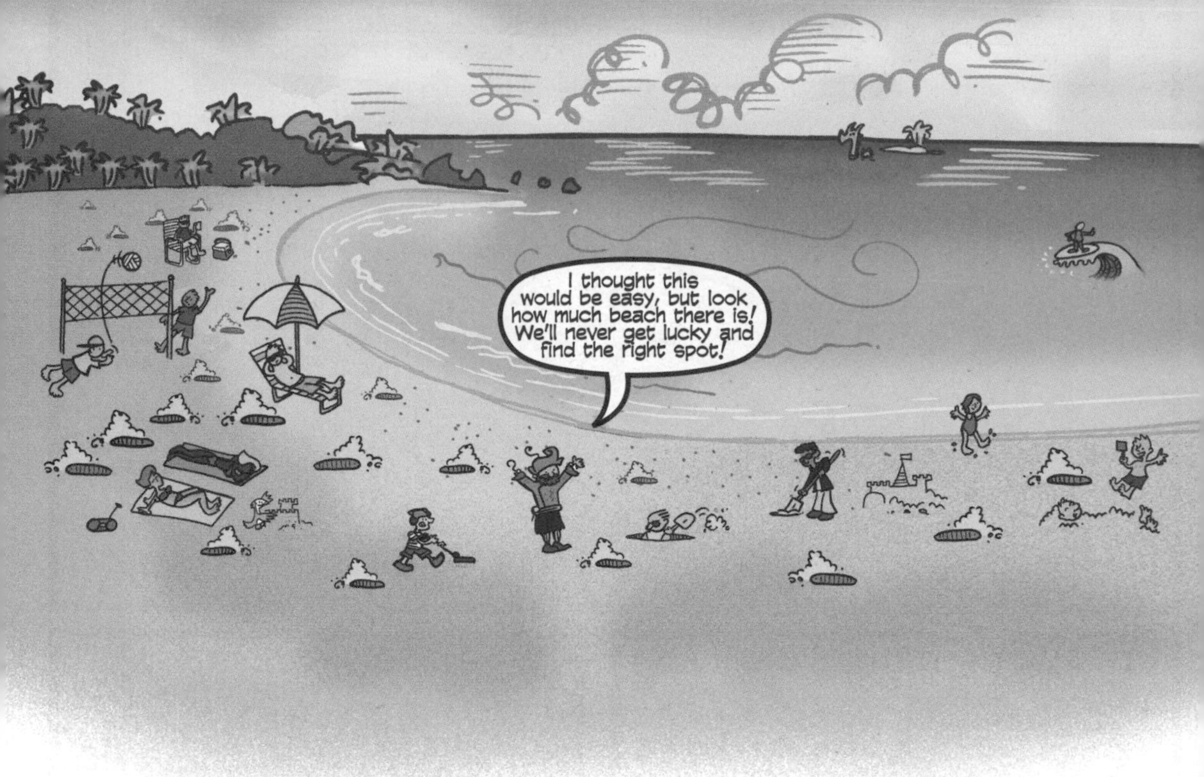
I thought this would be easy, but look how much beach there is! We'll never get lucky and find the right spot!

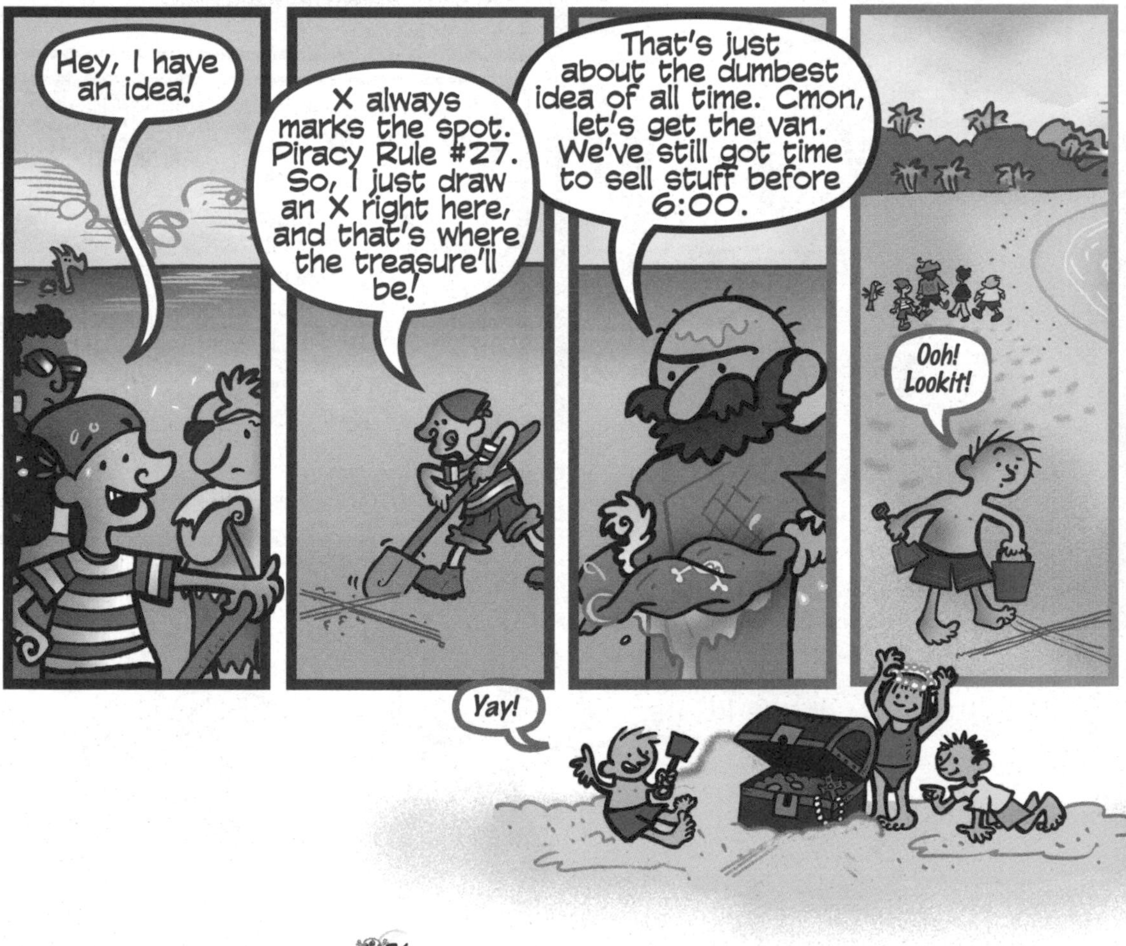
Hey, I have an idea!
X always marks the spot. Piracy Rule #27. So, I just draw an X right here, and that's where the treasure'll be!
That's just about the dumbest idea of all time. Cmon, let's get the van. We've still got time to sell stuff before 6:00.
Ooh! Lookit!
Yay!

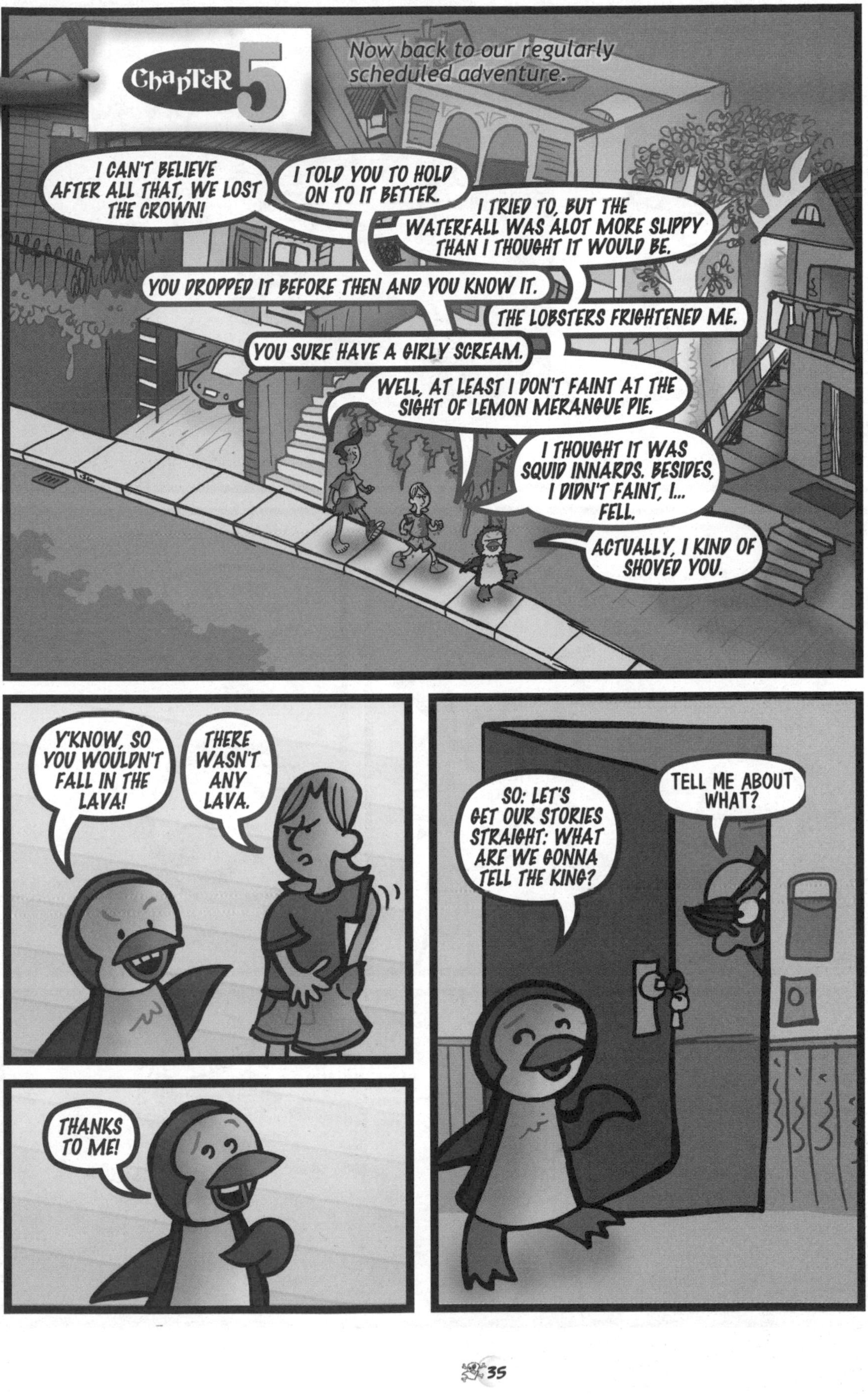
Chapter 5
Now back to our regularly scheduled adventure.
I CAN'T BELIEVE AFTER ALL THAT, WE LOST THE CROWN!
I TOLD YOU TO HOLD ON TO IT BETTER.
I TRIED TO, BUT THE WATERFALL WAS ALOT MORE SLIPPY THAN I THOUGHT IT WOULD BE.
YOU DROPPED IT BEFORE THEN AND YOU KNOW IT.
THE LOBSTERS FRIGHTENED ME.
YOU SURE HAVE A GIRLY SCREAM.
WELL, AT LEAST I DON'T FAINT AT THE SIGHT OF LEMON MERANGUE PIE.
I THOUGHT IT WAS SQUID INNARDS. BESIDES, I DIDN'T FAINT, I... FELL.
ACTUALLY, I KIND OF SHOVED YOU.
Y'KNOW, SO YOU WOULDN'T FALL IN THE LAVA!
THERE WASN'T ANY LAVA.
THANKS TO ME!
SO: LET'S GET OUR STORIES STRAIGHT: WHAT ARE WE GONNA TELL THE KING?
TELL ME ABOUT WHAT?

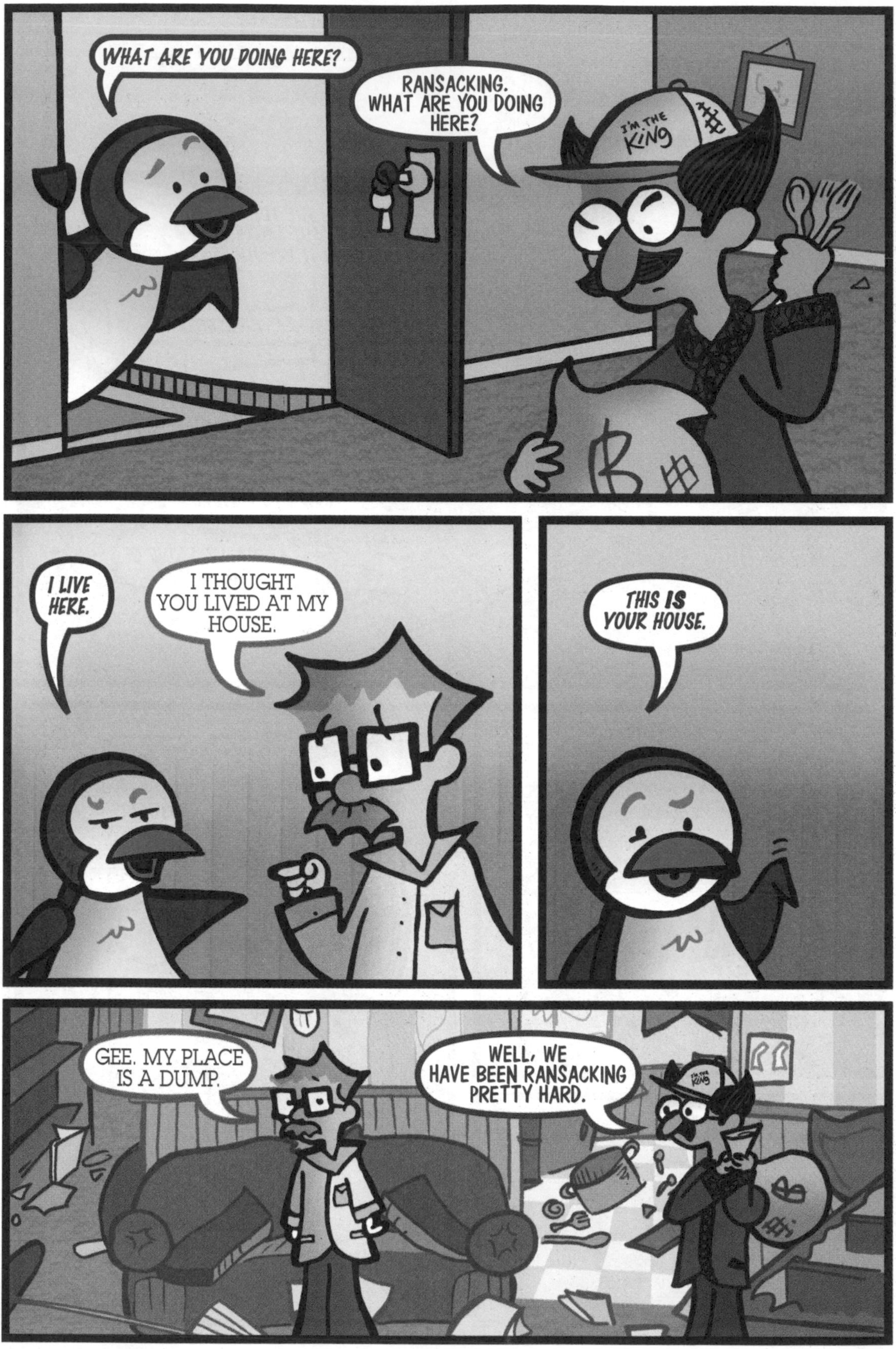
WHAT ARE YOU DOING HERE?
RANSACKING. WHAT ARE YOU DOING HERE?
I'M THE KING
I LIVE HERE.
I THOUGHT YOU LIVED AT MY HOUSE.
THIS IS YOUR HOUSE.
GEE. MY PLACE IS A DUMP.
WELL, WE HAVE BEEN RANSACKING PRETTY HARD.

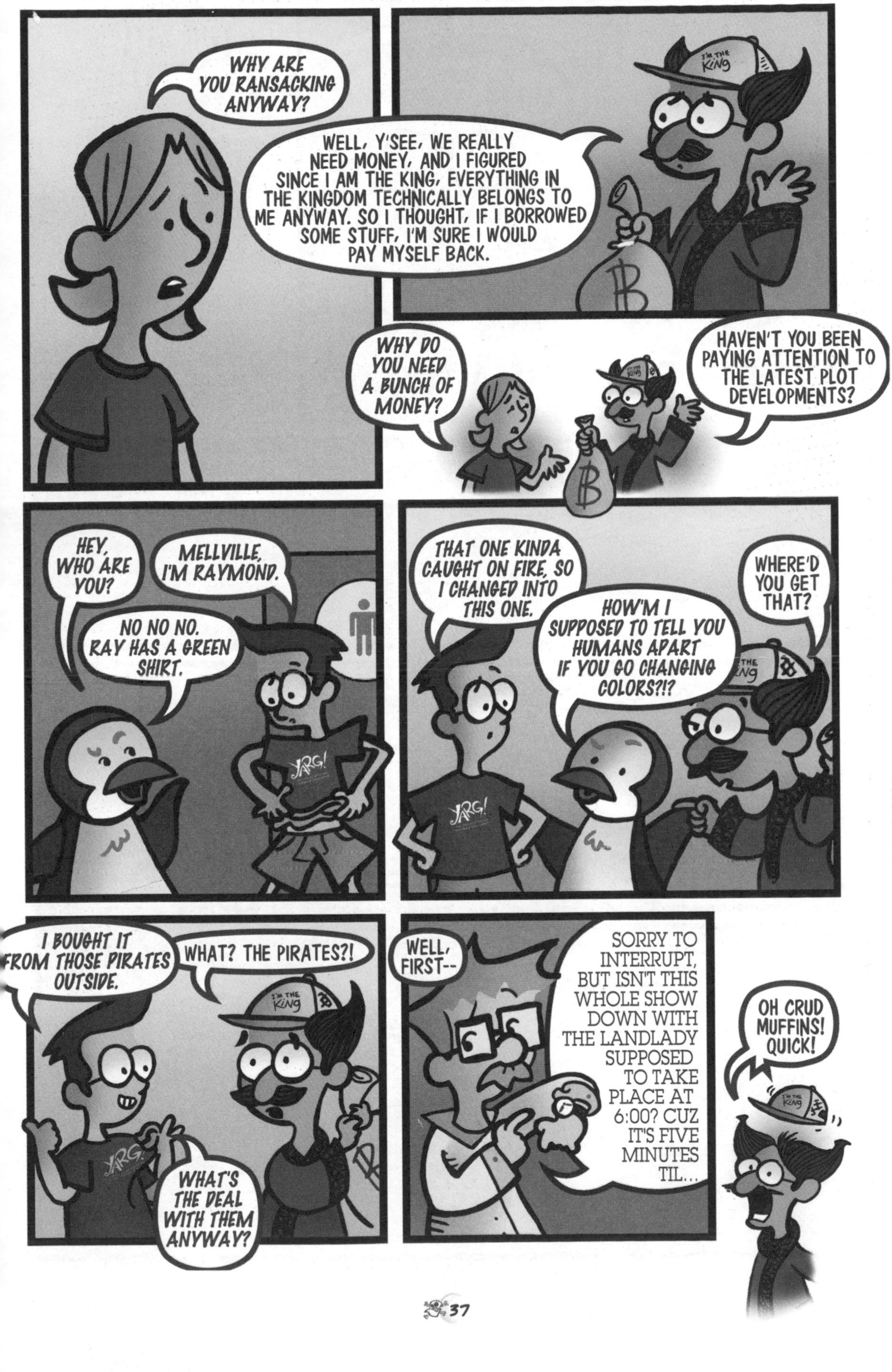
WHY ARE YOU RANSACKING ANYWAY?
WELL, Y'SEE, WE REALLY NEED MONEY, AND I FIGURED SINCE I AM THE KING, EVERYTHING IN THE KINGDOM TECHNICALLY BELONGS TO ME ANYWAY. SO I THOUGHT, IF I BORROWED SOME STUFF, I'M SURE I WOULD PAY MYSELF BACK.
I'M THE KING
WHY DO YOU NEED A BUNCH OF MONEY?
HAVEN'T YOU BEEN PAYING ATTENTION TO THE LATEST PLOT DEVELOPMENTS?
HEY, WHO ARE YOU?
MELLVILLE, I'M RAYMOND.
NO NO NO. RAY HAS A GREEN SHIRT.
YARG!
THAT ONE KINDA CAUGHT ON FIRE, SO I CHANGED INTO THIS ONE.
HOW'M I SUPPOSED TO TELL YOU HUMANS APART IF YOU GO CHANGING COLORS?!?
WHERE'D YOU GET THAT?
I BOUGHT IT FROM THOSE PIRATES OUTSIDE.
WHAT? THE PIRATES?!
WHAT'S THE DEAL WITH THEM ANYWAY?
WELL, FIRST--
SORRY TO INTERRUPT, BUT ISN'T THIS WHOLE SHOW DOWN WITH THE LANDLADY SUPPOSED TO TAKE PLACE AT 6:00? CUZ IT'S FIVE MINUTES TIL...
OH CRUD MUFFINS! QUICK!

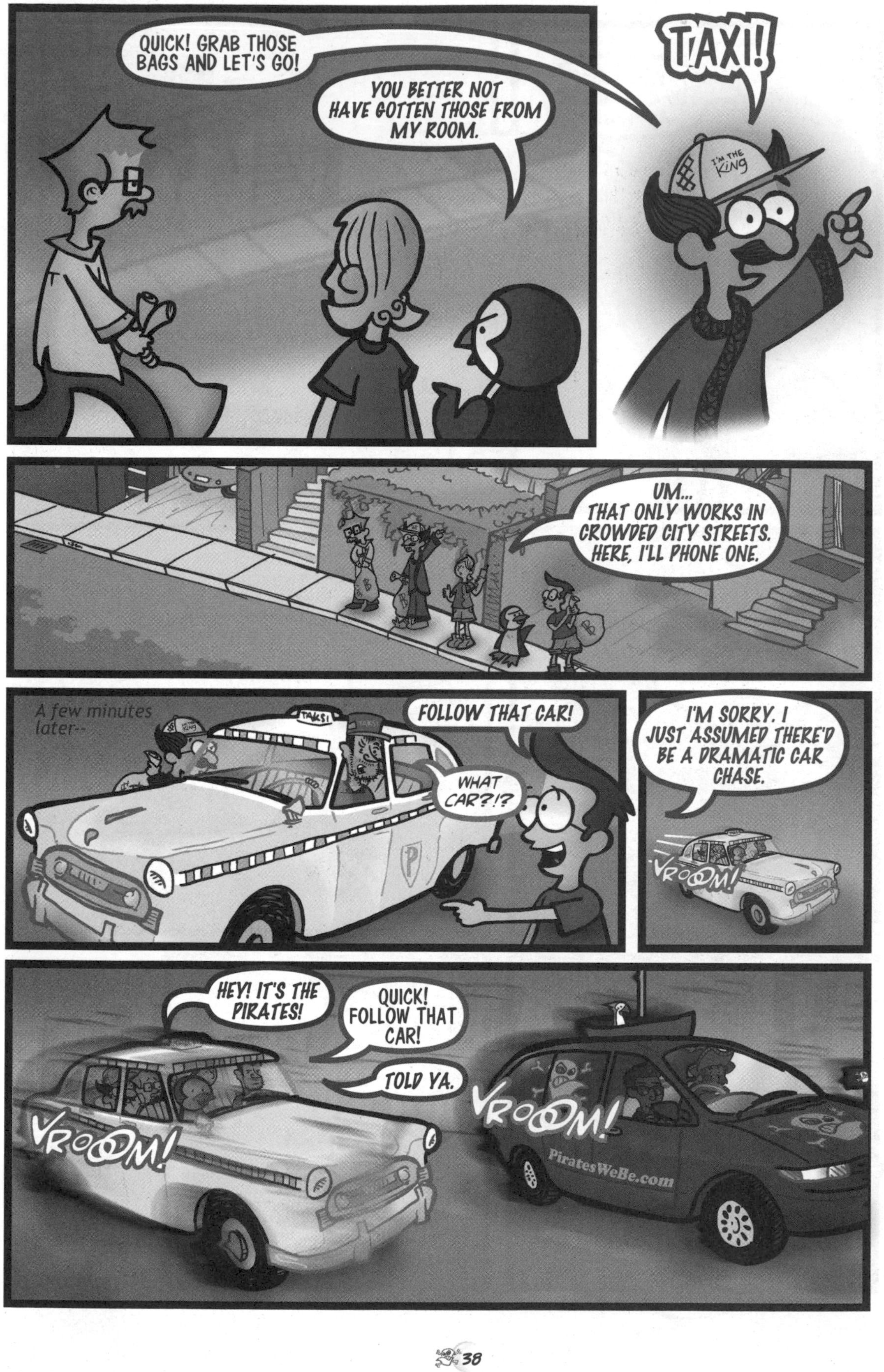
QUICK! GRAB THOSE BAGS AND LET'S GO!
YOU BETTER NOT HAVE GOTTEN THOSE FROM MY ROOM.
TAXI!
I'M THE King
UM... THAT ONLY WORKS IN CROWDED CITY STREETS. HERE, I'LL PHONE ONE.
A few minutes later--
TAKSI
FOLLOW THAT CAR!
WHAT CAR?!?
I'M SORRY. I JUST ASSUMED THERE'D BE A DRAMATIC CAR CHASE.
VROOM!
HEY! IT'S THE PIRATES!
QUICK! FOLLOW THAT CAR!
TOLD YA.
VROOM!
VROOM!
PiratesWeBe.com

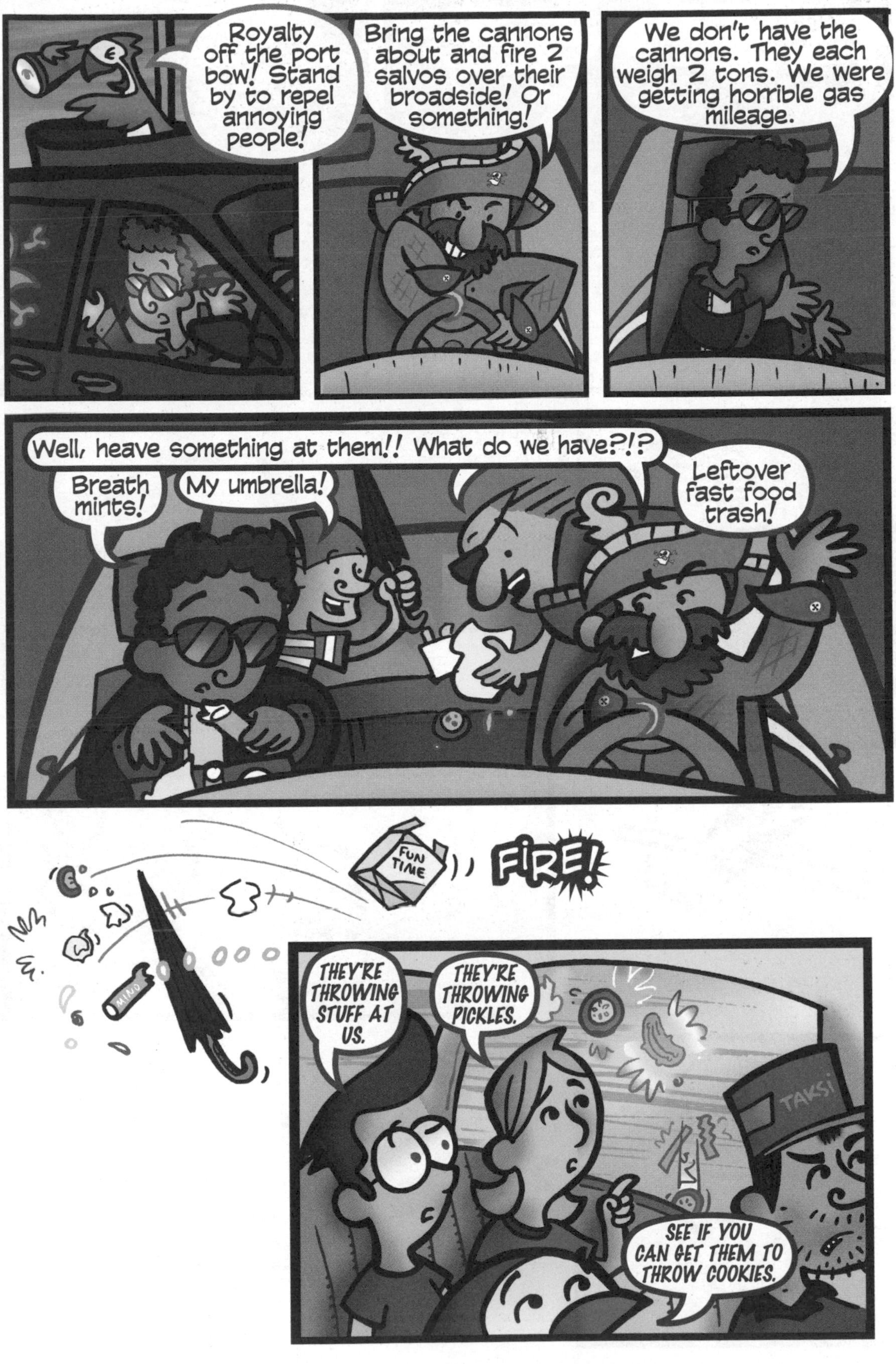
Royalty off the port bow! Stand by to repel annoying people!
Bring the cannons about and fire 2 salvos over their broadside! Or something!
We don't have the cannons. They each weigh 2 tons. We were getting horrible gas mileage.
Well, heave something at them!! What do we have?!?
Breath mints!
My umbrella!
Leftover fast food trash!
FUN TIME
FIRE!
MINO
THEY'RE THROWING STUFF AT US.
THEY'RE THROWING PICKLES.
TAKSI
SEE IF YOU CAN GET THEM TO THROW COOKIES.

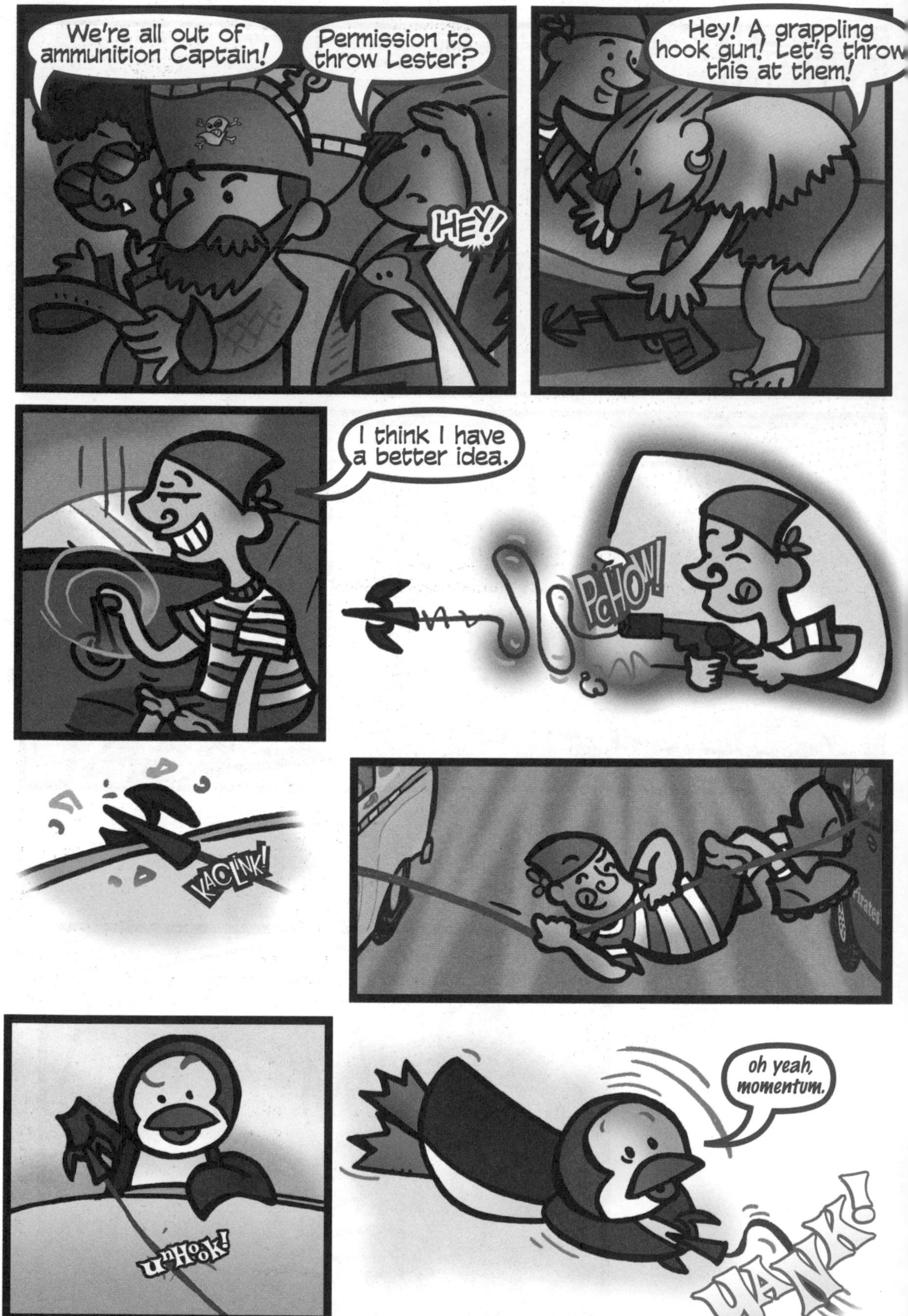
We're all out of ammunition Captain!
Permission to throw Lester?
HEY!
Hey! A grappling hook gun! Let's throw this at them!
I think I have a better idea.
POCHOW!
KACLINK!
Pirates
unHook!
oh yeah, momentum.
YANK!

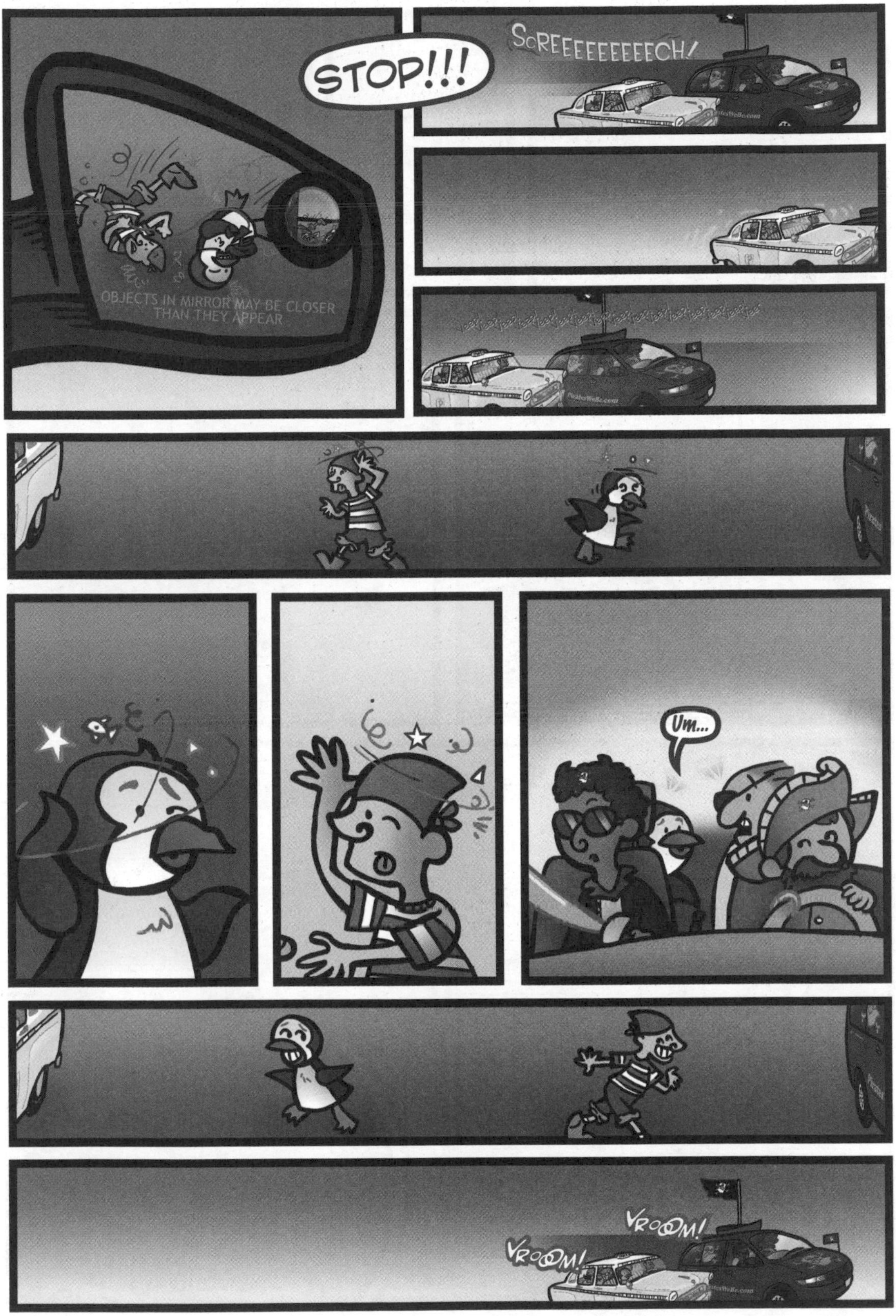
STOP!!!
OBJECTS IN MIRROR MAY BE CLOSER THAN THEY APPEAR
ScREEEEEEEEEECH!
Um...
VROOM!
VROOM!

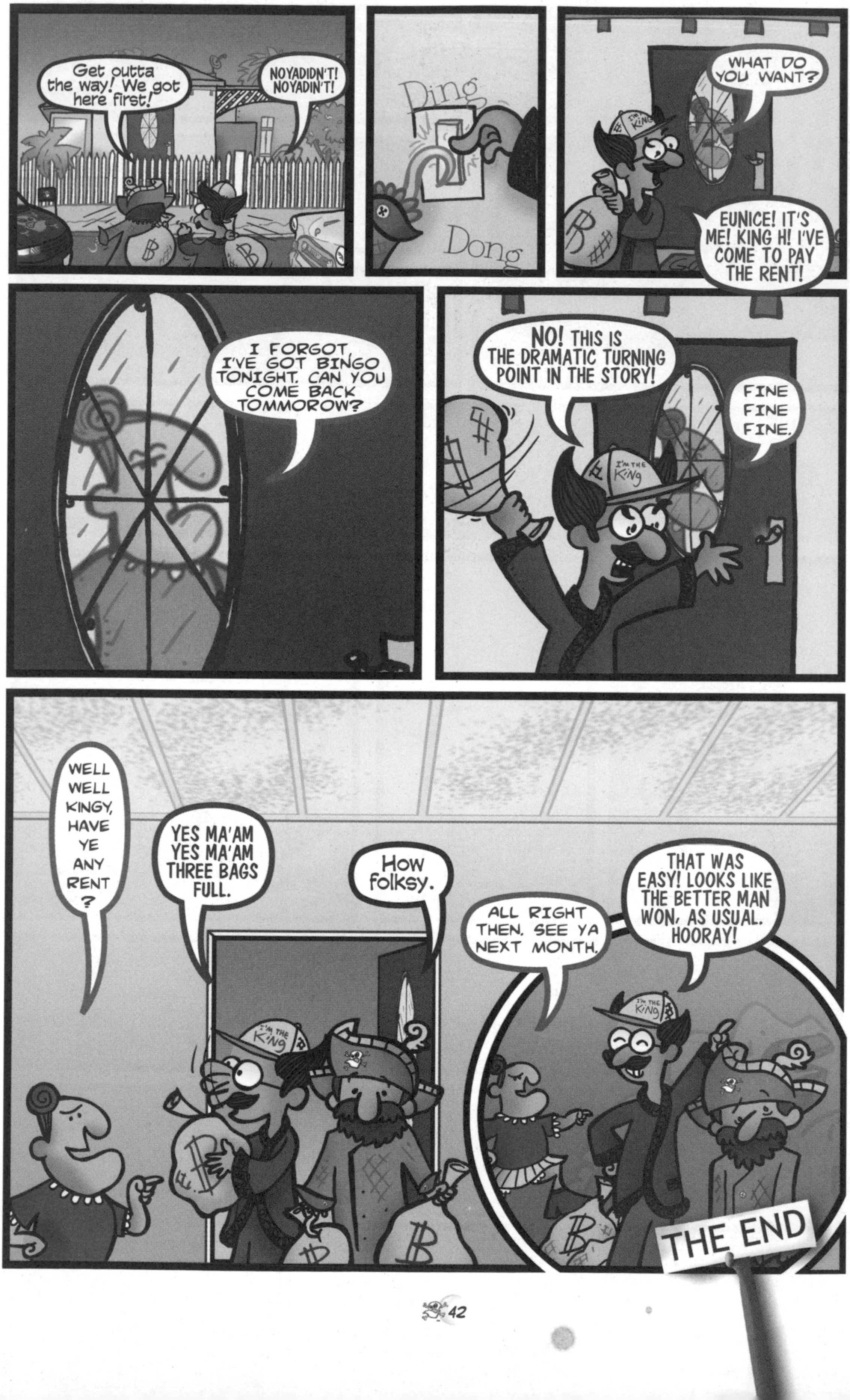
Get outta the way! We got here first!
NOYADIDN'T! NOYADIN'T!
Ding
Dong
WHAT DO YOU WANT?
EUNICE! IT'S ME! KING H! I'VE COME TO PAY THE RENT!
I FORGOT. I'VE GOT BINGO TONIGHT. CAN YOU COME BACK TOMMOROW?
NO! THIS IS THE DRAMATIC TURNING POINT IN THE STORY!
FINE FINE FINE.
WELL WELL KINGY, HAVE YE ANY RENT?
YES MA'AM YES MA'AM THREE BAGS FULL.
How folksy.
ALL RIGHT THEN. SEE YA NEXT MONTH.
THAT WAS EASY! LOOKS LIKE THE BETTER MAN WON, AS USUAL. HOORAY!
THE END

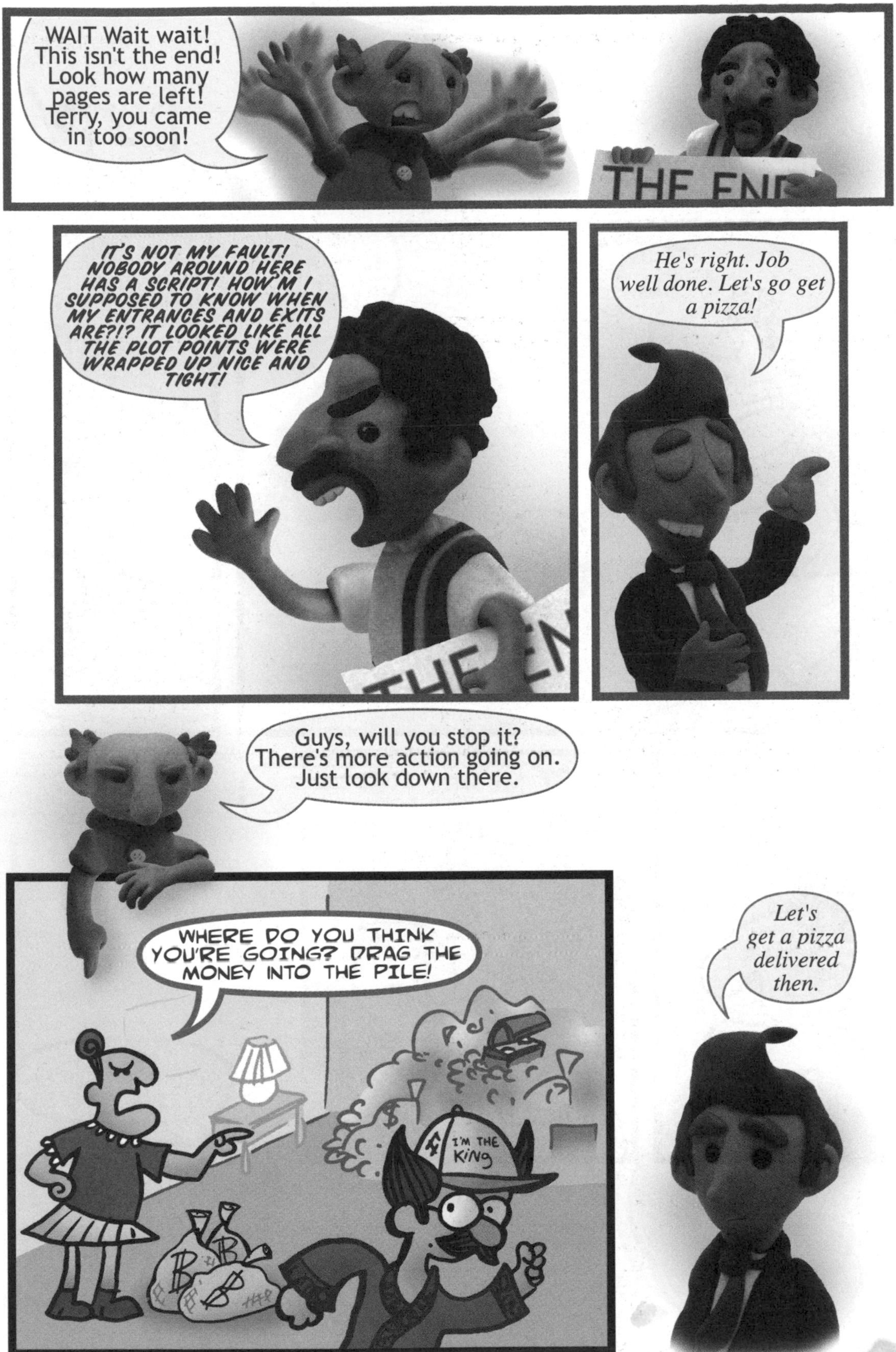

WAIT Wait wait! This isn't the end! Look how many pages are left! Terry, you came in too soon!
THE END
IT'S NOT MY FAULT! NOBODY AROUND HERE HAS A SCRIPT! HOW'M I SUPPOSED TO KNOW WHEN MY ENTRANCES AND EXITS ARE?!? IT LOOKED LIKE ALL THE PLOT POINTS WERE WRAPPED UP NICE AND TIGHT!
He's right. Job well done. Let's go get a pizza!
Guys, will you stop it? There's more action going on. Just look down there.
WHERE DO YOU THINK YOU'RE GOING? DRAG THE MONEY INTO THE PILE!
I'M THE KING
Let's get a pizza delivered then.

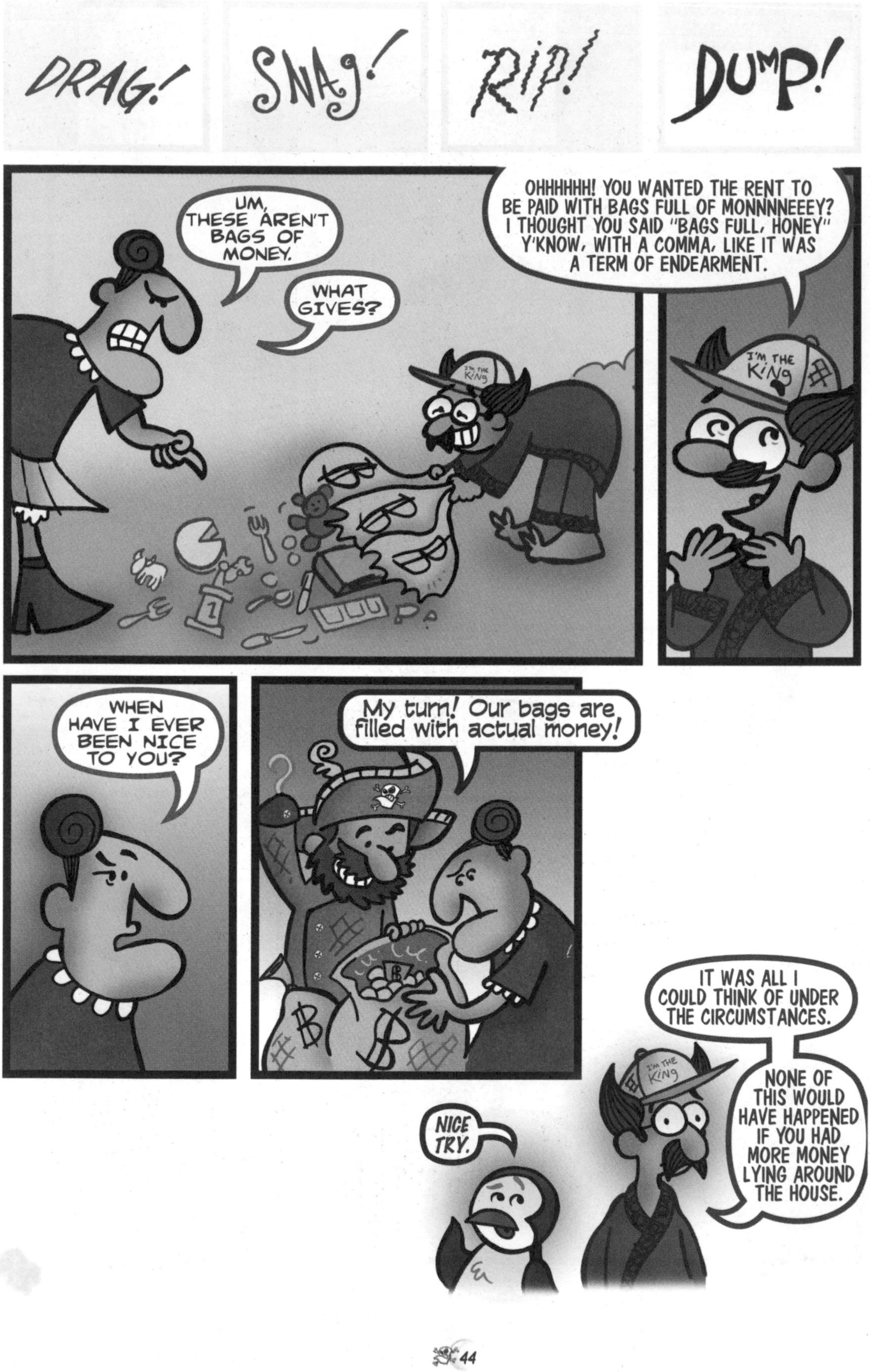
DRAG!
SNAG!
RIP!
DUMP!
UM, THESE AREN'T BAGS OF MONEY.
WHAT GIVES?
I'M THE KING
OHHHHHH! YOU WANTED THE RENT TO BE PAID WITH BAGS FULL OF MONNNNEEEY? I THOUGHT YOU SAID "BAGS FULL, HONEY" Y'KNOW, WITH A COMMA, LIKE IT WAS A TERM OF ENDEARMENT.
I'M THE KING
WHEN HAVE I EVER BEEN NICE TO YOU?
My turn! Our bags are filled with actual money!
IT WAS ALL I COULD THINK OF UNDER THE CIRCUMSTANCES.
NONE OF THIS WOULD HAVE HAPPENED IF YOU HAD MORE MONEY LYING AROUND THE HOUSE.
I'M THE KING
NICE TRY.

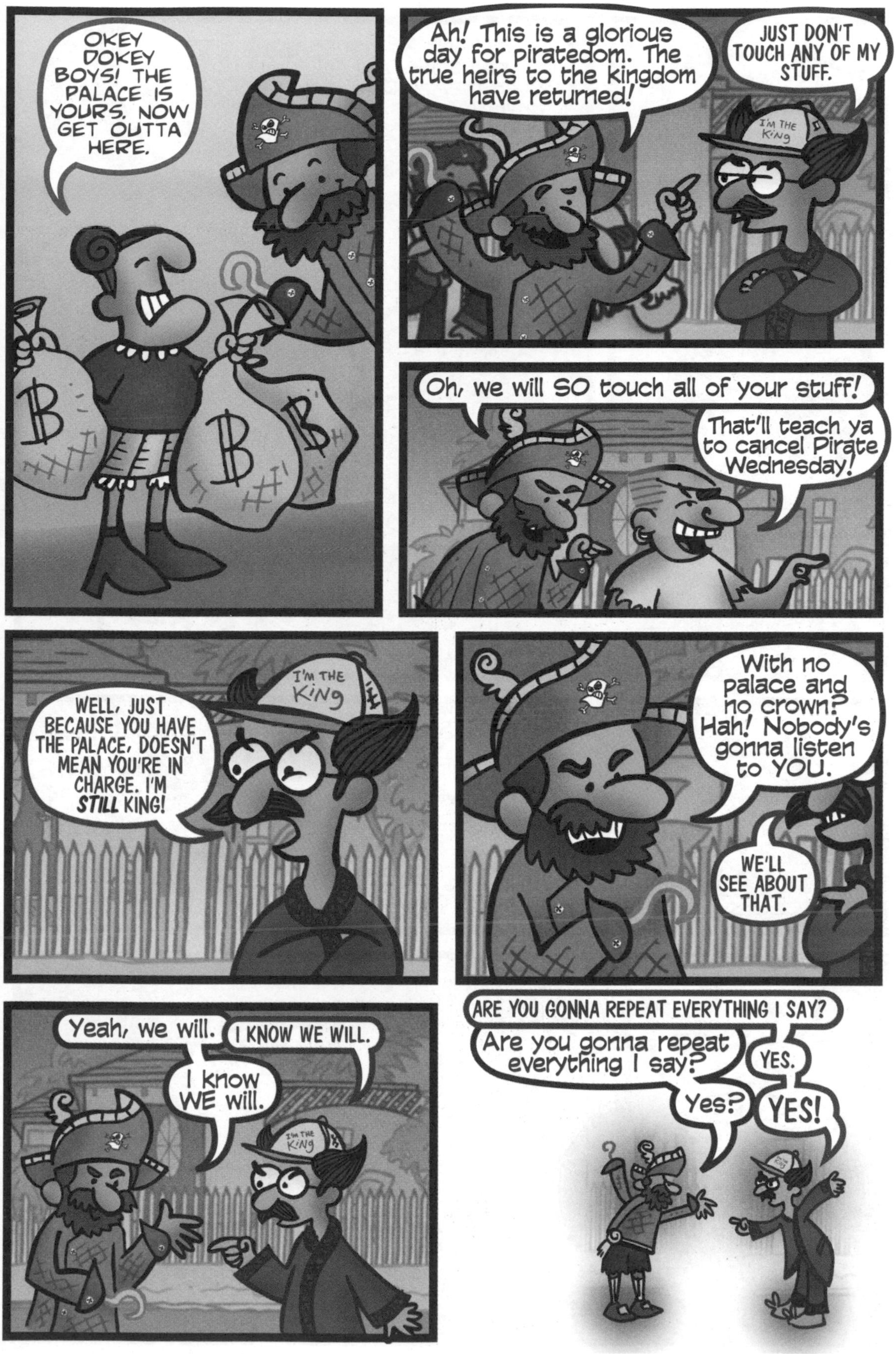
OKEY DOKEY BOYS! THE PALACE IS YOURS. NOW GET OUTTA HERE.
Ah! This is a glorious day for piratedom. The true heirs to the kingdom have returned!
JUST DON'T TOUCH ANY OF MY STUFF.
I'M THE KING
Oh, we will SO touch all of your stuff!
That'll teach ya to cancel Pirate Wednesday!
I'M THE KING
WELL, JUST BECAUSE YOU HAVE THE PALACE, DOESN'T MEAN YOU'RE IN CHARGE. I'M STILL KING!
With no palace and no crown? Hah! Nobody's gonna listen to YOU.
WE'LL SEE ABOUT THAT.
Yeah, we will.
I KNOW WE WILL.
I know WE will.
ARE YOU GONNA REPEAT EVERYTHING I SAY?
Are you gonna repeat everything I say?
YES.
Yes?
YES!

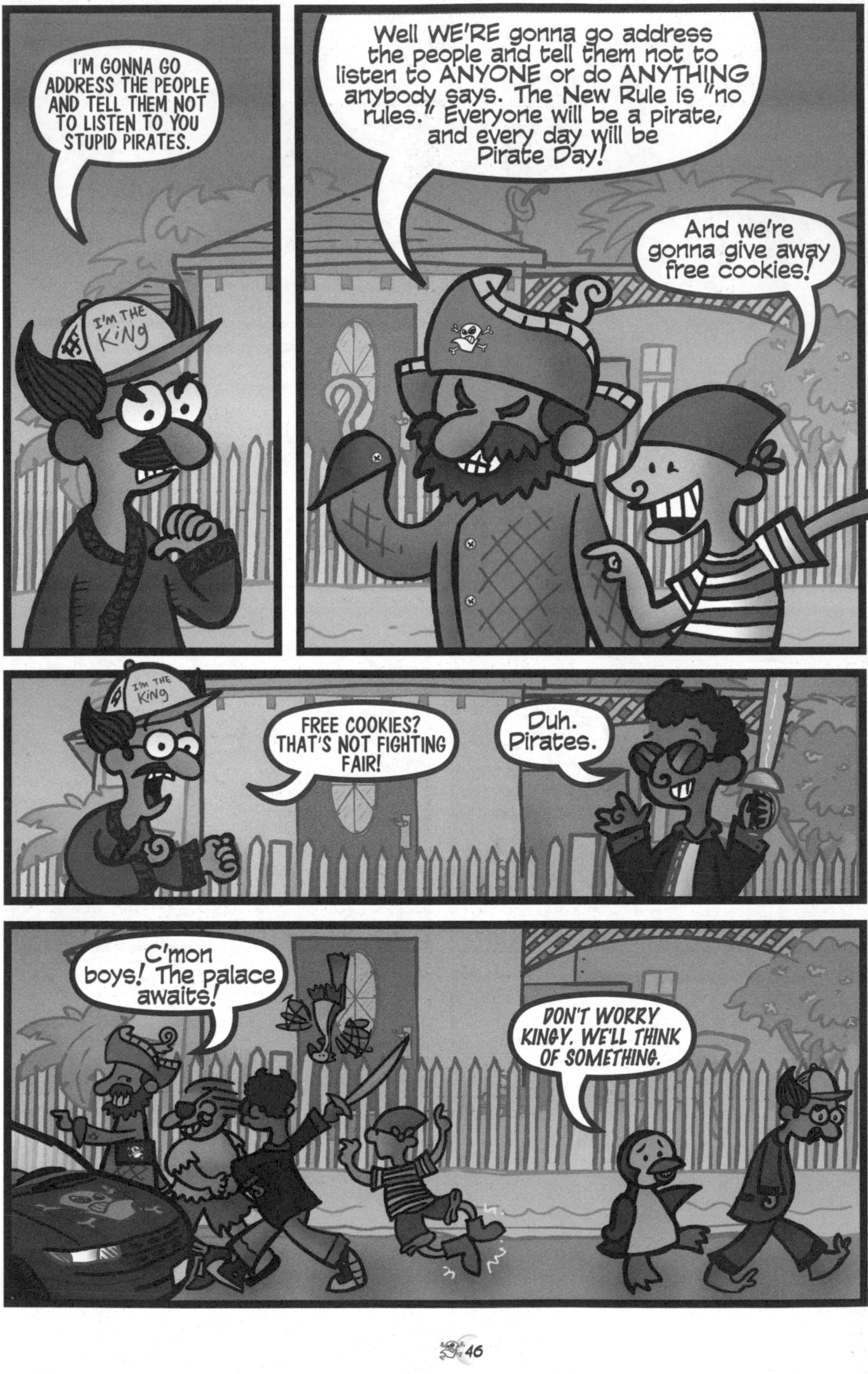
I'M GONNA GO ADDRESS THE PEOPLE AND TELL THEM NOT TO LISTEN TO YOU STUPID PIRATES.
I'M THE KING
Well WE'RE gonna go address the people and tell them not to listen to ANYONE or do ANYTHING anybody says. The New Rule is "no rules." Everyone will be a pirate, and every day will be Pirate Day!
And we're gonna give away free cookies!
I'M THE KING
FREE COOKIES? THAT'S NOT FIGHTING FAIR!
Duh. Pirates.
C'mon boys! The palace awaits!
DON'T WORRY KINGY. WE'LL THINK OF SOMETHING.

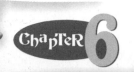

# Chapter 6

In which the pirates get to work.

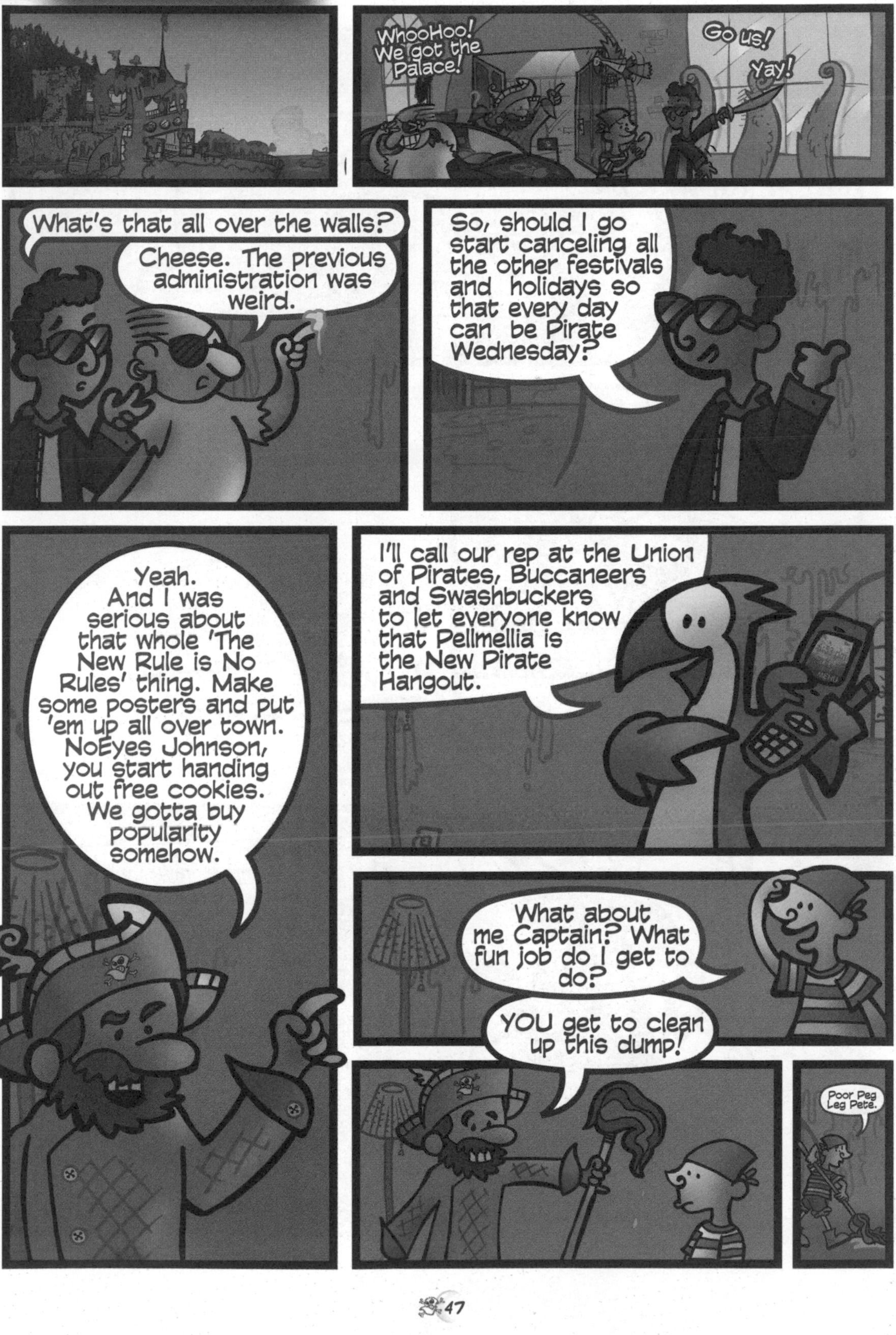
WhooHoo! We got the Palace!
Go us!
Yay!
What's that all over the walls?
Cheese. The previous administration was weird.
So, should I go start canceling all the other festivals and holidays so that every day can be Pirate Wednesday?
Yeah. And I was serious about that whole 'The New Rule is No Rules' thing. Make some posters and put 'em up all over town. NoEyes Johnson, you start handing out free cookies. We gotta buy popularity somehow.
I'll call our rep at the Union of Pirates, Buccaneers and Swashbuckers to let everyone know that Pellmellia is the New Pirate Hangout.
What about me Captain? What fun job do I get to do?
YOU get to clean up this dump!
Poor Peg Leg Pete.

# Chapter 7

In which the king doesn't ~~gets to work.~~

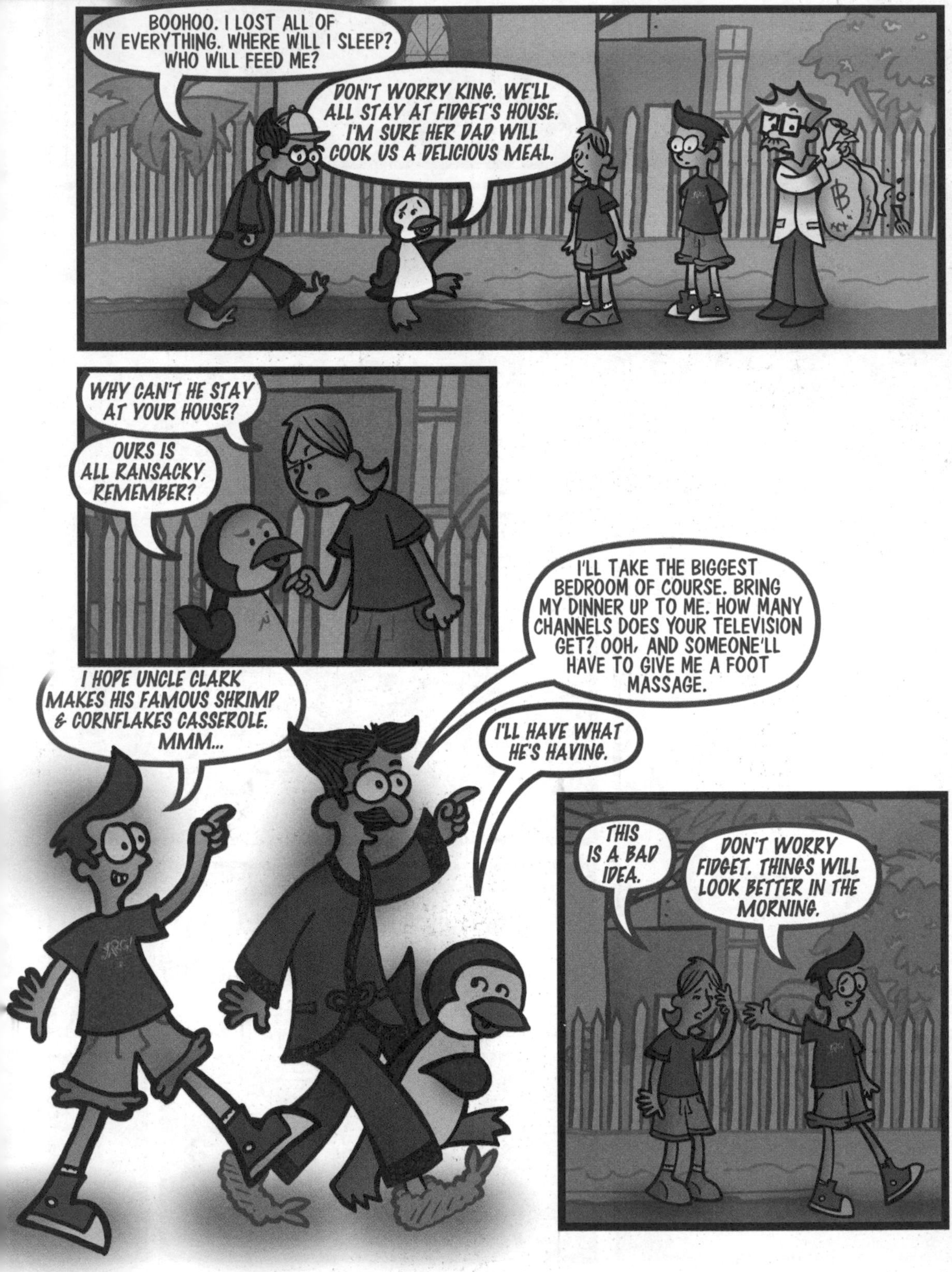

BOOHOO. I LOST ALL OF MY EVERYTHING. WHERE WILL I SLEEP? WHO WILL FEED ME?
DON'T WORRY KING. WE'LL ALL STAY AT FIDGET'S HOUSE. I'M SURE HER DAD WILL COOK US A DELICIOUS MEAL.
WHY CAN'T HE STAY AT YOUR HOUSE?
OURS IS ALL RANSACKY, REMEMBER?
I'LL TAKE THE BIGGEST BEDROOM OF COURSE. BRING MY DINNER UP TO ME. HOW MANY CHANNELS DOES YOUR TELEVISION GET? OOH, AND SOMEONE'LL HAVE TO GIVE ME A FOOT MASSAGE.
I HOPE UNCLE CLARK MAKES HIS FAMOUS SHRIMP & CORNFLAKES CASSEROLE. MMM...
I'LL HAVE WHAT HE'S HAVING.
THIS IS A BAD IDEA.
DON'T WORRY FIDGET. THINGS WILL LOOK BETTER IN THE MORNING.

*The next morning...*

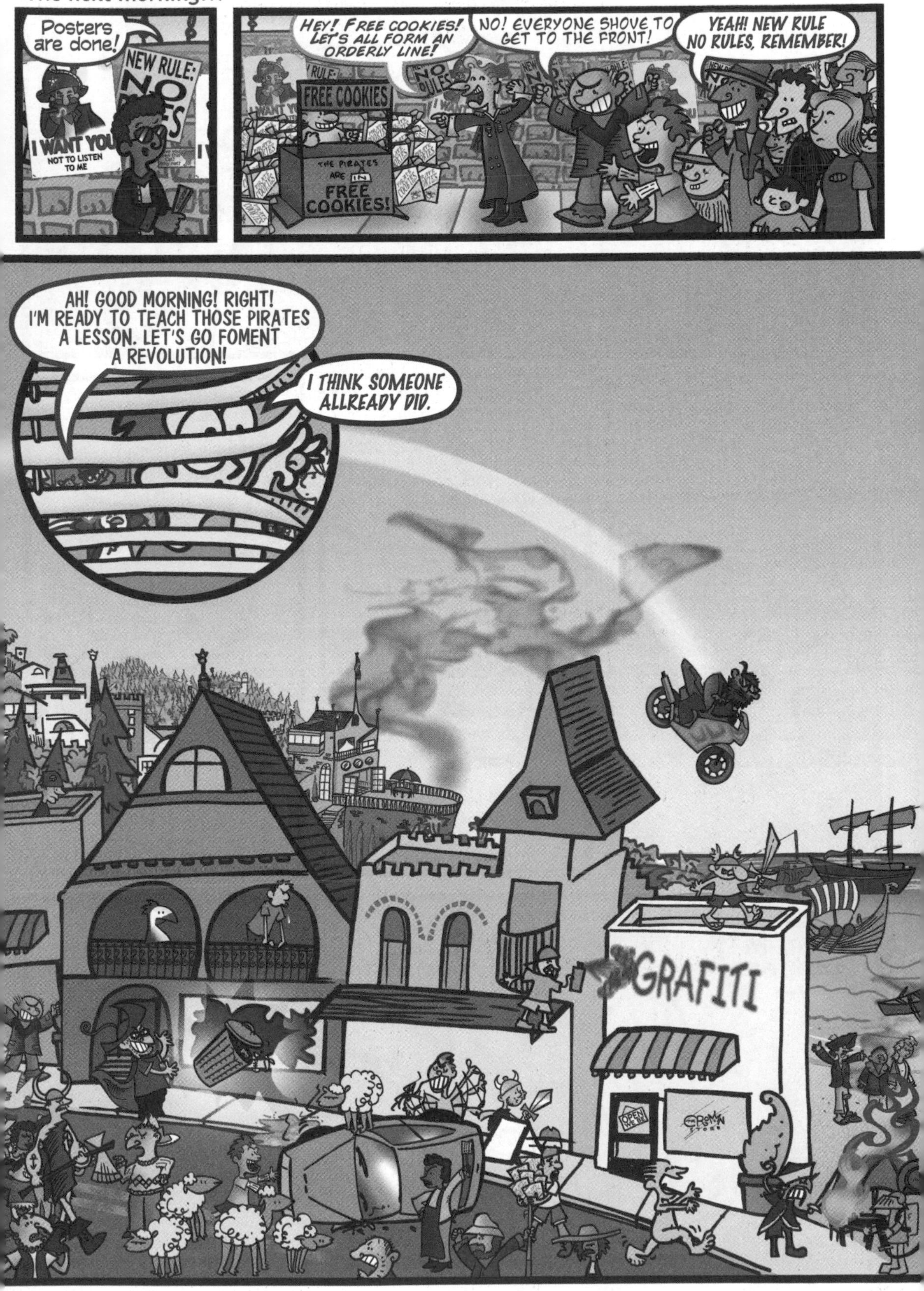
Posters are done!
NEW RULE: NO RULES
I WANT YOU NOT TO LISTEN TO ME
HEY! FREE COOKIES! LET'S ALL FORM AN ORDERLY LINE!
NO! EVERYONE SHOVE TO GET TO THE FRONT!
YEAH! NEW RULE NO RULES, REMEMBER!
FREE COOKIES
THE PIRATES ARE IN FREE COOKIES!
AH! GOOD MORNING! RIGHT! I'M READY TO TEACH THOSE PIRATES A LESSON. LET'S GO FOMENT A REVOLUTION!
I THINK SOMEONE ALLREADY DID.
GRAFITI

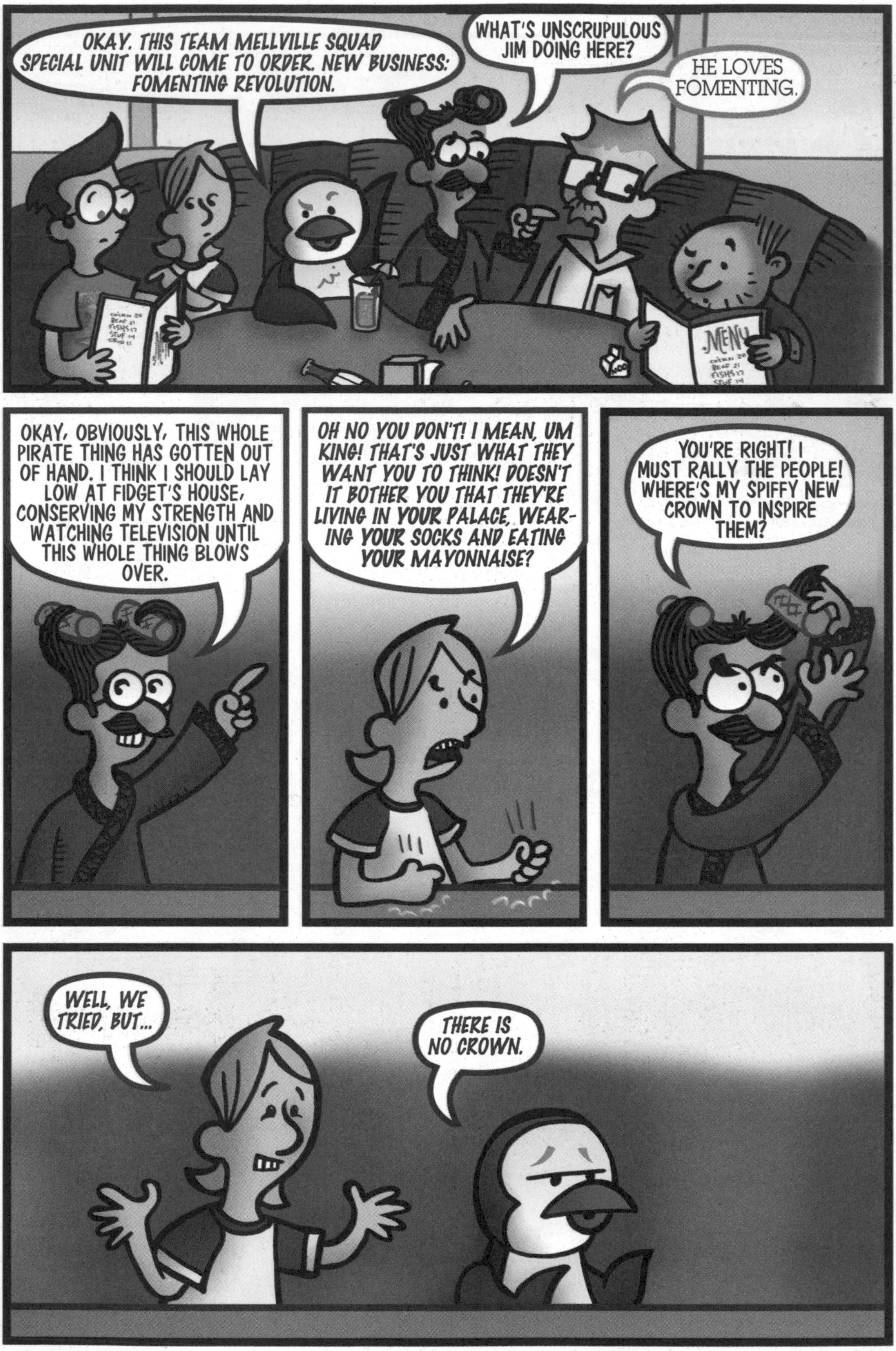
OKAY. THIS TEAM MELLVILLE SQUAD SPECIAL UNIT WILL COME TO ORDER. NEW BUSINESS: FOMENTING REVOLUTION.
WHAT'S UNSCRUPULOUS JIM DOING HERE?
HE LOVES FOMENTING.
MENU
OKAY, OBVIOUSLY, THIS WHOLE PIRATE THING HAS GOTTEN OUT OF HAND. I THINK I SHOULD LAY LOW AT FIDGET'S HOUSE, CONSERVING MY STRENGTH AND WATCHING TELEVISION UNTIL THIS WHOLE THING BLOWS OVER.
OH NO YOU DON'T! I MEAN, UM KING! THAT'S JUST WHAT THEY WANT YOU TO THINK! DOESN'T IT BOTHER YOU THAT THEY'RE LIVING IN YOUR PALACE, WEARING YOUR SOCKS AND EATING YOUR MAYONNAISE?
YOU'RE RIGHT! I MUST RALLY THE PEOPLE! WHERE'S MY SPIFFY NEW CROWN TO INSPIRE THEM?
WELL, WE TRIED, BUT...
THERE IS NO CROWN.

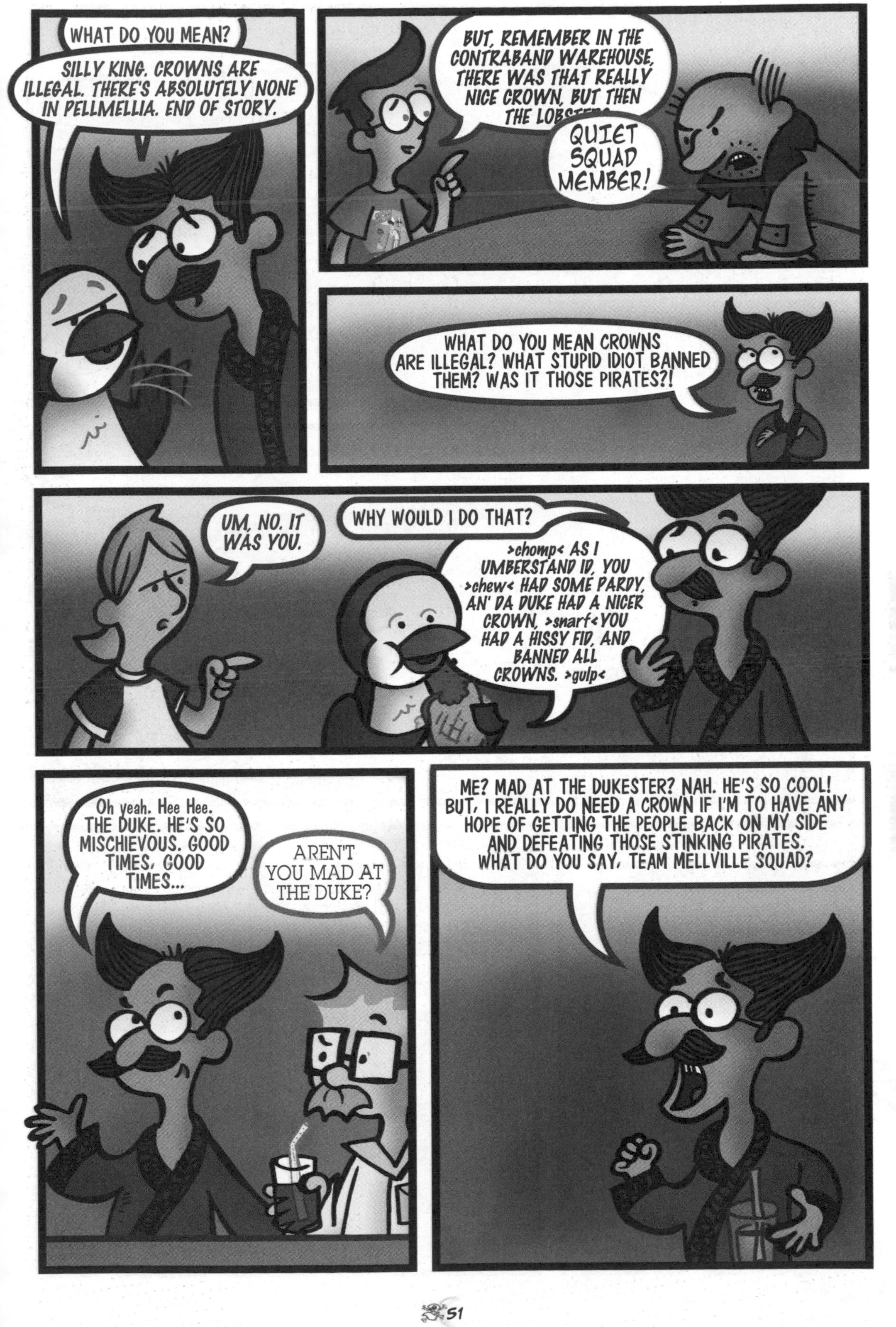
WHAT DO YOU MEAN?
SILLY KING. CROWNS ARE ILLEGAL. THERE'S ABSOLUTELY NONE IN PELLMELLIA. END OF STORY.
BUT, REMEMBER IN THE CONTRABAND WAREHOUSE, THERE WAS THAT REALLY NICE CROWN, BUT THEN THE LOBST
QUIET SQUAD MEMBER!
WHAT DO YOU MEAN CROWNS ARE ILLEGAL? WHAT STUPID IDIOT BANNED THEM? WAS IT THOSE PIRATES?!
UM, NO. IT WAS YOU.
WHY WOULD I DO THAT?
>chomp< AS I UMBERSTAND ID, YOU >chew< HAD SOME PARDY, AN' DA DUKE HAD A NICER CROWN, >snarf<YOU HAD A HISSY FID, AND BANNED ALL CROWNS. >gulp<
Oh yeah. Hee Hee. THE DUKE. HE'S SO MISCHIEVOUS. GOOD TIMES, GOOD TIMES...
AREN'T YOU MAD AT THE DUKE?
ME? MAD AT THE DUKESTER? NAH. HE'S SO COOL! BUT, I REALLY DO NEED A CROWN IF I'M TO HAVE ANY HOPE OF GETTING THE PEOPLE BACK ON MY SIDE AND DEFEATING THOSE STINKING PIRATES. WHAT DO YOU SAY, TEAM MELLVILLE SQUAD?

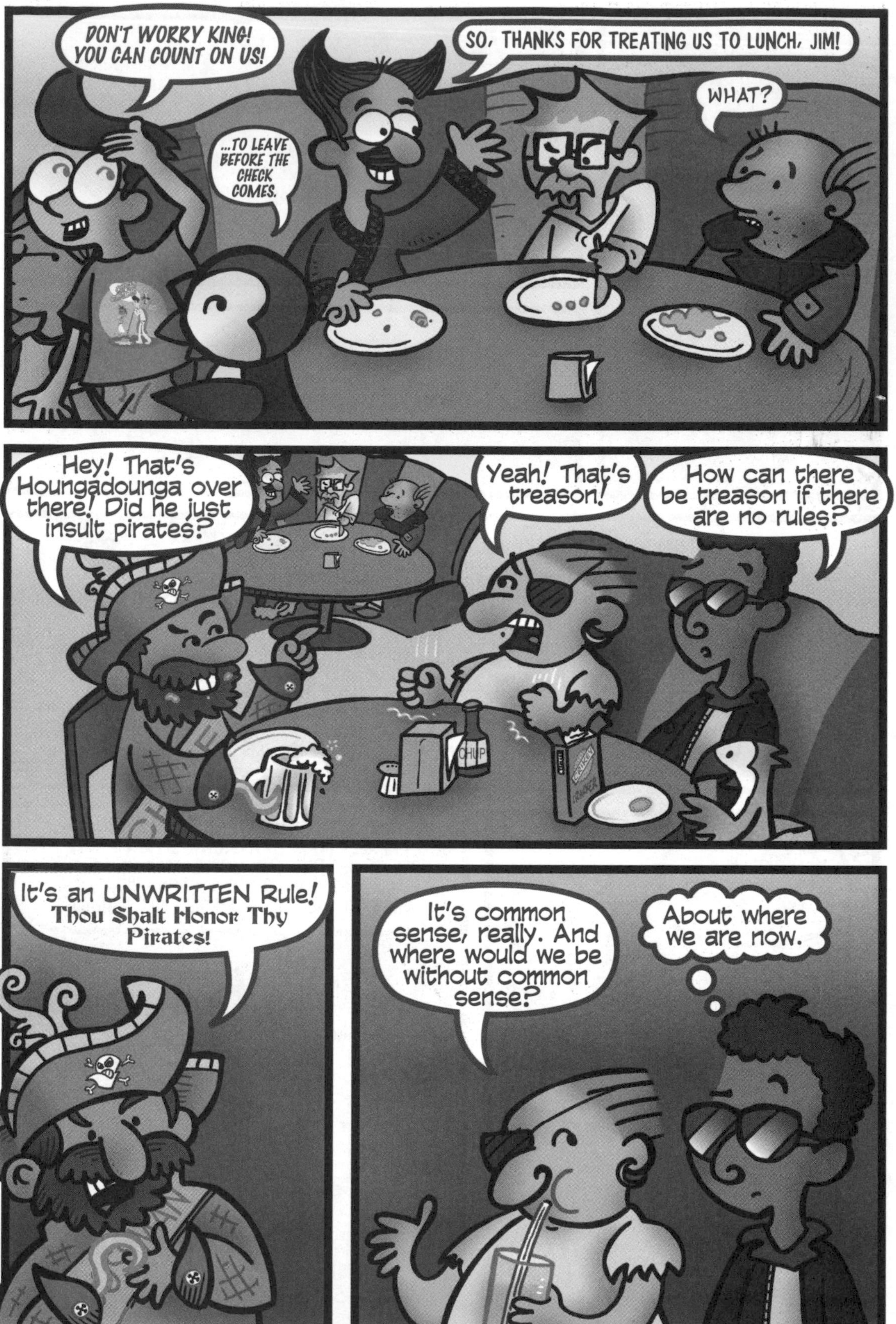
DON'T WORRY KING! YOU CAN COUNT ON US!
SO, THANKS FOR TREATING US TO LUNCH, JIM!
...TO LEAVE BEFORE THE CHECK COMES.
WHAT?
Hey! That's Houngadounga over there! Did he just insult pirates?
Yeah! That's treason!
How can there be treason if there are no rules?
It's an UNWRITTEN Rule! Thou Shalt Honor Thy Pirates!
It's common sense, really. And where would we be without common sense?
About where we are now.

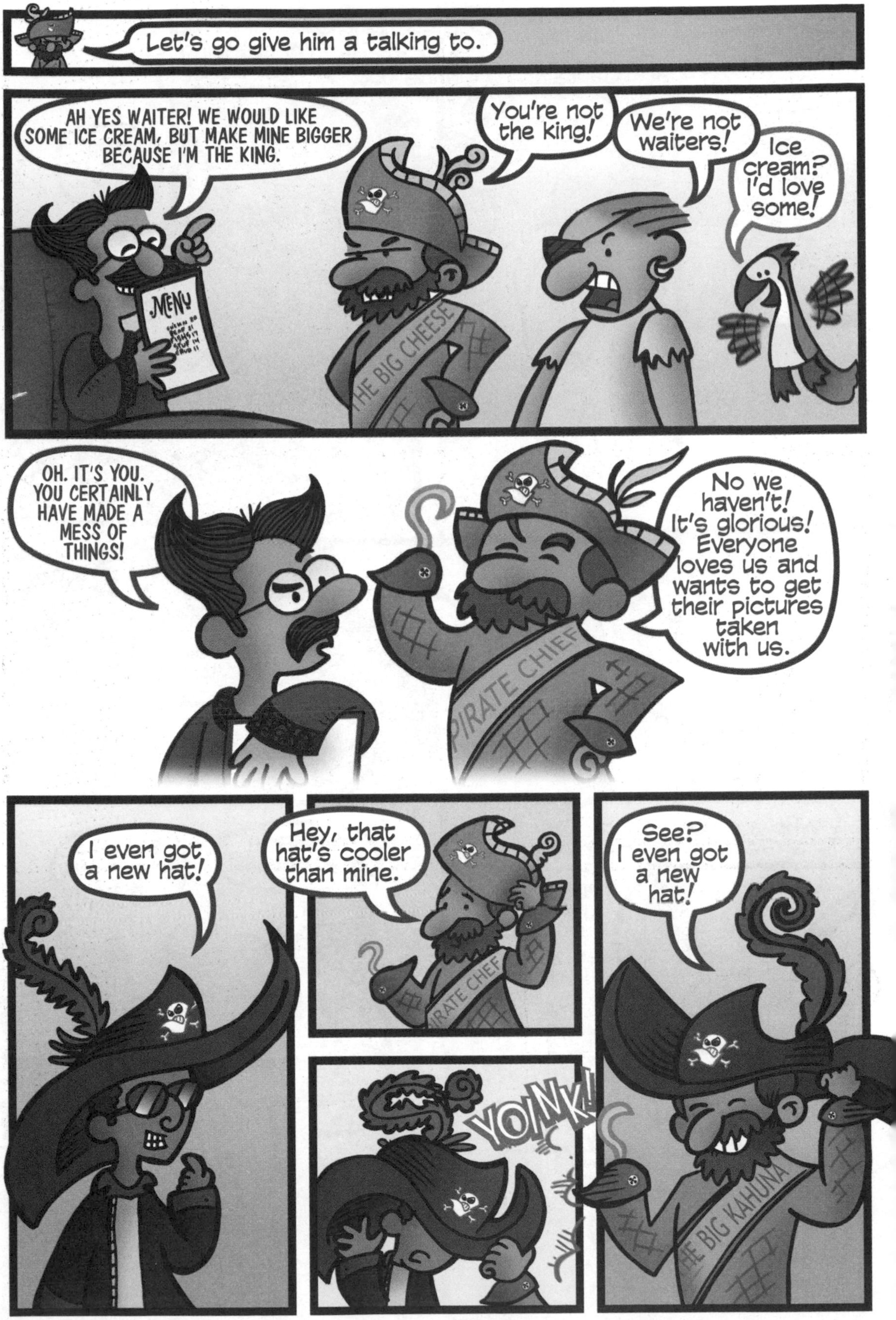
Let's go give him a talking to.
AH YES WAITER! WE WOULD LIKE SOME ICE CREAM, BUT MAKE MINE BIGGER BECAUSE I'M THE KING.
You're not the king!
We're not waiters!
Ice cream? I'd love some!
MENU
THE BIG CHEESE
OH. IT'S YOU. YOU CERTAINLY HAVE MADE A MESS OF THINGS!
No we haven't! It's glorious! Everyone loves us and wants to get their pictures taken with us.
PIRATE CHIEF
I even got a new hat!
Hey, that hat's cooler than mine.
PIRATE CHEF
YOINK!
See? I even got a new hat!
THE BIG KAHUNA

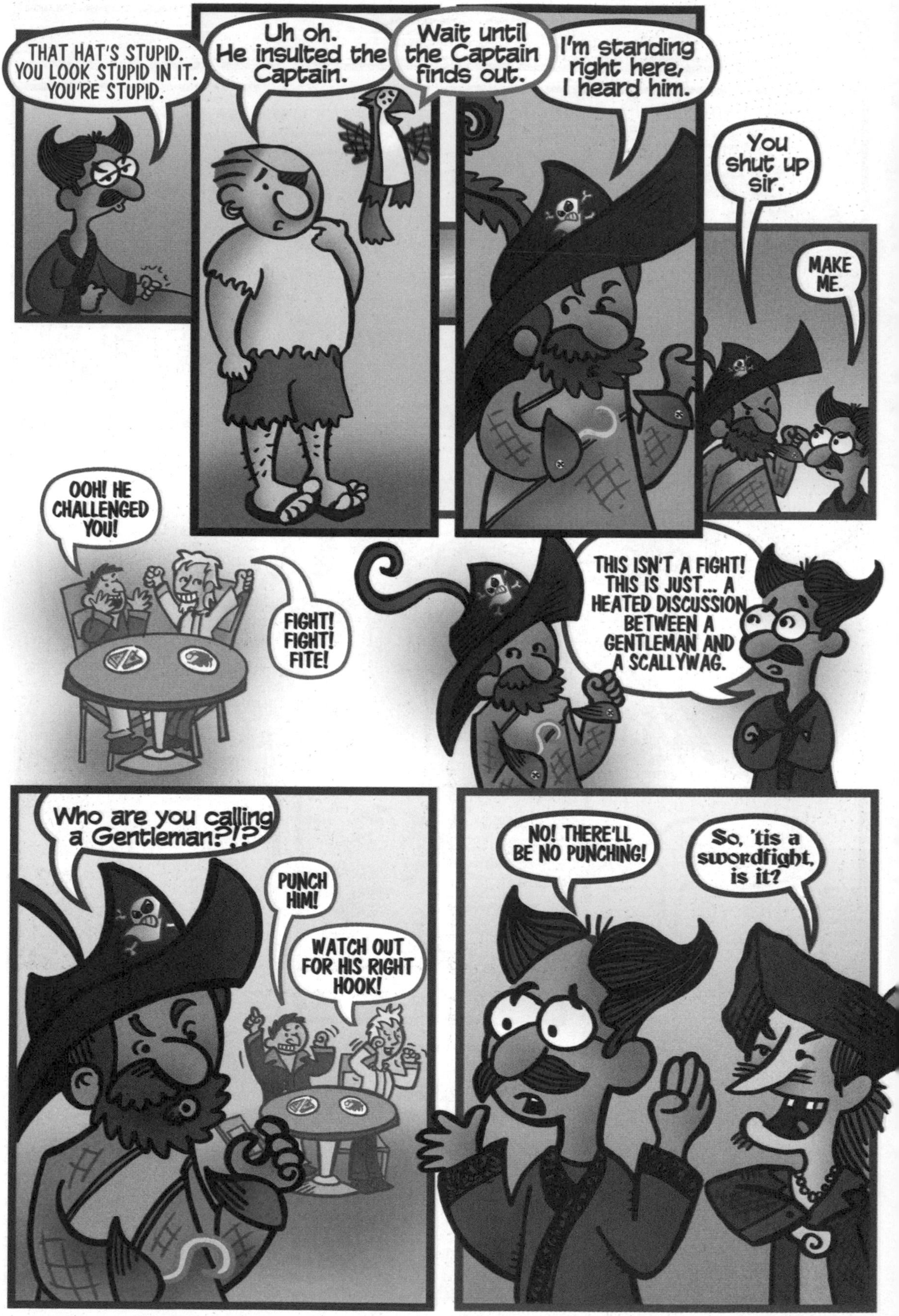
THAT HAT'S STUPID. YOU LOOK STUPID IN IT. YOU'RE STUPID.
Uh oh. He insulted the Captain.
Wait until the Captain finds out.
I'm standing right here, I heard him.
You shut up sir.
MAKE ME.
OOH! HE CHALLENGED YOU!
FIGHT! FIGHT! FITE!
THIS ISN'T A FIGHT! THIS IS JUST... A HEATED DISCUSSION BETWEEN A GENTLEMAN AND A SCALLYWAG.
Who are you calling a Gentleman?!?
PUNCH HIM!
WATCH OUT FOR HIS RIGHT HOOK!
NO! THERE'LL BE NO PUNCHING!
So, 'tis a swordfight, is it?

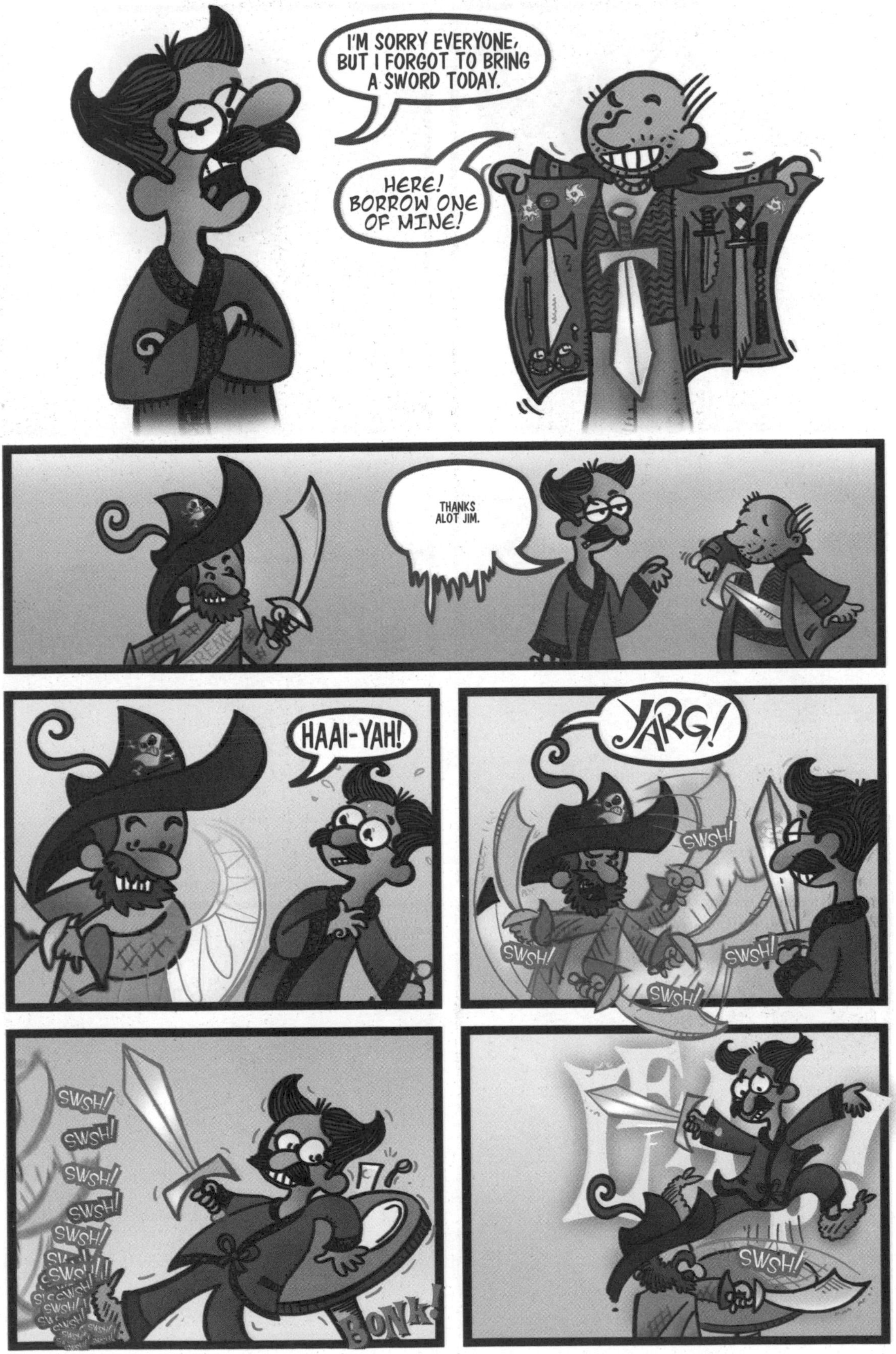
I'M SORRY EVERYONE, BUT I FORGOT TO BRING A SWORD TODAY.
HERE! BORROW ONE OF MINE!
THANKS ALOT JIM.
HAAI-YAH!
YARG!
SWSH!
SWSH!
SWSH!
SWSH!
SWSH!
SWSH!
SWSH!
SWSH!
SWSH!
BONK!
SWSH!

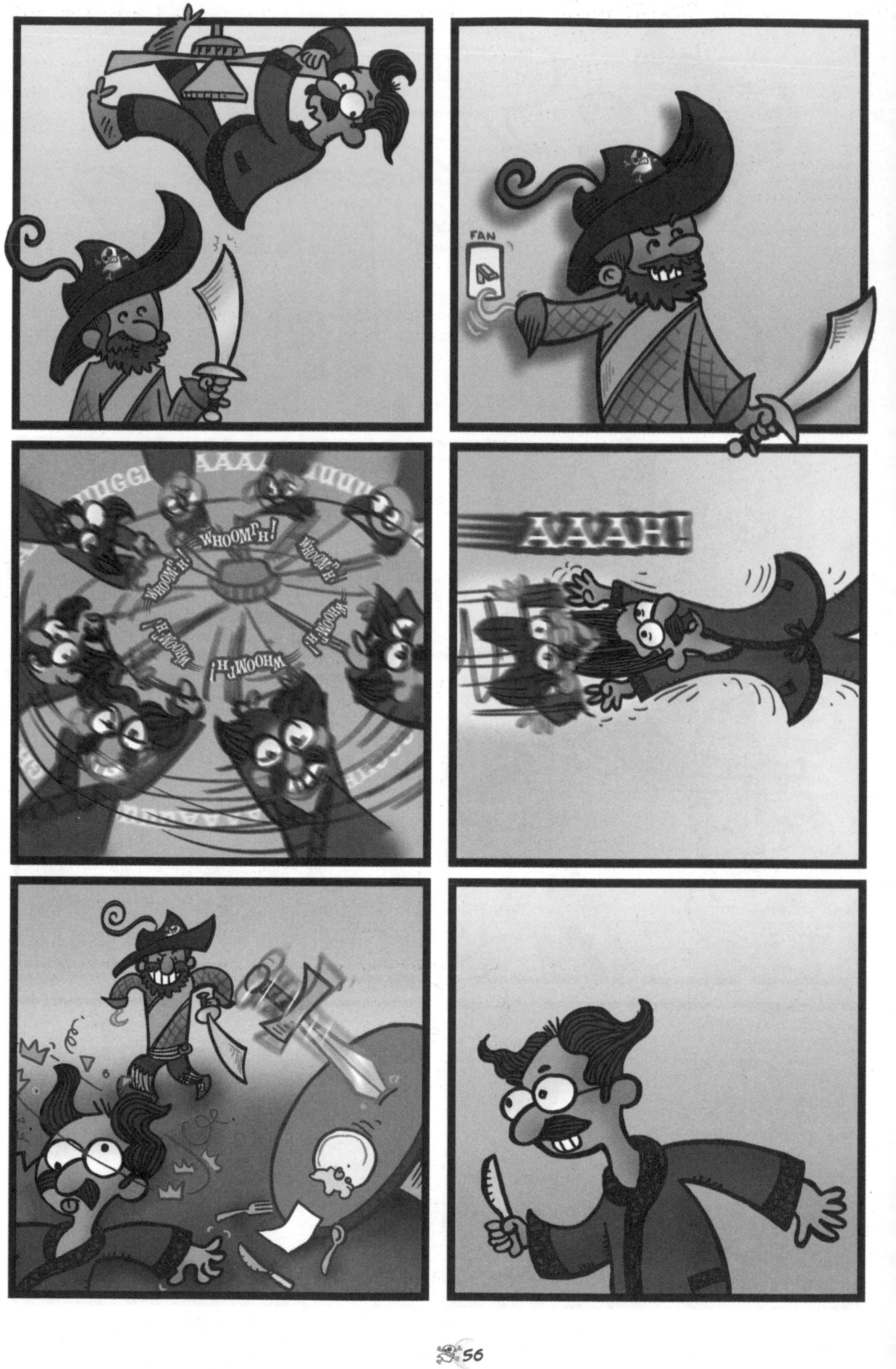
FAN
WHOOMPH!
WHOOMPH!
WHOOMPH!
WHOOMPH!
WHOOMPH!
WHOOMPH!
AAAH!

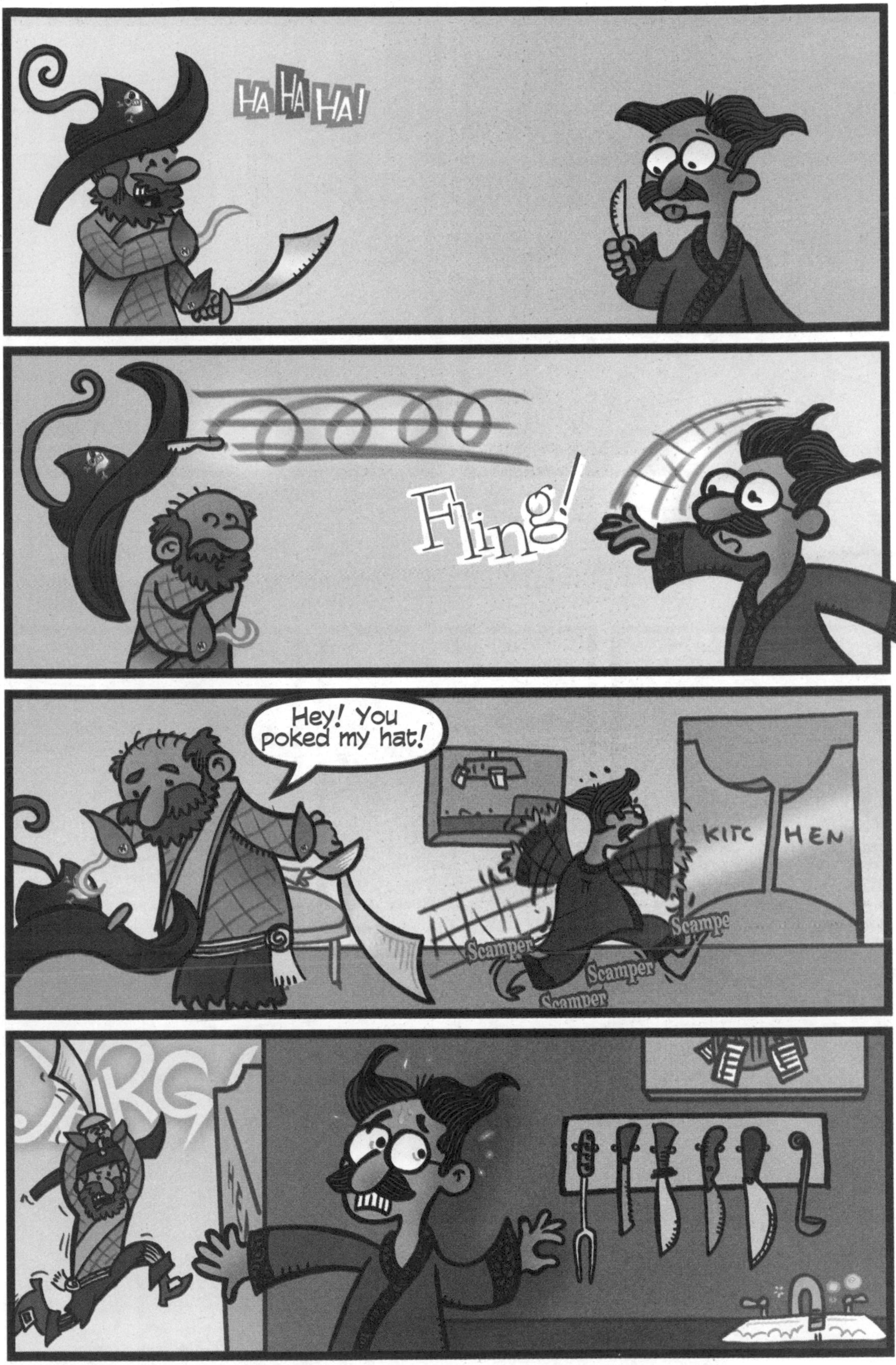
HA HA HA!
Fling!
Hey! You poked my hat!
KITC HEN
Scamper
Scamper
Scampe

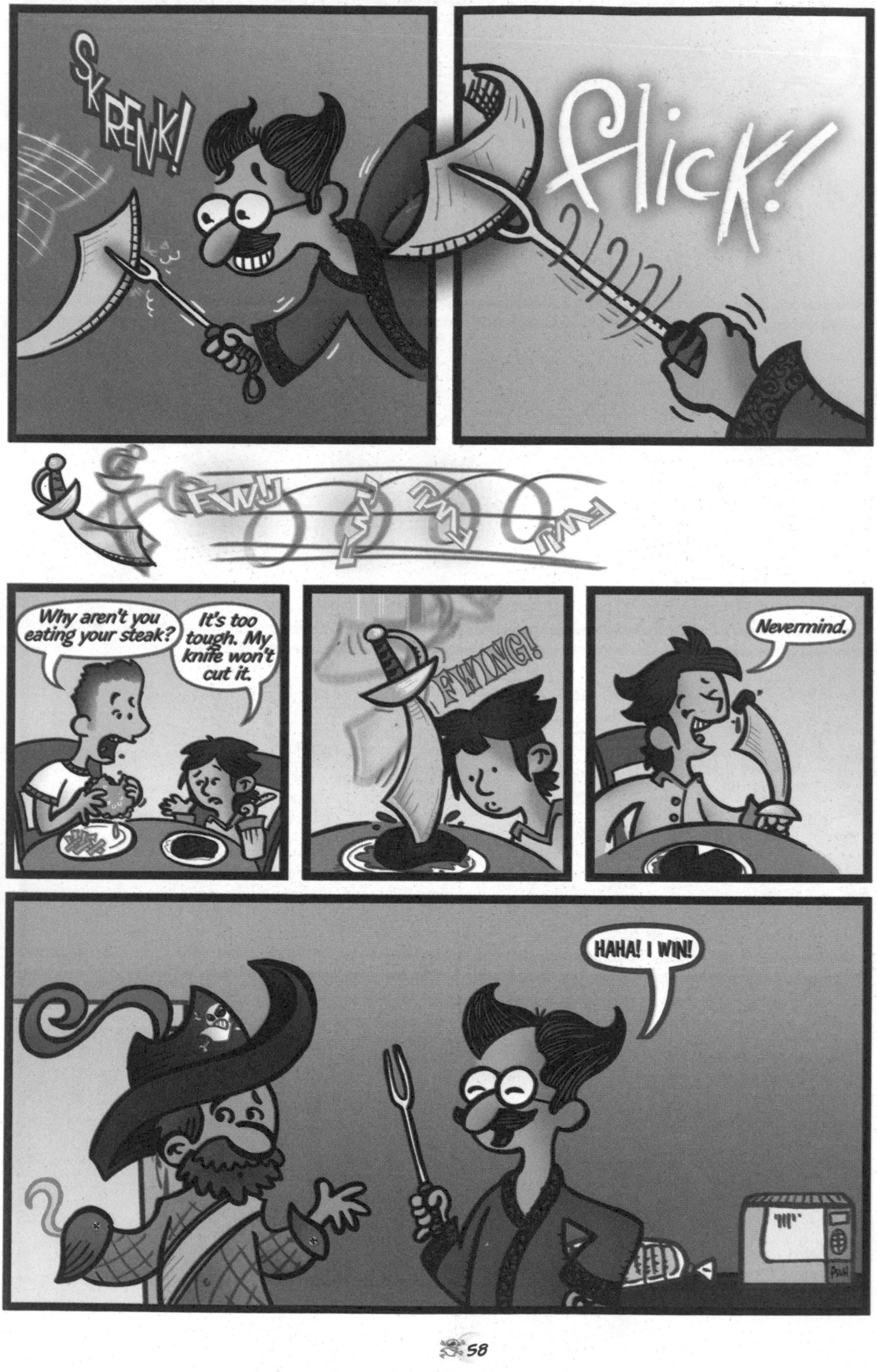
SKRENK!
flick!
Why aren't you eating your steak?
It's too tough. My knife won't cut it.
FWING!
Nevermind.
HAHA! I WIN!

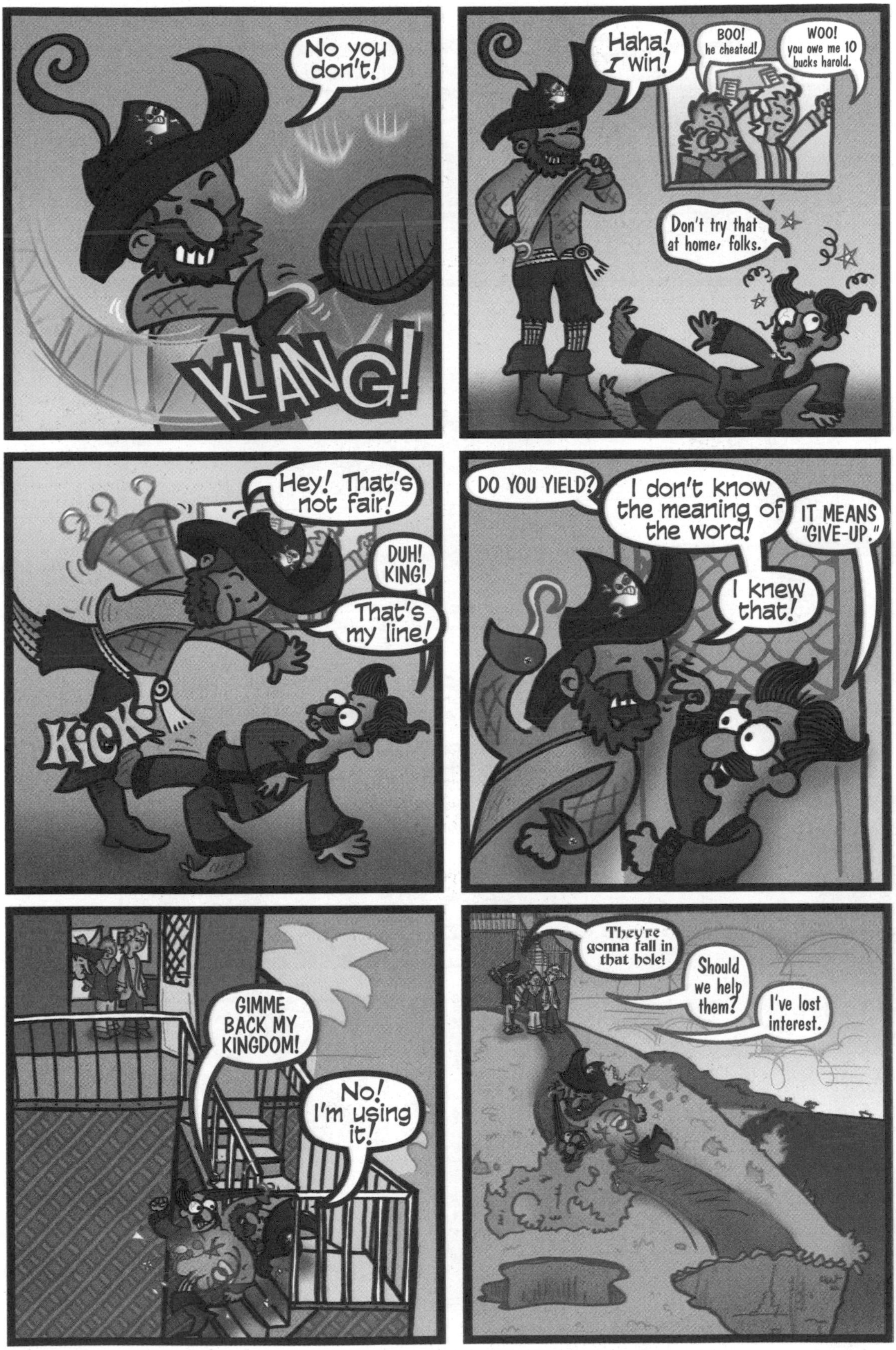
No you don't!
KLANG!
Haha! I win!
BOO! he cheated!
WOO! you owe me 10 bucks harold.
Don't try that at home, folks.
Hey! That's not fair!
DUH! KING!
That's my line!
KICK!
DO YOU YIELD?
I don't know the meaning of the word!
IT MEANS "GIVE-UP."
I knew that!
GIMME BACK MY KINGDOM!
No! I'm using it!
They're gonna fall in that hole!
Should we help them?
I've lost interest.

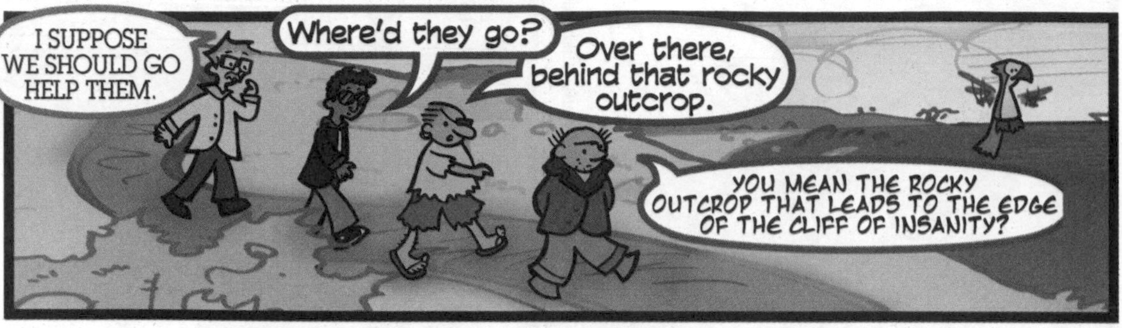
I SUPPOSE WE SHOULD GO HELP THEM.
Where'd they go?
Over there, behind that rocky outcrop.
YOU MEAN THE ROCKY OUTCROP THAT LEADS TO THE EDGE OF THE CLIFF OF INSANITY?

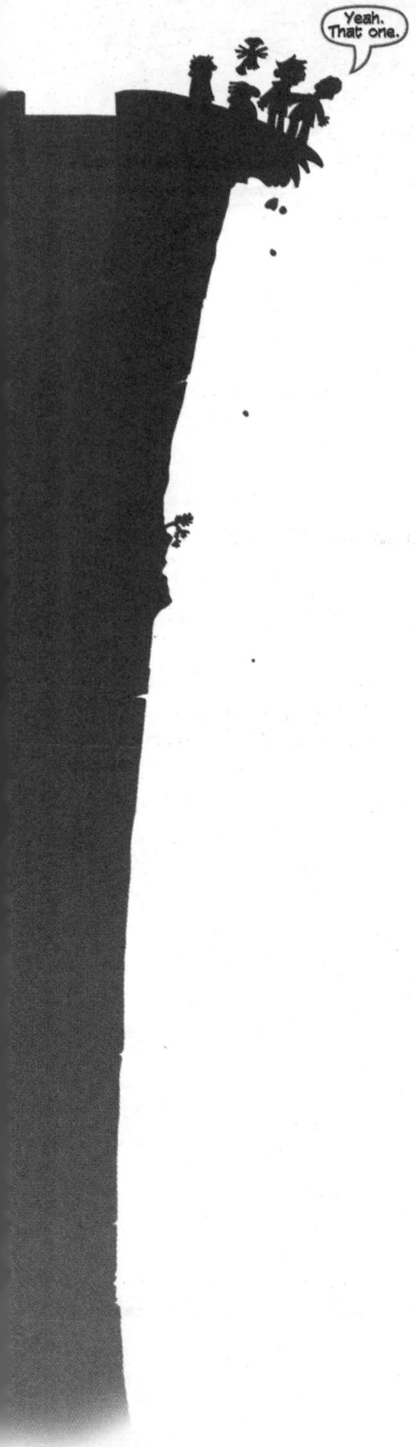
Yeah. That one.

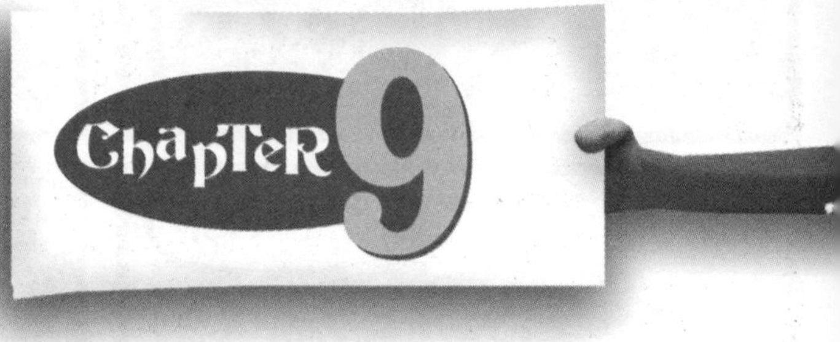
ChapTeR 9

Meanwhile!
Everything else is going on.

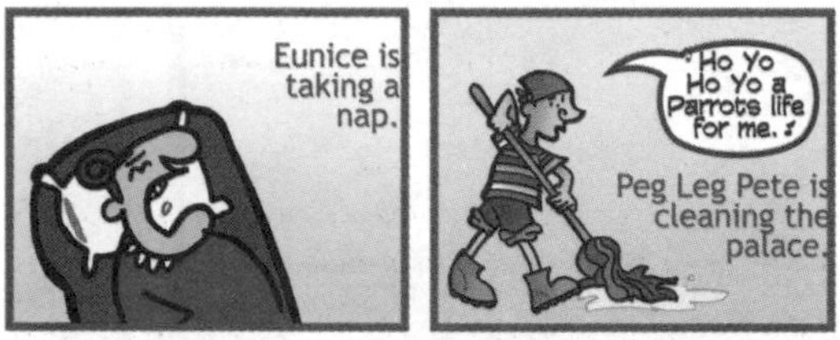
Eunice is taking a nap.
Ho Yo Ho Yo a Parrots life for me.
Peg Leg Pete is cleaning the palace.

The Pirates are running amok.

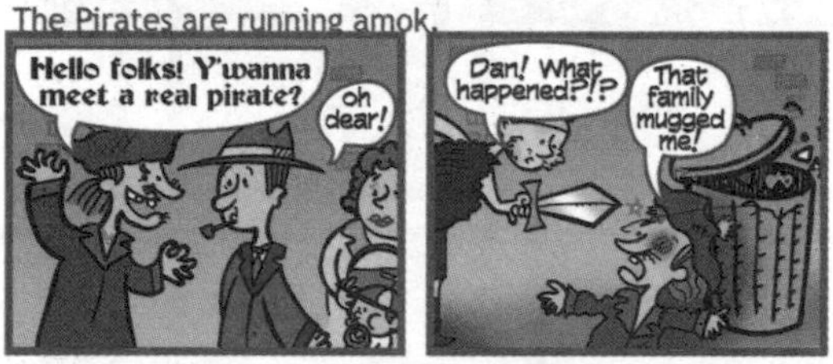
Hello folks! Y'wanna meet a real pirate?
oh dear!
Dan! What happened?!?
That family mugged me!

The Townsfolk are running amok.

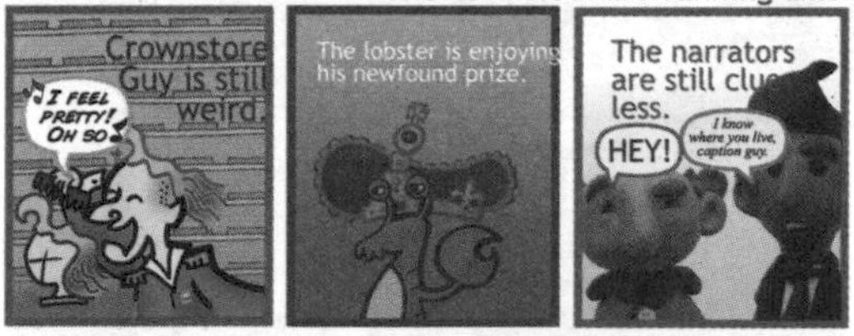
Crownstore Guy is still weird.
I FEEL PRETTY! OH SO
The lobster is enjoying his newfound prize.
The narrators are still clue less.
HEY!
I know where you live, caption guy.

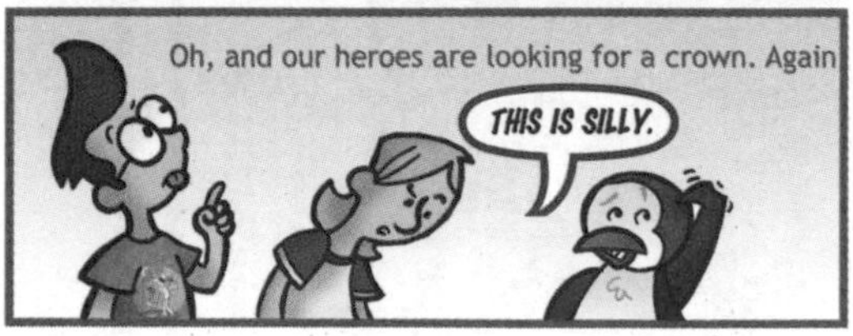
Oh, and our heroes are looking for a crown. Again
THIS IS SILLY.

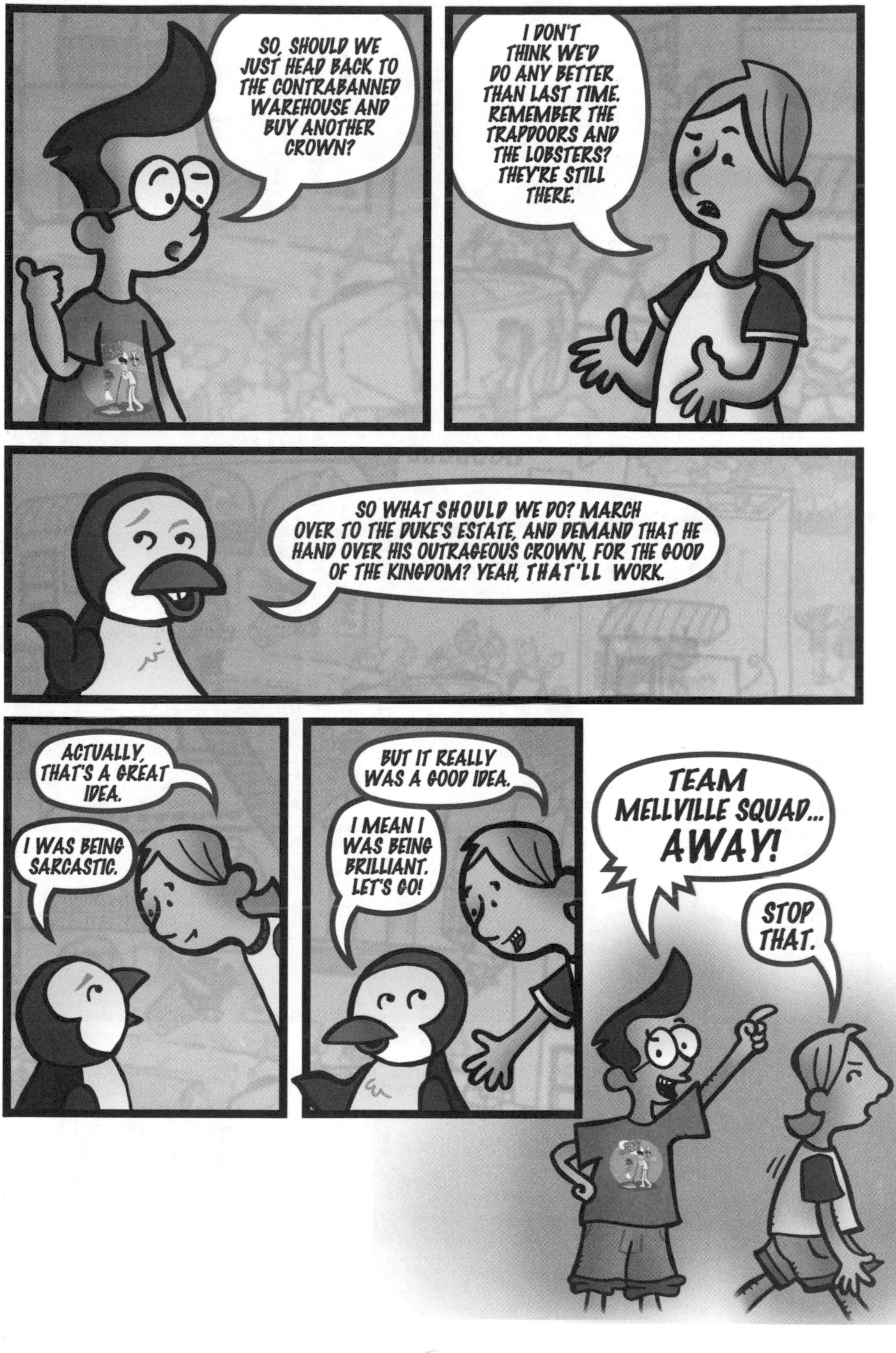
SO, SHOULD WE JUST HEAD BACK TO THE CONTRABANNED WAREHOUSE AND BUY ANOTHER CROWN?
I DON'T THINK WE'D DO ANY BETTER THAN LAST TIME. REMEMBER THE TRAPDOORS AND THE LOBSTERS? THEY'RE STILL THERE.
SO WHAT SHOULD WE DO? MARCH OVER TO THE DUKE'S ESTATE, AND DEMAND THAT HE HAND OVER HIS OUTRAGEOUS CROWN, FOR THE GOOD OF THE KINGDOM? YEAH, THAT'LL WORK.
ACTUALLY, THAT'S A GREAT IDEA.
I WAS BEING SARCASTIC.
BUT IT REALLY WAS A GOOD IDEA.
I MEAN I WAS BEING BRILLIANT. LET'S GO!
TEAM MELLVILLE SQUAD... AWAY!
STOP THAT.

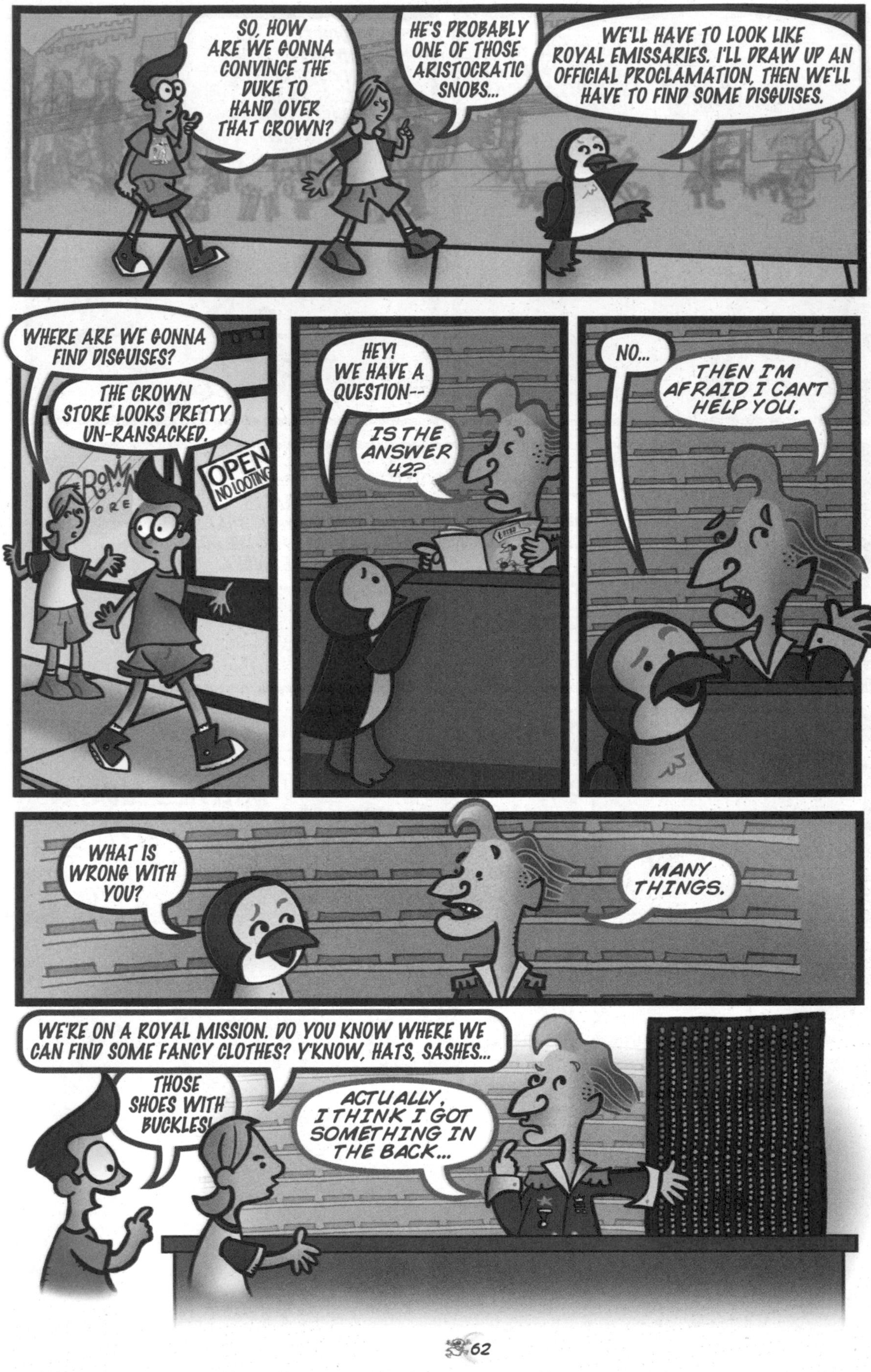
SO, HOW ARE WE GONNA CONVINCE THE DUKE TO HAND OVER THAT CROWN?
HE'S PROBABLY ONE OF THOSE ARISTOCRATIC SNOBS...
WE'LL HAVE TO LOOK LIKE ROYAL EMISSARIES. I'LL DRAW UP AN OFFICIAL PROCLAMATION, THEN WE'LL HAVE TO FIND SOME DISGUISES.
WHERE ARE WE GONNA FIND DISGUISES?
THE CROWN STORE LOOKS PRETTY UN-RANSACKED.
OPEN NO LOOTING
HEY! WE HAVE A QUESTION--
IS THE ANSWER 42?
NO...
THEN I'M AFRAID I CAN'T HELP YOU.
WHAT IS WRONG WITH YOU?
MANY THINGS.
WE'RE ON A ROYAL MISSION. DO YOU KNOW WHERE WE CAN FIND SOME FANCY CLOTHES? Y'KNOW, HATS, SASHES...
THOSE SHOES WITH BUCKLES!
ACTUALLY, I THINK I GOT SOMETHING IN THE BACK...

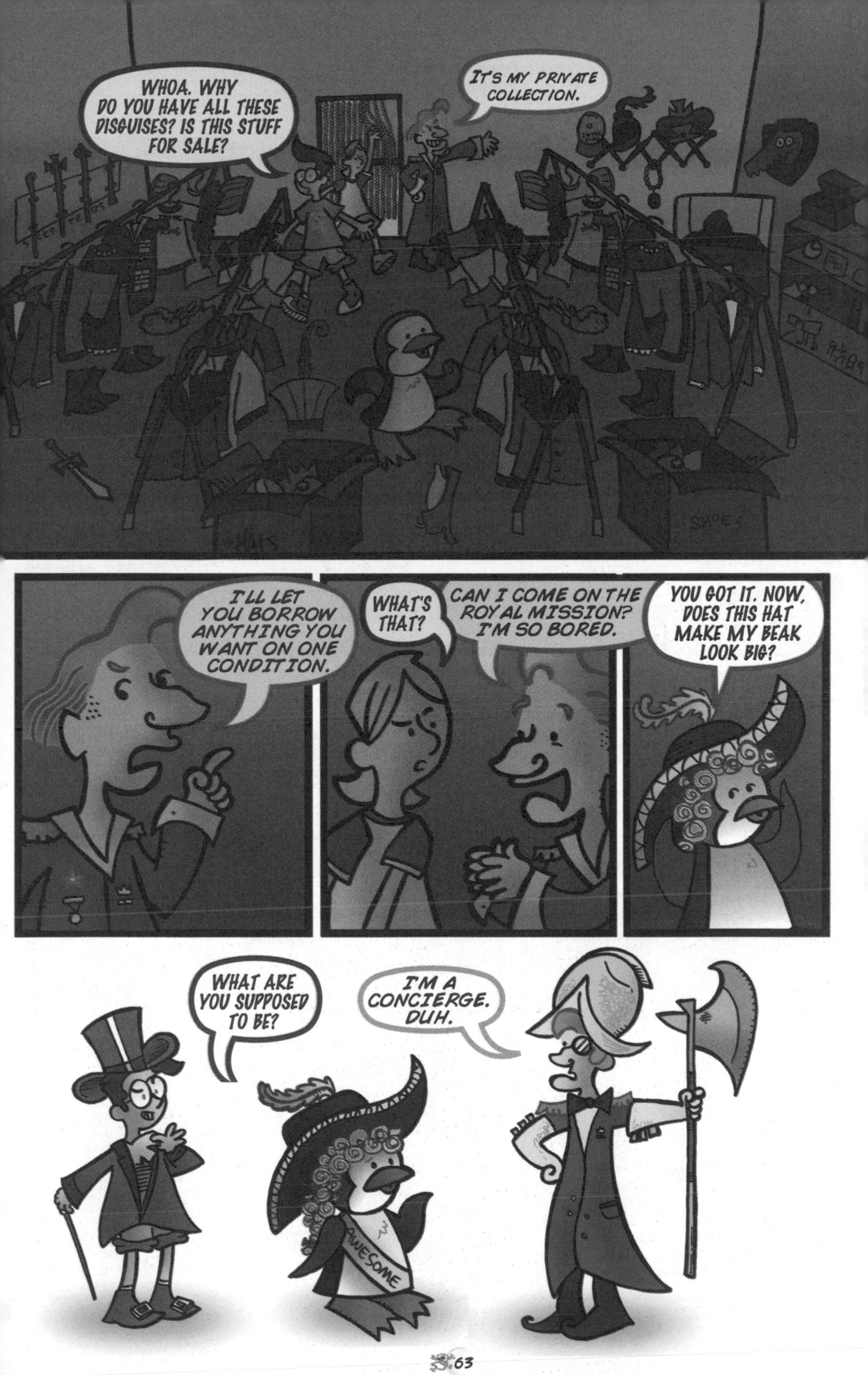
WHOA. WHY DO YOU HAVE ALL THESE DISGUISES? IS THIS STUFF FOR SALE?
IT'S MY PRIVATE COLLECTION.
I'LL LET YOU BORROW ANYTHING YOU WANT ON ONE CONDITION.
WHAT'S THAT?
CAN I COME ON THE ROYAL MISSION? I'M SO BORED.
YOU GOT IT. NOW, DOES THIS HAT MAKE MY BEAK LOOK BIG?
WHAT ARE YOU SUPPOSED TO BE?
I'M A CONCIERGE. DUH.
AWESOME

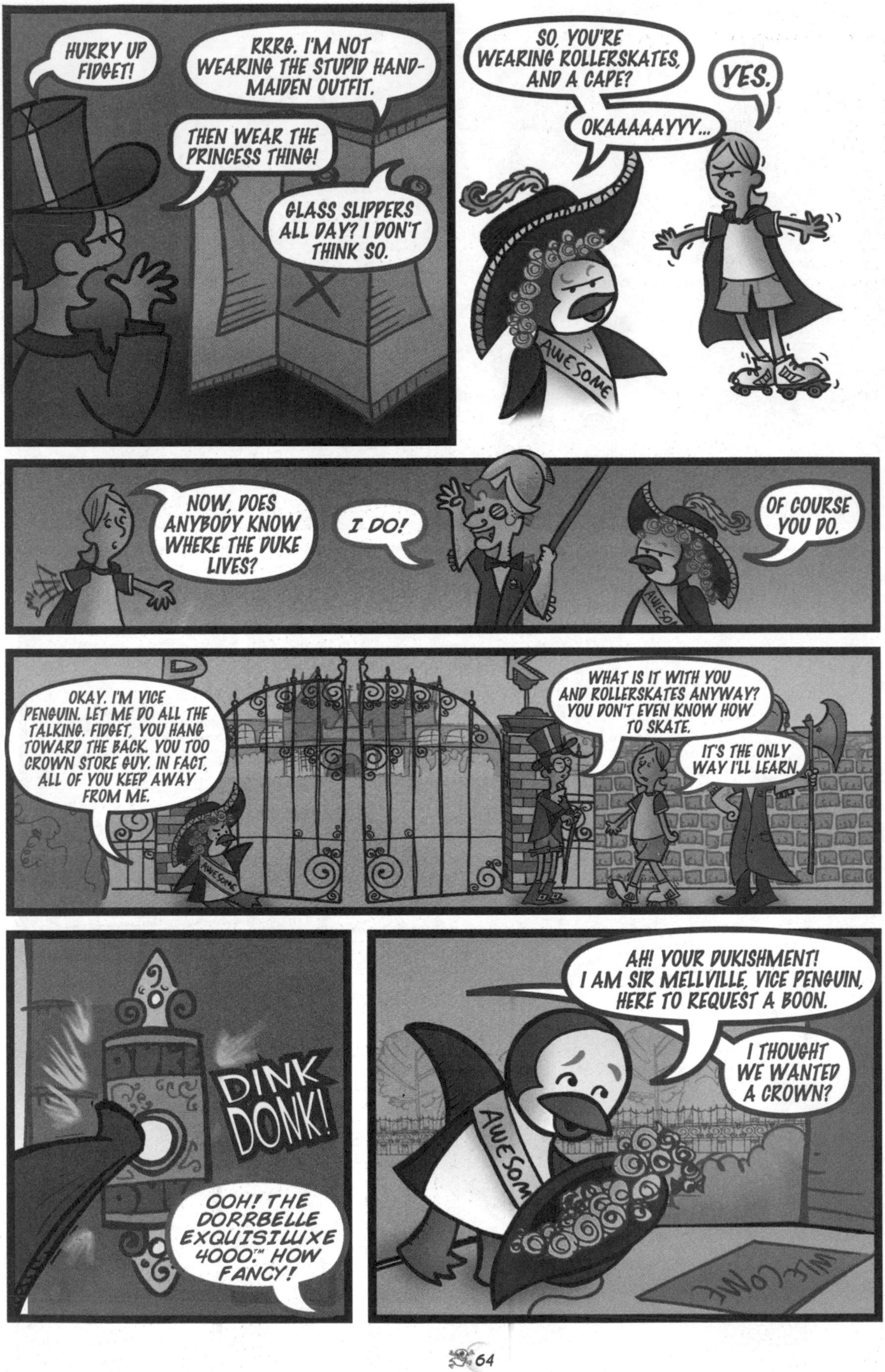

HURRY UP FIDGET!
RRRG. I'M NOT WEARING THE STUPID HAND-MAIDEN OUTFIT.
THEN WEAR THE PRINCESS THING!
GLASS SLIPPERS ALL DAY? I DON'T THINK SO.
SO, YOU'RE WEARING ROLLERSKATES, AND A CAPE?
YES.
OKAAAAAYYY...
AWESOME
NOW, DOES ANYBODY KNOW WHERE THE DUKE LIVES?
I DO!
OF COURSE YOU DO.
OKAY. I'M VICE PENGUIN. LET ME DO ALL THE TALKING. FIDGET, YOU HANG TOWARD THE BACK. YOU TOO CROWN STORE GUY. IN FACT, ALL OF YOU KEEP AWAY FROM ME.
WHAT IS IT WITH YOU AND ROLLERSKATES ANYWAY? YOU DON'T EVEN KNOW HOW TO SKATE.
IT'S THE ONLY WAY I'LL LEARN.
DINK DONK!
OOH! THE DORRBELLE EXQUISILUXE 4000™ HOW FANCY!
AH! YOUR DUKISHMENT! I AM SIR MELLVILLE, VICE PENGUIN, HERE TO REQUEST A BOON.
I THOUGHT WE WANTED A CROWN?
WELCOME

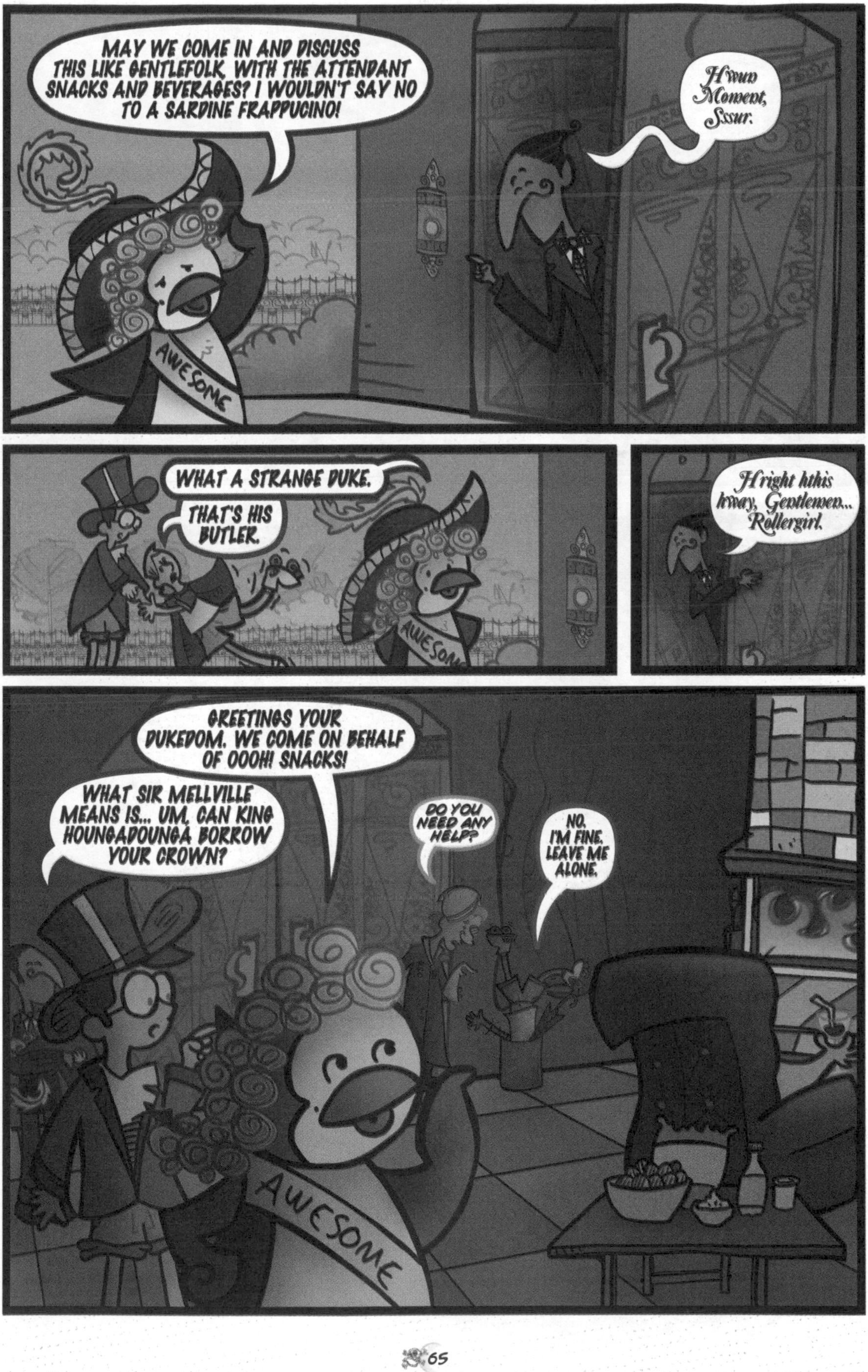
MAY WE COME IN AND DISCUSS THIS LIKE GENTLEFOLK, WITH THE ATTENDANT SNACKS AND BEVERAGES? I WOULDN'T SAY NO TO A SARDINE FRAPPUCINO!
Hwun Moment, Sssur.
AWESOME
WHAT A STRANGE DUKE.
THAT'S HIS BUTLER.
AWESOME
Hright hthis hway, Gentlemen... Rollergirl.
GREETINGS YOUR DUKEDOM. WE COME ON BEHALF OF OOOH! SNACKS!
WHAT SIR MELLVILLE MEANS IS... UM, CAN KING HOUNGADOUNGA BORROW YOUR CROWN?
DO YOU NEED ANY HELP?
NO. I'M FINE. LEAVE ME ALONE.
AWESOME

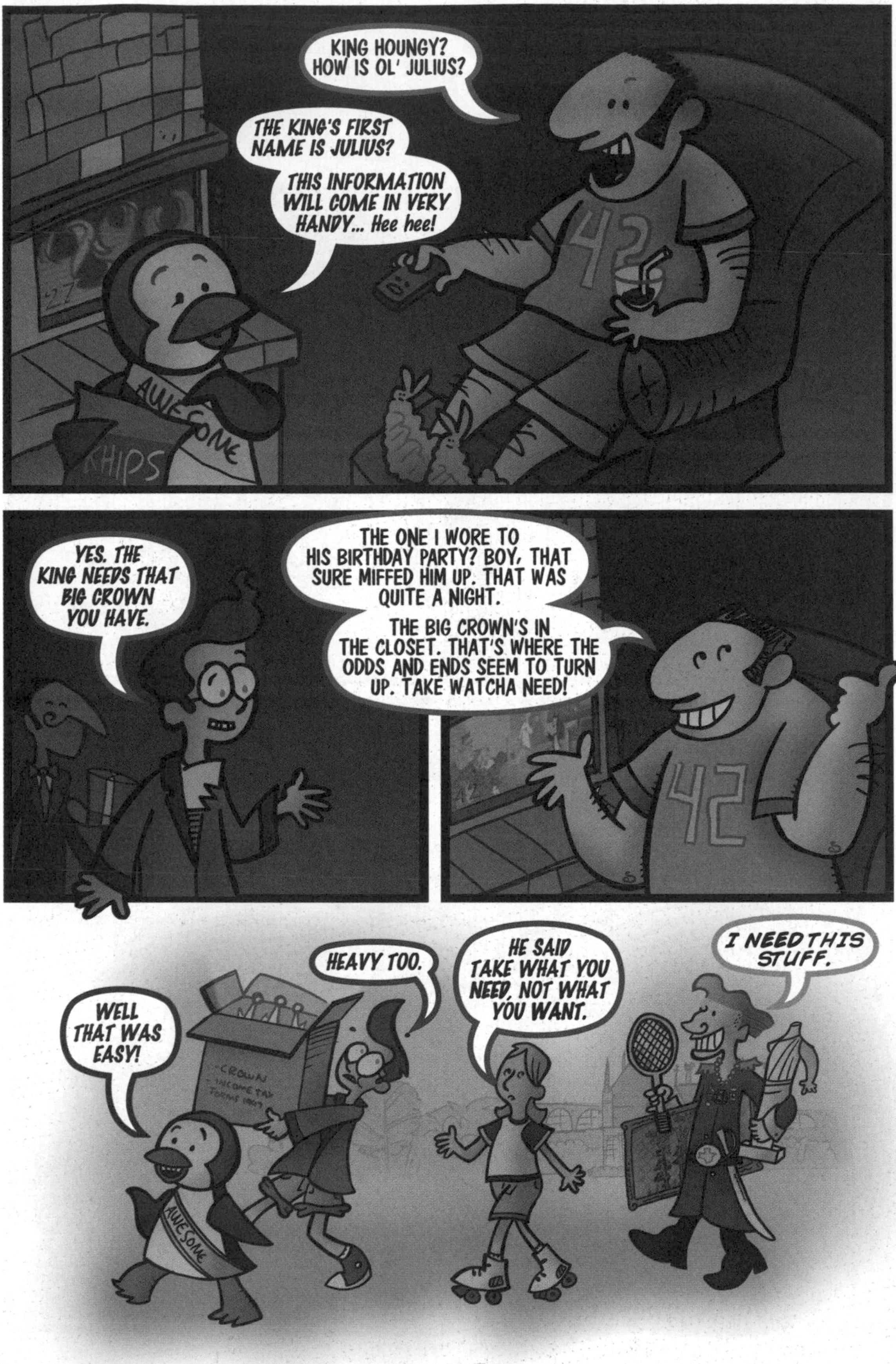

KING HOUNGY? HOW IS OL' JULIUS?
THE KING'S FIRST NAME IS JULIUS?
THIS INFORMATION WILL COME IN VERY HANDY... Hee hee!
YES. THE KING NEEDS THAT BIG CROWN YOU HAVE.
THE ONE I WORE TO HIS BIRTHDAY PARTY? BOY, THAT SURE MIFFED HIM UP. THAT WAS QUITE A NIGHT.
THE BIG CROWN'S IN THE CLOSET. THAT'S WHERE THE ODDS AND ENDS SEEM TO TURN UP. TAKE WATCHA NEED!
WELL THAT WAS EASY!
HEAVY TOO.
HE SAID TAKE WHAT YOU NEED, NOT WHAT YOU WANT.
I NEED THIS STUFF.

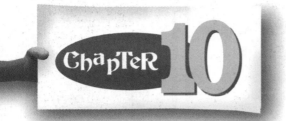

# Chapter 10

In which the various subplots converge toward the conclusion of this thrilling tale, and I, the Caption Guy, will go home I guess. Stupid Narrators. Never invite me to the post book party.

I don't like those guys. Grumble Mumble

Back at the palace, at least someone knows what they're doing.

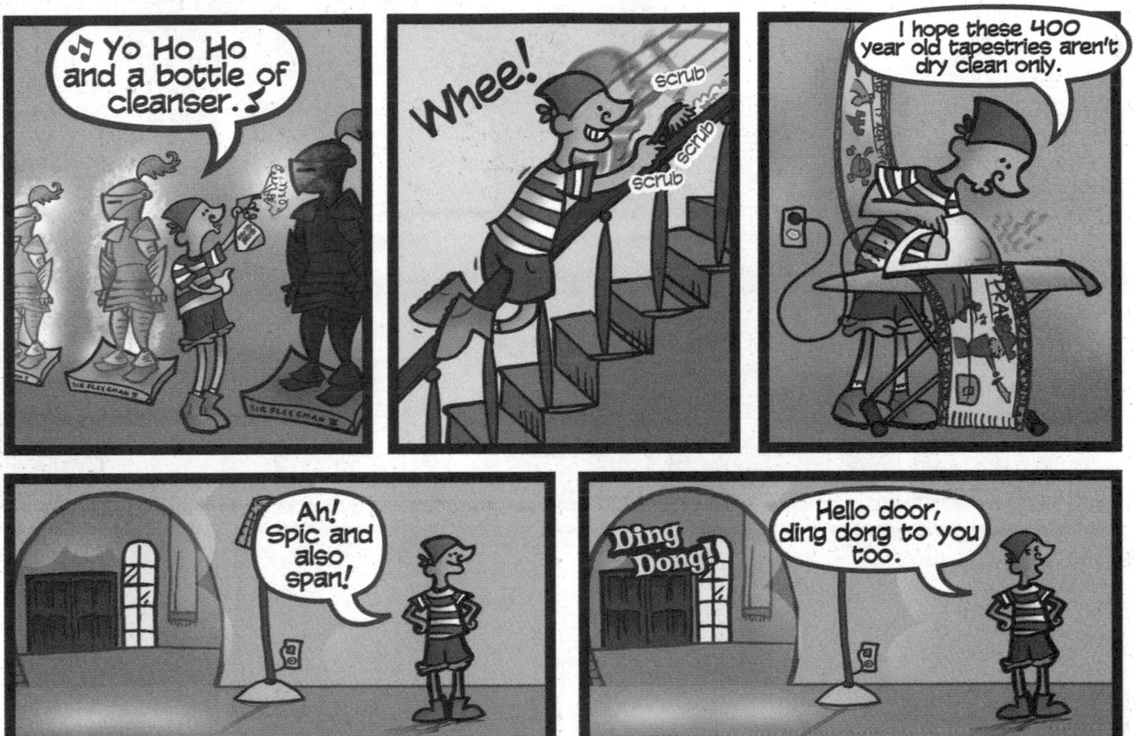

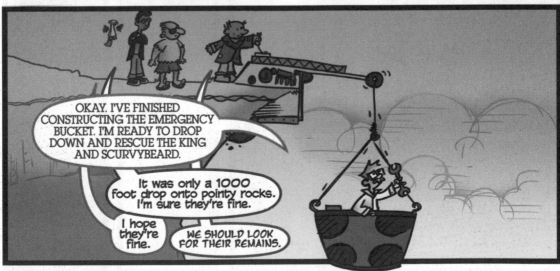

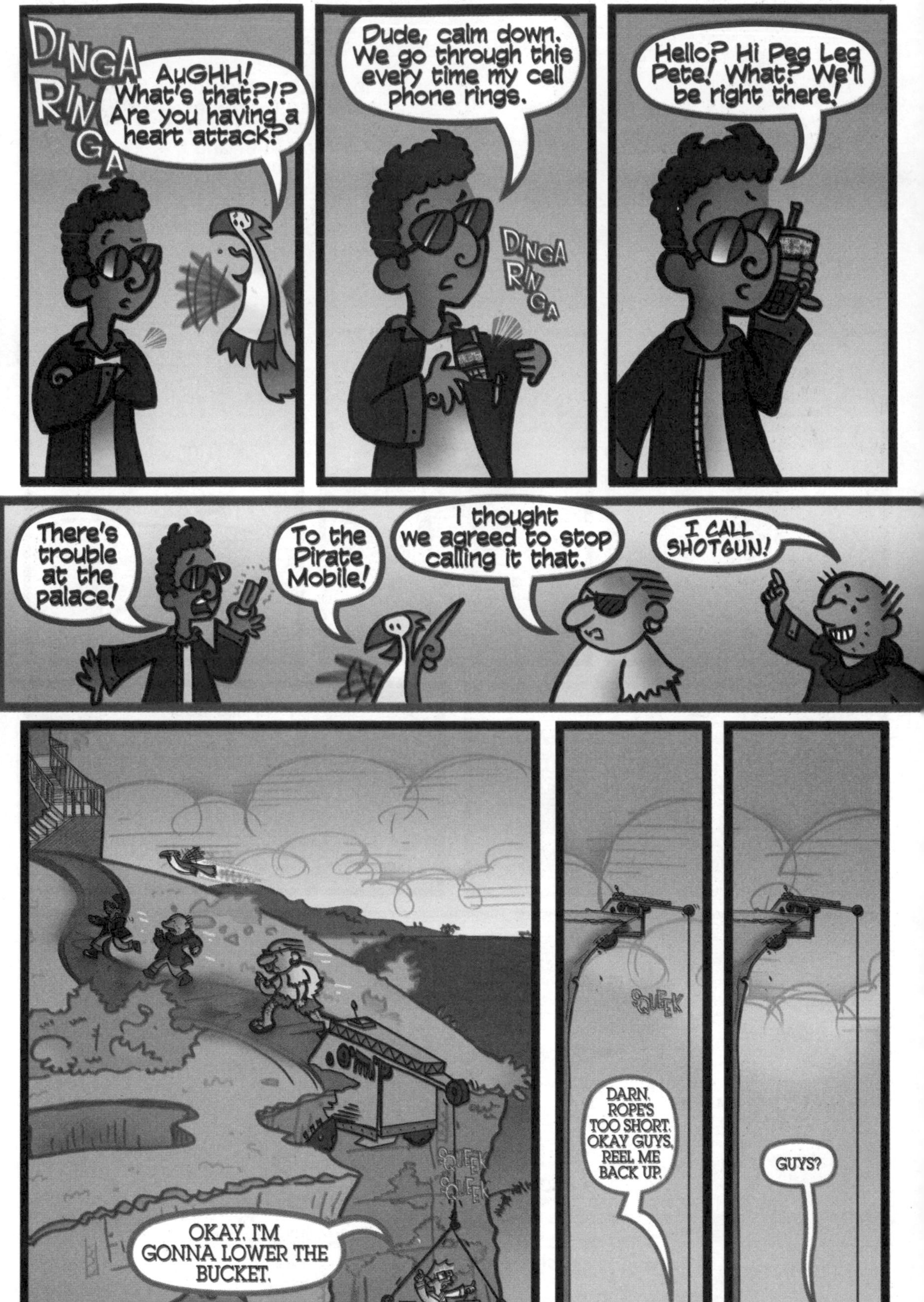
DINGA RINGA
AUGHH! What's that?!? Are you having a heart attack?
Dude, calm down. We go through this every time my cell phone rings.
DINGA RINGA
Hello? Hi Peg Leg Pete! What? We'll be right there!
There's trouble at the palace!
To the Pirate Mobile!
I thought we agreed to stop calling it that.
I CALL SHOTGUN!
SQUEEK SQUEEK
OKAY. I'M GONNA LOWER THE BUCKET.
SQUEEK
DARN. ROPE'S TOO SHORT. OKAY GUYS, REEL ME BACK UP.
GUYS?

At the palace, trouble...

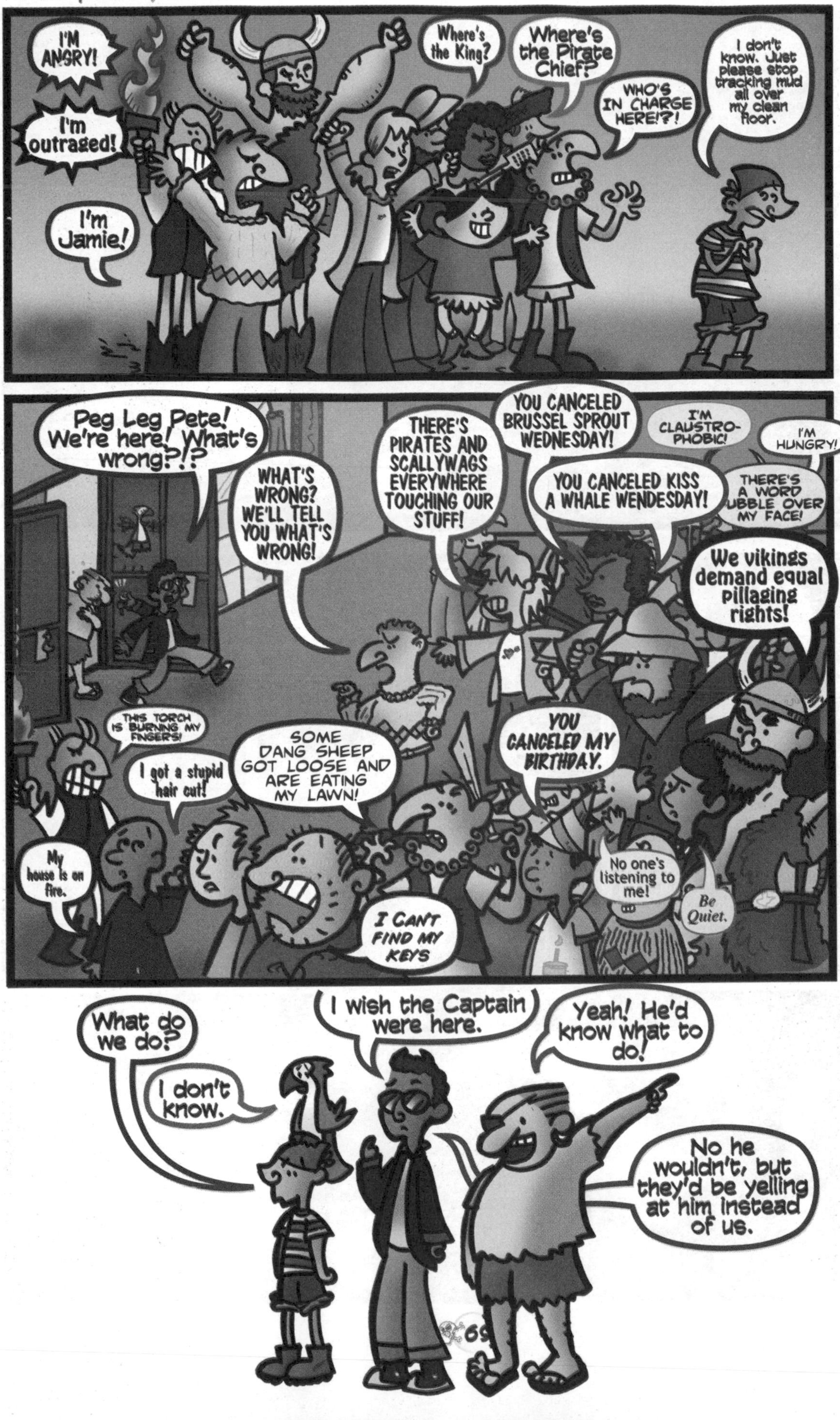
I'M ANGRY!
I'm outraged!
I'm Jamie!
Where's the King?
Where's the Pirate Chief?
WHO'S IN CHARGE HERE!?!
I don't know. Just please stop tracking mud all over my clean floor.
Peg Leg Pete! We're here! What's wrong?!?
WHAT'S WRONG? WE'LL TELL YOU WHAT'S WRONG!
THERE'S PIRATES AND SCALLYWAGS EVERYWHERE TOUCHING OUR STUFF!
YOU CANCELED BRUSSEL SPROUT WEDNESDAY!
YOU CANCELED KISS A WHALE WENDESDAY!
I'M CLAUSTRO-PHOBIC!
I'M HUNGRY!
THERE'S A WORD UBBLE OVER MY FACE!
We vikings demand equal pillaging rights!
THIS TORCH IS BURNING MY FINGERS!
I got a stupid hair cut!
SOME DANG SHEEP GOT LOOSE AND ARE EATING MY LAWN!
YOU CANCELED MY BIRTHDAY.
My house is on fire.
I CAN'T FIND MY KEYS
No one's listening to me!
Be Quiet.
What do we do?
I don't know.
I wish the Captain were here.
Yeah! He'd know what to do!
No he wouldn't, but they'd be yelling at him instead of us.

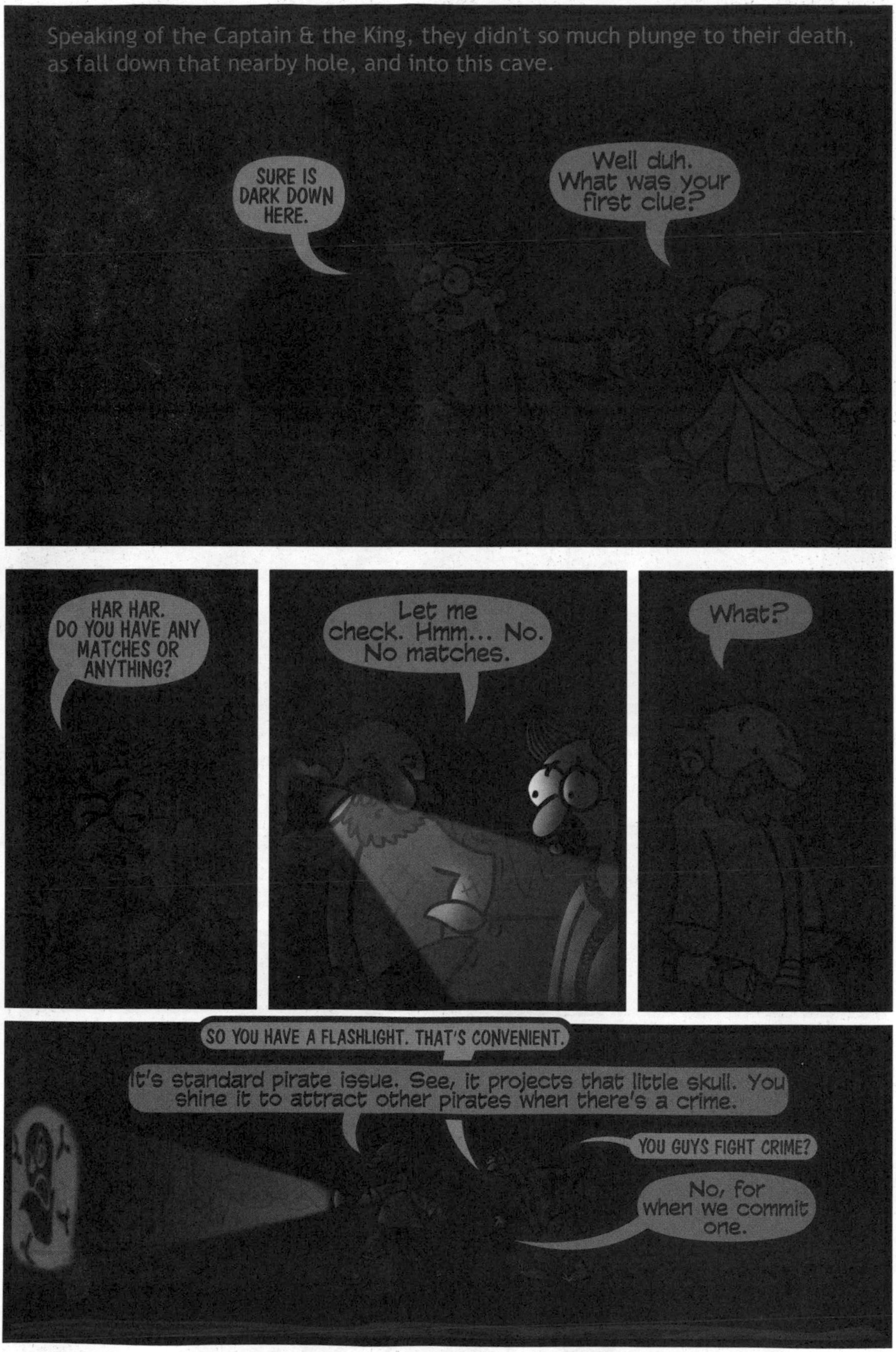

Speaking of the Captain & the King, they didn't so much plunge to their death, as fall down that nearby hole, and into this cave.
SURE IS DARK DOWN HERE.
Well duh. What was your first clue?
HAR HAR. DO YOU HAVE ANY MATCHES OR ANYTHING?
Let me check. Hmm... No. No matches.
What?
SO YOU HAVE A FLASHLIGHT. THAT'S CONVENIENT.
It's standard pirate issue. See, it projects that little skull. You shine it to attract other pirates when there's a crime.
YOU GUYS FIGHT CRIME?
No, for when we commit one.

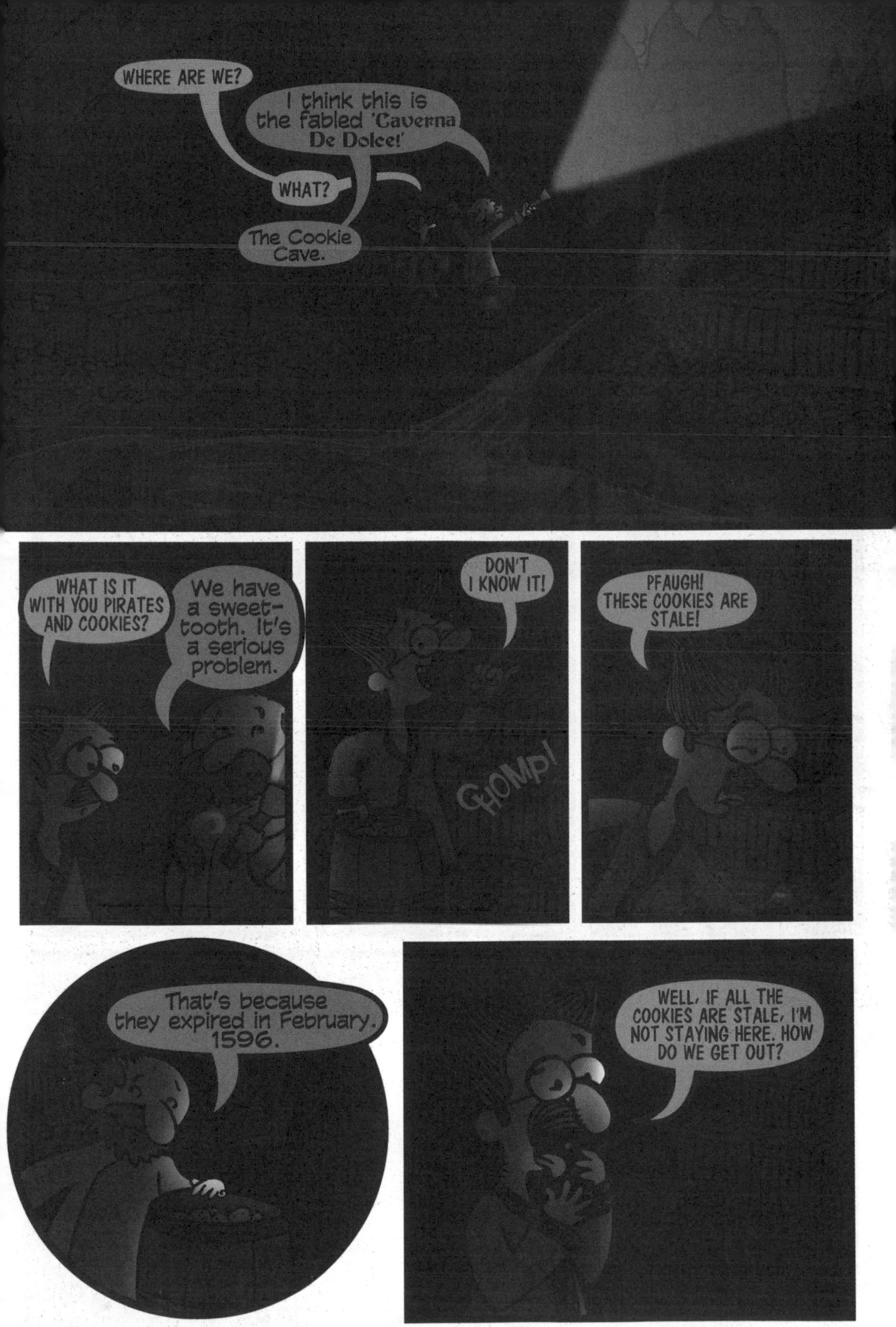
WHERE ARE WE?
I think this is the fabled 'Caverna De Dolce!'
WHAT?
The Cookie Cave.
WHAT IS IT WITH YOU PIRATES AND COOKIES?
We have a sweet-tooth. It's a serious problem.
DON'T I KNOW IT!
CHOMP!
PFAUGH! THESE COOKIES ARE STALE!
That's because they expired in February. 1596.
WELL, IF ALL THE COOKIES ARE STALE, I'M NOT STAYING HERE. HOW DO WE GET OUT?

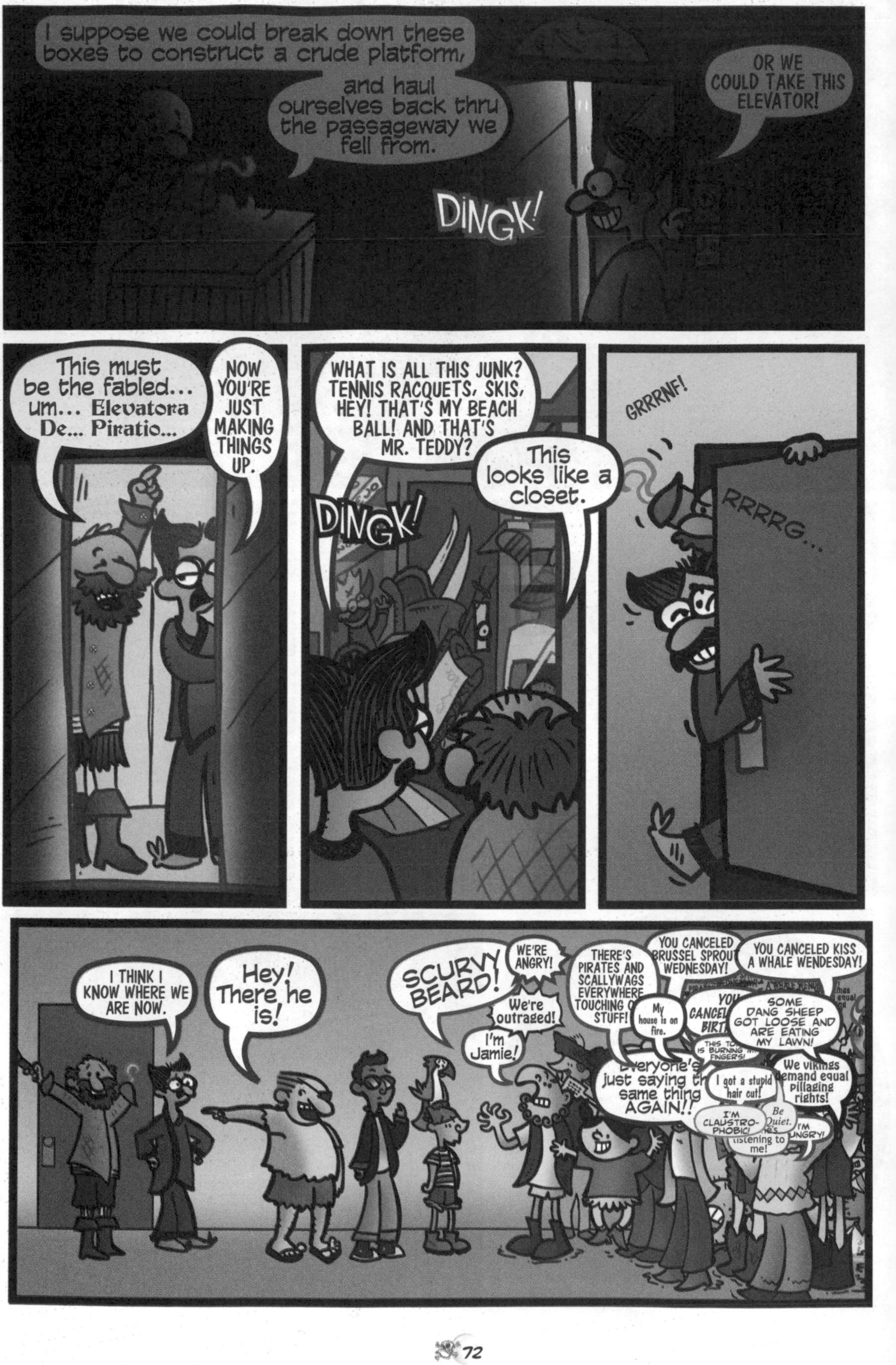
I suppose we could break down these boxes to construct a crude platform,
and haul ourselves back thru the passageway we fell from.
OR WE COULD TAKE THIS ELEVATOR!
DINGK!
This must be the fabled... um... Elevatora De... Piratio...
NOW YOU'RE JUST MAKING THINGS UP.
WHAT IS ALL THIS JUNK? TENNIS RACQUETS, SKIS, HEY! THAT'S MY BEACH BALL! AND THAT'S MR. TEDDY?
This looks like a closet.
DINGK!
GRRRNF!
RRRRG...
I THINK I KNOW WHERE WE ARE NOW.
Hey! There he is!
SCURVY BEARD!
WE'RE ANGRY!
We're outraged!
I'm Jamie!
THERE'S PIRATES AND SCALLYWAGS EVERYWHERE
STUFF!
YOU CANCELED BRUSSEL SPROUT WEDNESDAY!
YOU CANCELED KISS A WHALE WENDESDAY!
My house is on fire.
SOME DANG SHEEP GOT LOOSE AND ARE EATING MY LAWN!
just saying
same thing AGAIN!!
I got a stupid hair cut!
We vikings demand equal pillaging rights!
I'M CLAUSTRO-PHOBIC!
Be Quiet.
me!

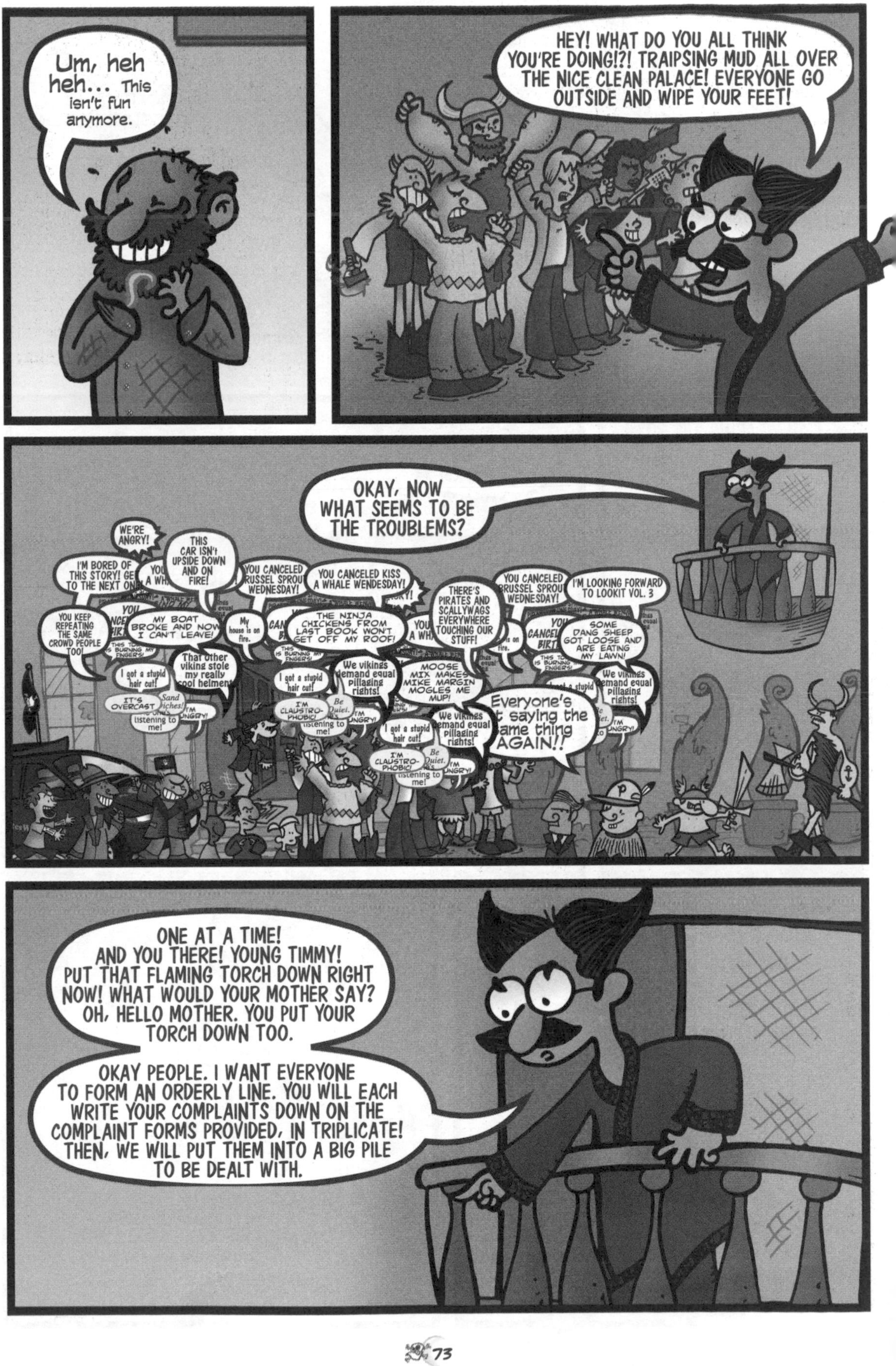

Um, heh heh... This isn't fun anymore.
HEY! WHAT DO YOU ALL THINK YOU'RE DOING!?! TRAIPSING MUD ALL OVER THE NICE CLEAN PALACE! EVERYONE GO OUTSIDE AND WIPE YOUR FEET!
OKAY, NOW WHAT SEEMS TO BE THE TROUBLEMS?
WE'RE ANGRY!
THIS CAR ISN't UPSIDE DOWN AND ON FIRE!
YOU CANCELED KISS A WHALE WENDESDAY!
YOU CANCELED BRUSSEL SPROUT WEDNESDAY!
I'M LOOKING FORWARD TO LOOKIT VOL. 3
YOU KEEP REPEATING THE SAME CROWD PEOPLE TOO!
MY BOAT BROKE AND NOW I CAN'T LEAVE!
My house is on fire.
THE NINJA CHICKENS FROM LAST BOOK WON'T GET OFF MY ROOF!
THERE'S PIRATES AND SCALLYWAGS EVERYWHERE TOUCHING OUR STUFF!
SOME DANG SHEEP GOT LOOSE AND ARE EATING MY LAWN!
That other viking stole my really cool helmen
I got a stupid hair cut!
We vikings demand equal pillaging rights!
MOOSE MIX MAKES MIKE MARGIN MOGLES ME MUP!
IT'S OVERCAST
I'M CLAUSTRO-PHOBIC!
Be Quiet.
Everyone's …t saying the …ame thing AGAIN!!
ONE AT A TIME! AND YOU THERE! YOUNG TIMMY! PUT THAT FLAMING TORCH DOWN RIGHT NOW! WHAT WOULD YOUR MOTHER SAY? OH, HELLO MOTHER. YOU PUT YOUR TORCH DOWN TOO.
OKAY PEOPLE. I WANT EVERYONE TO FORM AN ORDERLY LINE. YOU WILL EACH WRITE YOUR COMPLAINTS DOWN ON THE COMPLAINT FORMS PROVIDED, IN TRIPLICATE! THEN, WE WILL PUT THEM INTO A BIG PILE TO BE DEALT WITH.

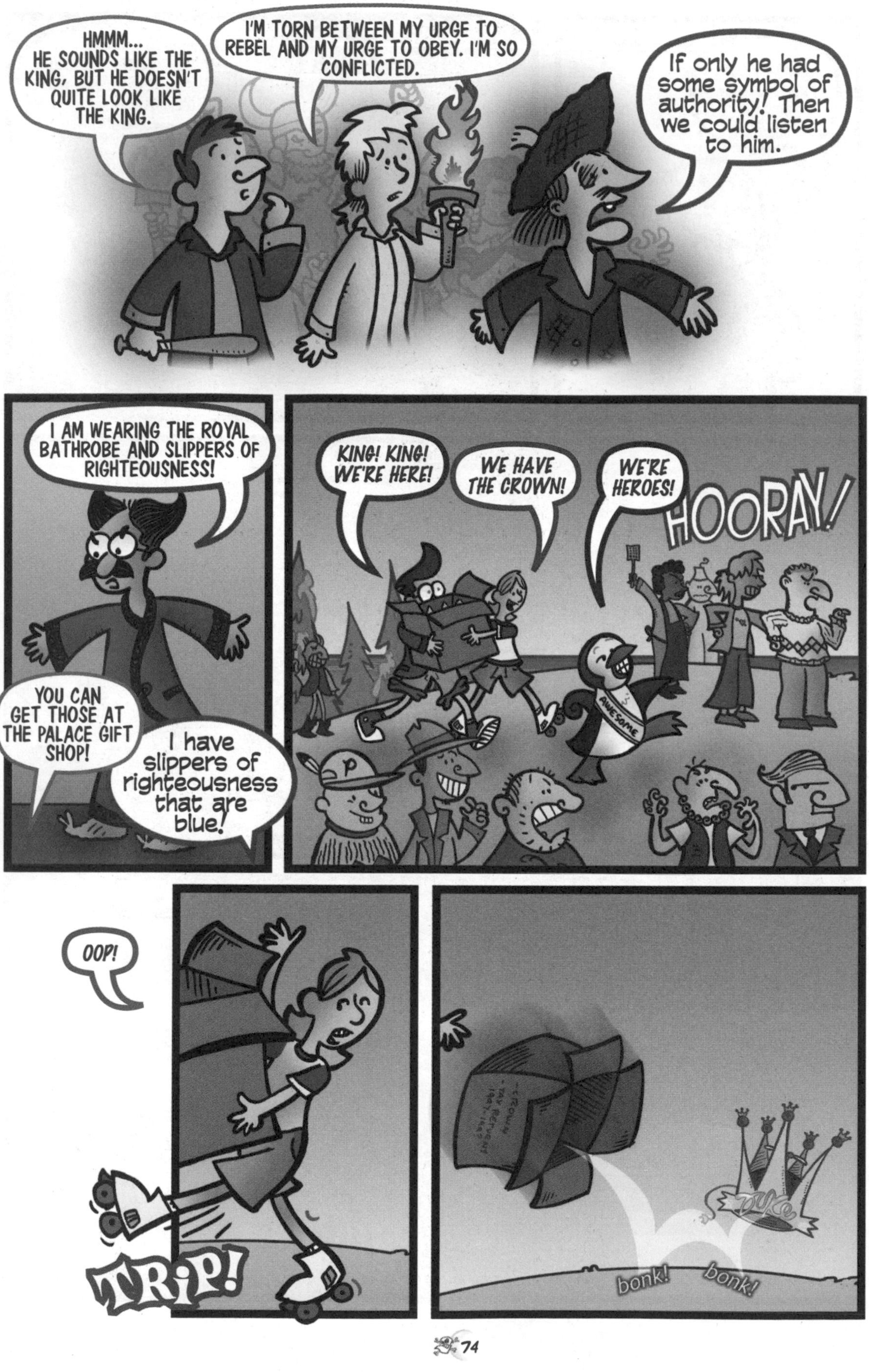
HMMM... HE SOUNDS LIKE THE KING, BUT HE DOESN'T QUITE LOOK LIKE THE KING.
I'M TORN BETWEEN MY URGE TO REBEL AND MY URGE TO OBEY. I'M SO CONFLICTED.
If only he had some symbol of authority! Then we could listen to him.
I AM WEARING THE ROYAL BATHROBE AND SLIPPERS OF RIGHTEOUSNESS!
YOU CAN GET THOSE AT THE PALACE GIFT SHOP!
I have slippers of righteousness that are blue!
KING! KING! WE'RE HERE!
WE HAVE THE CROWN!
WE'RE HEROES!
HOORAY!
AWESOME
OOP!
TRIP!
DUKE
bonk!
bonk!

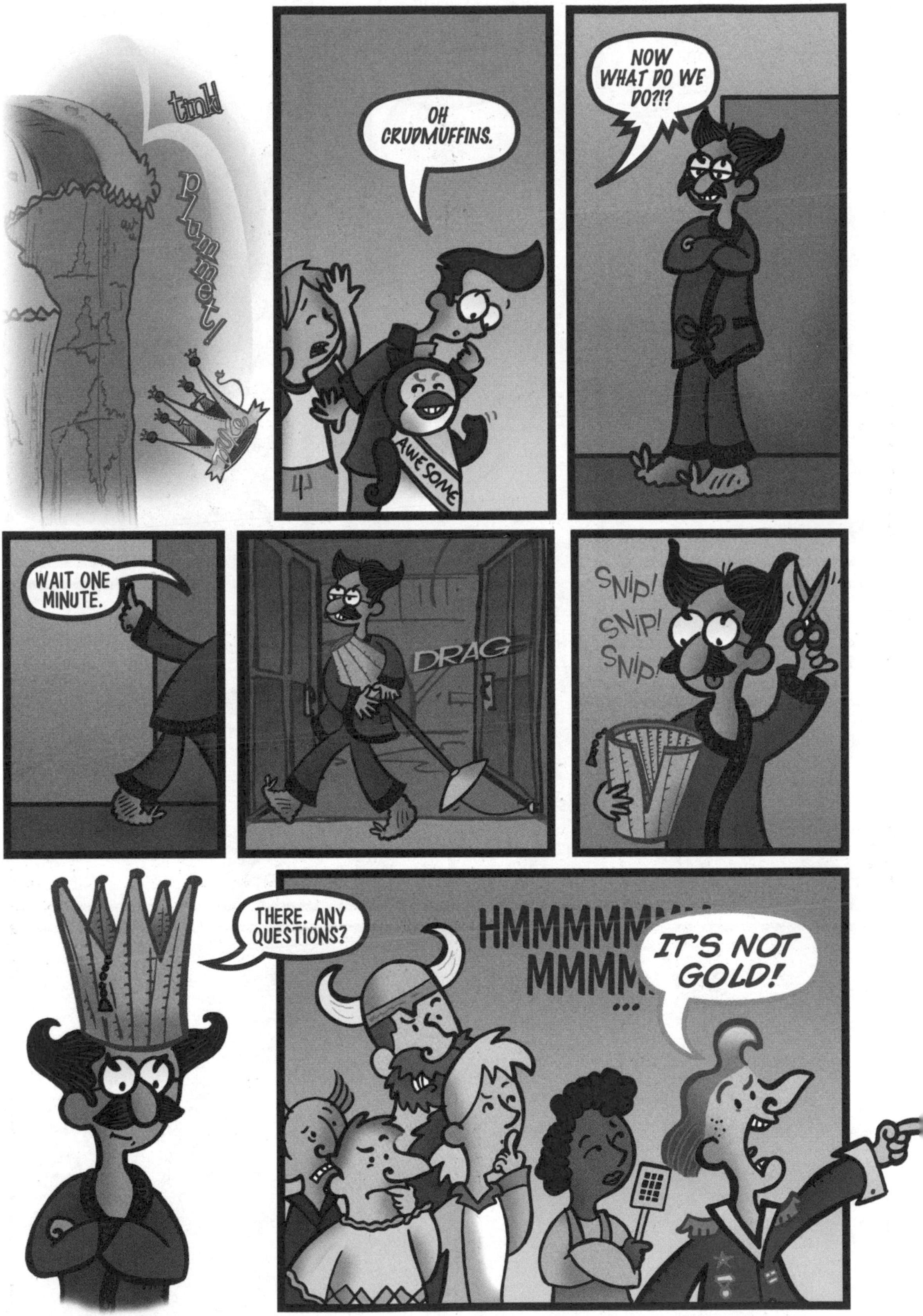
tink!
plummet!
OH CRUDMUFFINS.
AWESOME
NOW WHAT DO WE DO?!?
WAIT ONE MINUTE.
DRAG
SNIP! SNIP! SNIP!
THERE. ANY QUESTIONS?
HMMMMMM MMMM...
IT'S NOT GOLD!

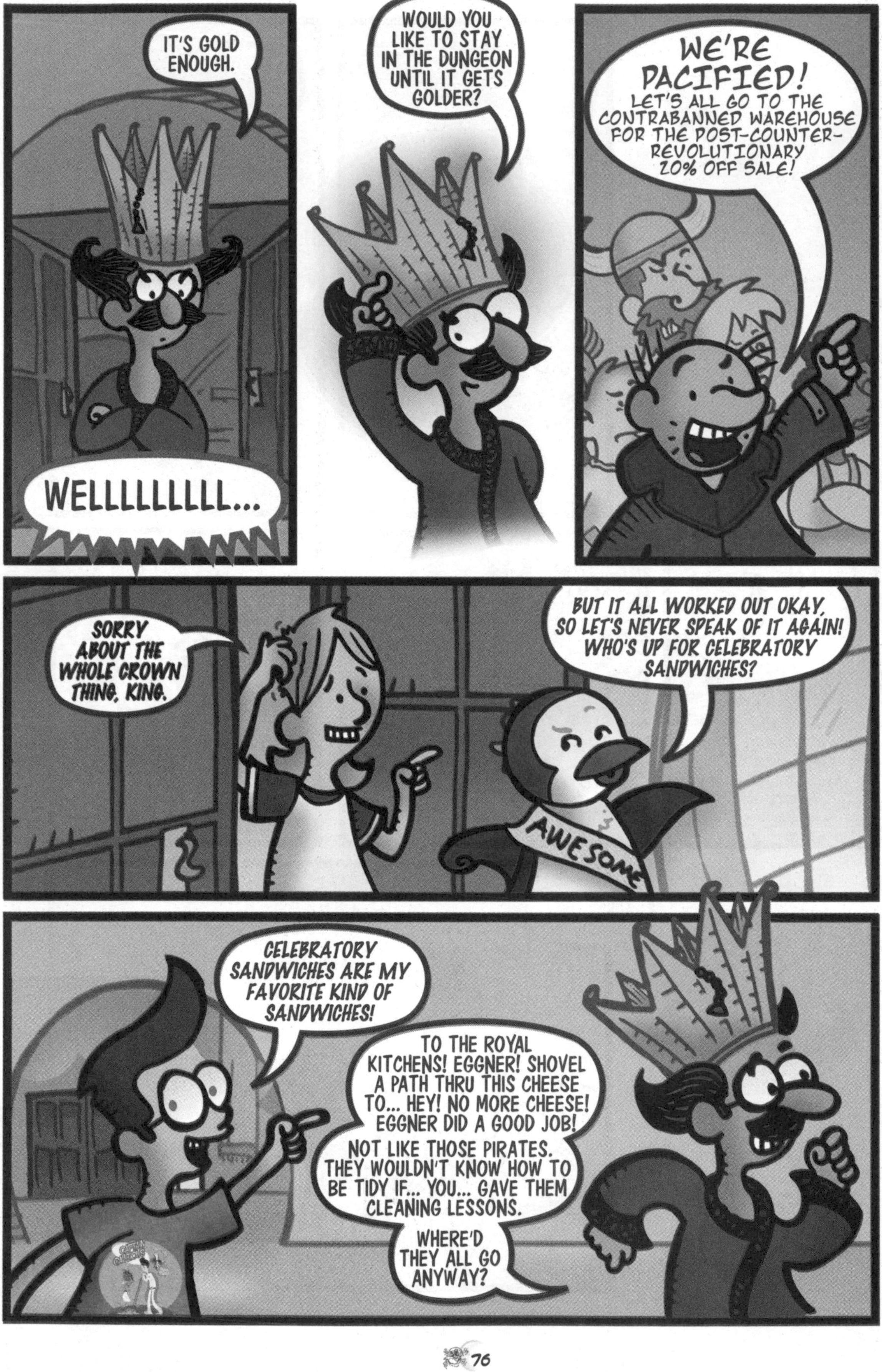
IT'S GOLD ENOUGH.
WELLLLLLLLL...
WOULD YOU LIKE TO STAY IN THE DUNGEON UNTIL IT GETS GOLDER?
WE'RE PACIFIED! LET'S ALL GO TO THE CONTRABANNED WAREHOUSE FOR THE POST-COUNTER-REVOLUTIONARY 20% OFF SALE!
SORRY ABOUT THE WHOLE CROWN THING, KING.
BUT IT ALL WORKED OUT OKAY, SO LET'S NEVER SPEAK OF IT AGAIN! WHO'S UP FOR CELEBRATORY SANDWICHES?
AWESOME
CELEBRATORY SANDWICHES ARE MY FAVORITE KIND OF SANDWICHES!
TO THE ROYAL KITCHENS! EGGNER! SHOVEL A PATH THRU THIS CHEESE TO... HEY! NO MORE CHEESE! EGGNER DID A GOOD JOB!
NOT LIKE THOSE PIRATES. THEY WOULDN'T KNOW HOW TO BE TIDY IF... YOU... GAVE THEM CLEANING LESSONS.
WHERE'D THEY ALL GO ANYWAY?

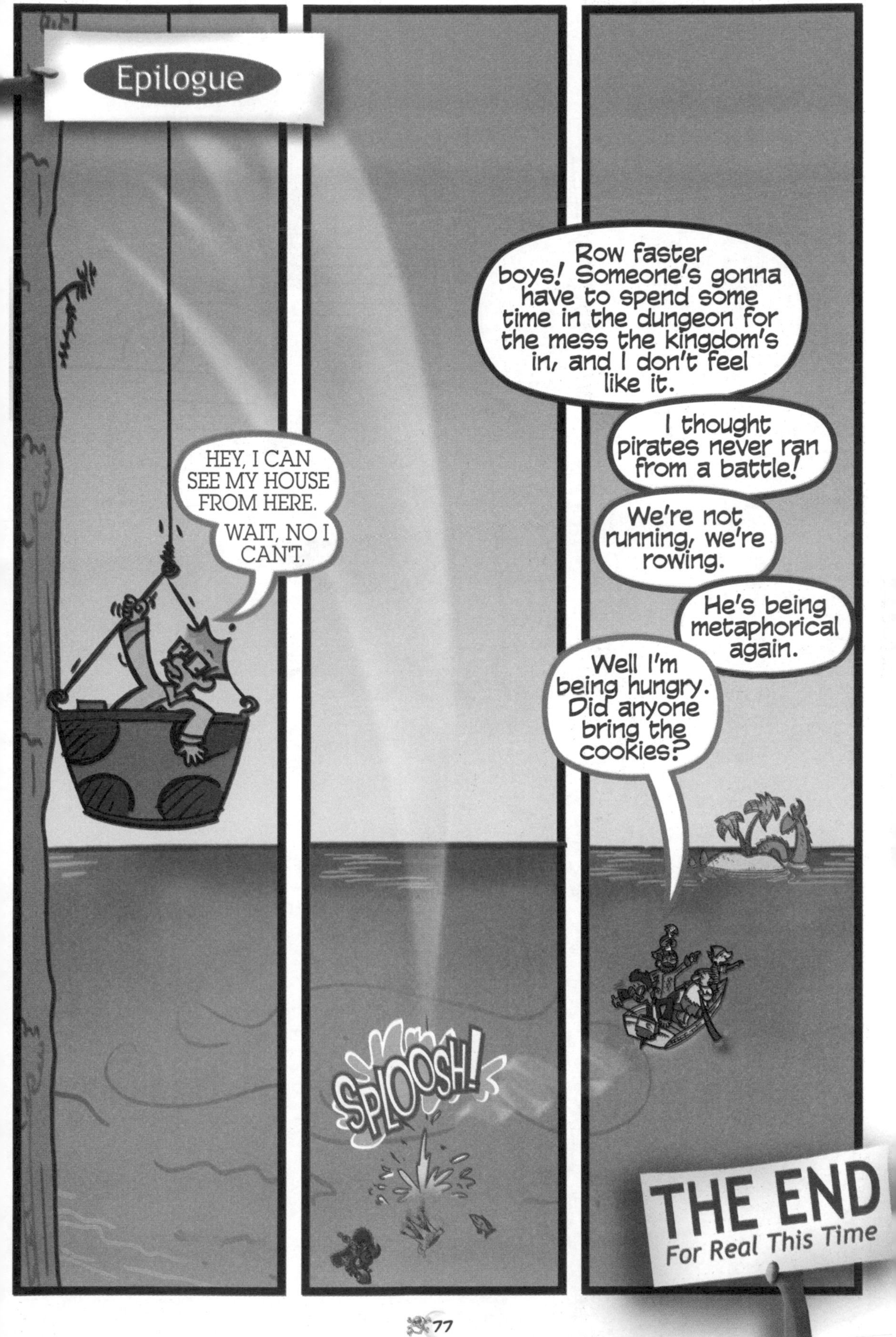

Epilogue
HEY, I CAN SEE MY HOUSE FROM HERE.
WAIT, NO I CAN'T.
SPLOOSH!
Row faster boys! Someone's gonna have to spend some time in the dungeon for the mess the kingdom's in, and I don't feel like it.
I thought pirates never ran from a battle!
We're not running, we're rowing.
He's being metaphorical again.
Well I'm being hungry. Did anyone bring the cookies?
THE END
For Real This Time

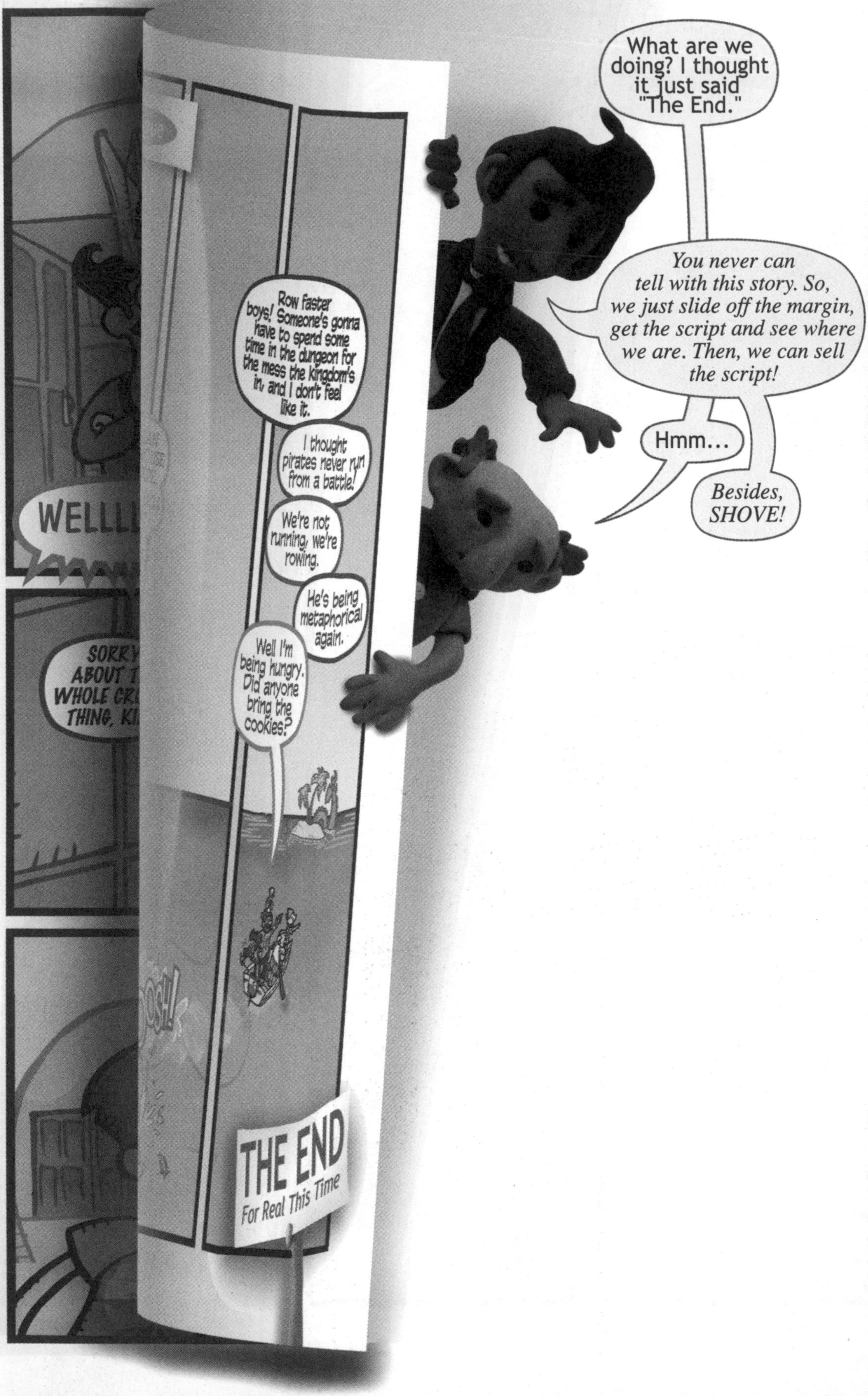
What are we doing? I thought it just said "The End."
You never can tell with this story. So, we just slide off the margin, get the script and see where we are. Then, we can sell the script!
Hmm...
Besides, SHOVE!
Row faster boys! Someone's gonna have to spend some time in the dungeon for the mess the kingdom's in, and I don't feel like it.
I thought pirates never run from a battle!
We're not running, we're rowing.
He's being metaphorical again.
Well I'm being hungry. Did anyone bring the cookies?
THE END
For Real This Time

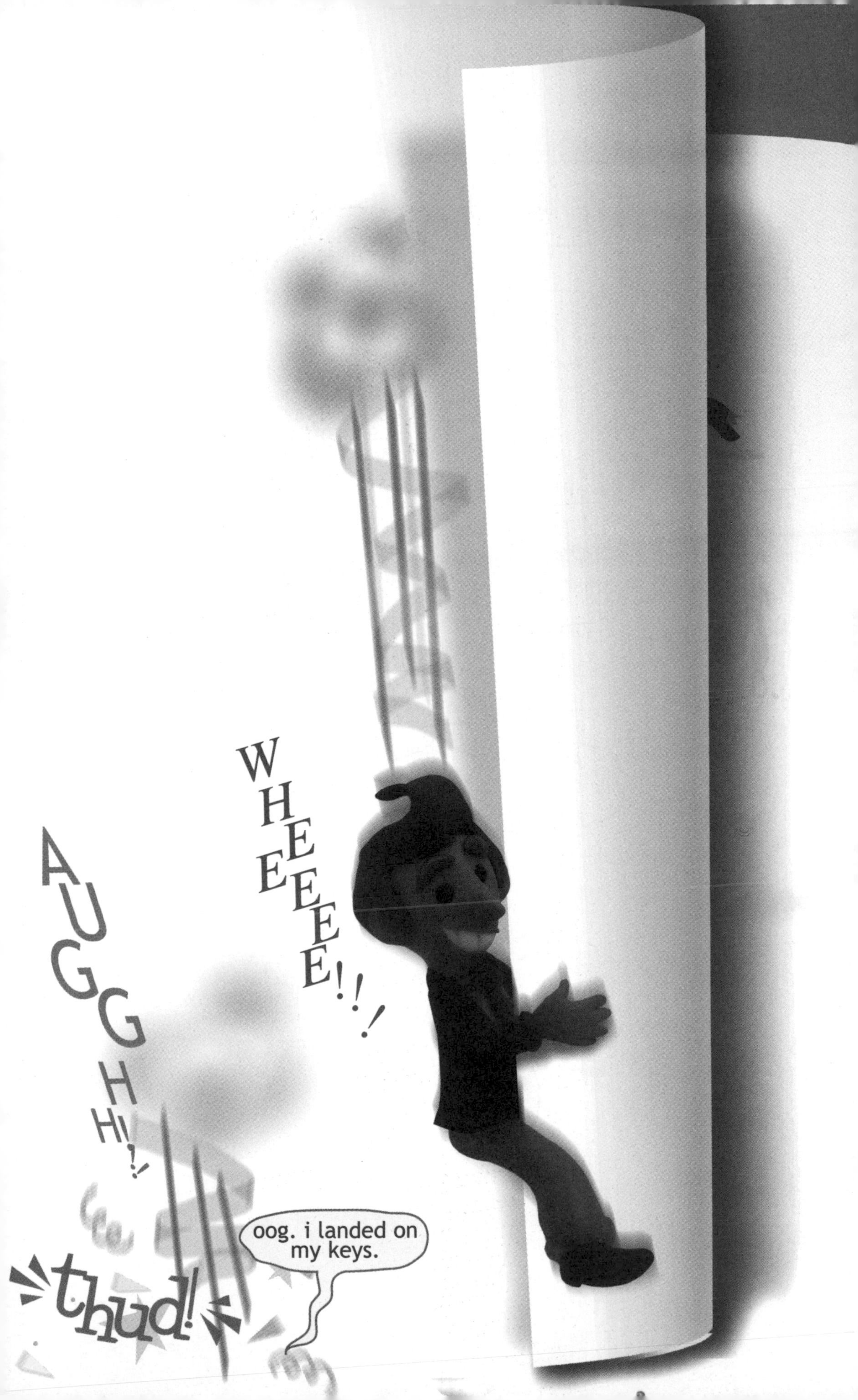
WHEEEEE!!!
AUGGHH!!!
thud!
oog. i landed on my keys.

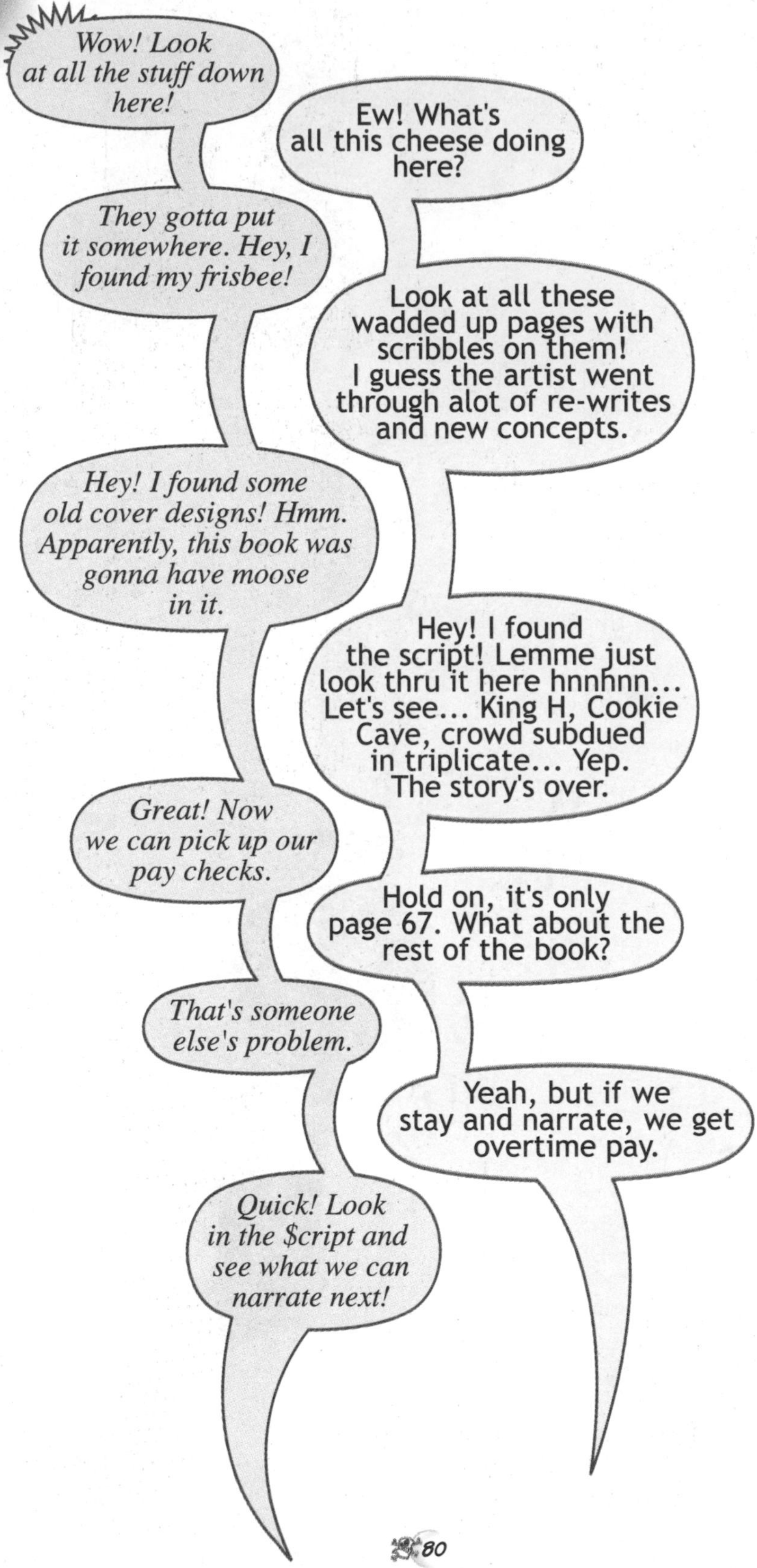
Wow! Look at all the stuff down here!
Ew! What's all this cheese doing here?
They gotta put it somewhere. Hey, I found my frisbee!
Look at all these wadded up pages with scribbles on them! I guess the artist went through alot of re-writes and new concepts.
Hey! I found some old cover designs! Hmm. Apparently, this book was gonna have moose in it.
Hey! I found the script! Lemme just look thru it here hnnhnn... Let's see... King H, Cookie Cave, crowd subdued in triplicate... Yep. The story's over.
Great! Now we can pick up our pay checks.
Hold on, it's only page 67. What about the rest of the book?
That's someone else's problem.
Yeah, but if we stay and narrate, we get overtime pay.
Quick! Look in the $cript and see what we can narrate next!

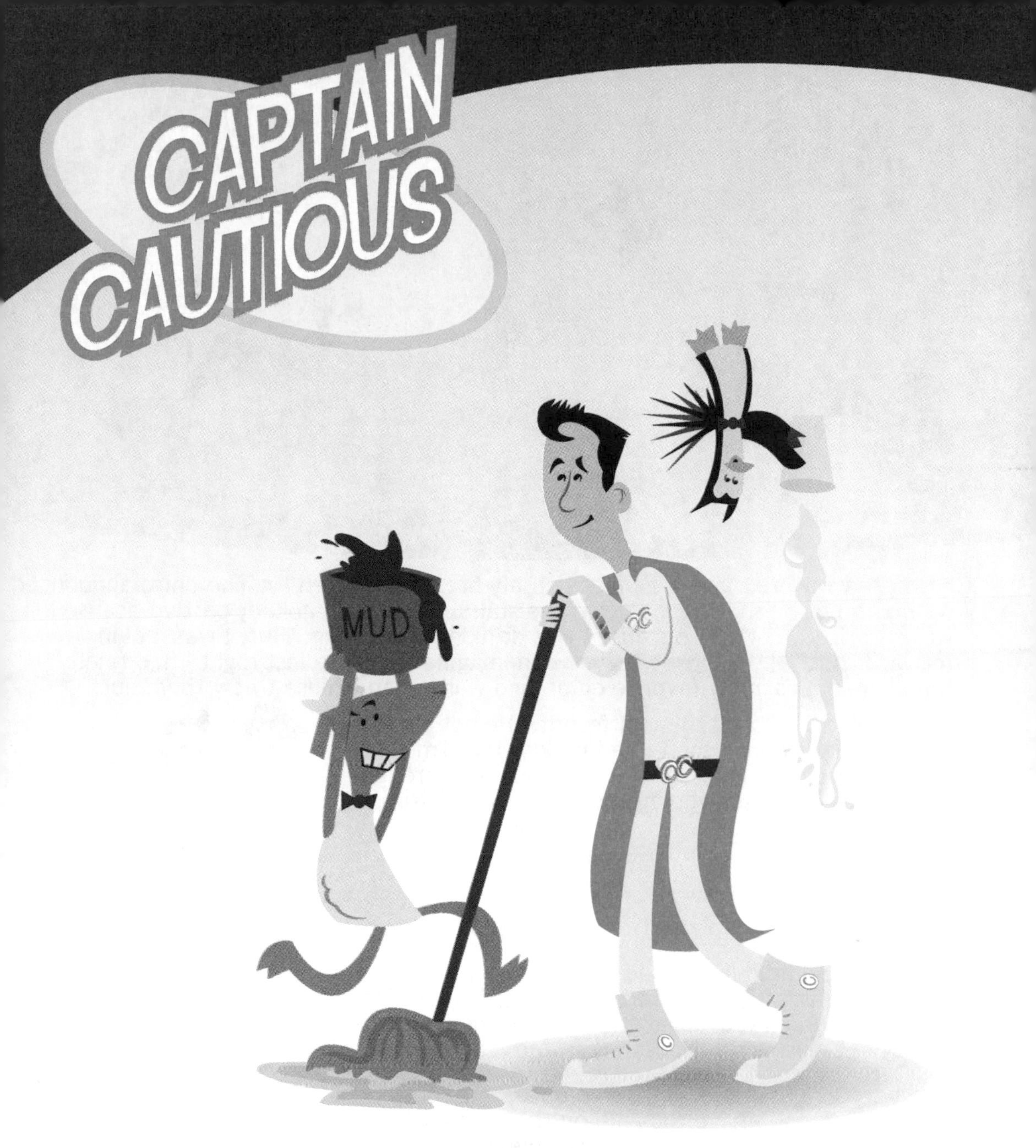
CAPTAIN CAUTIOUS
MUD

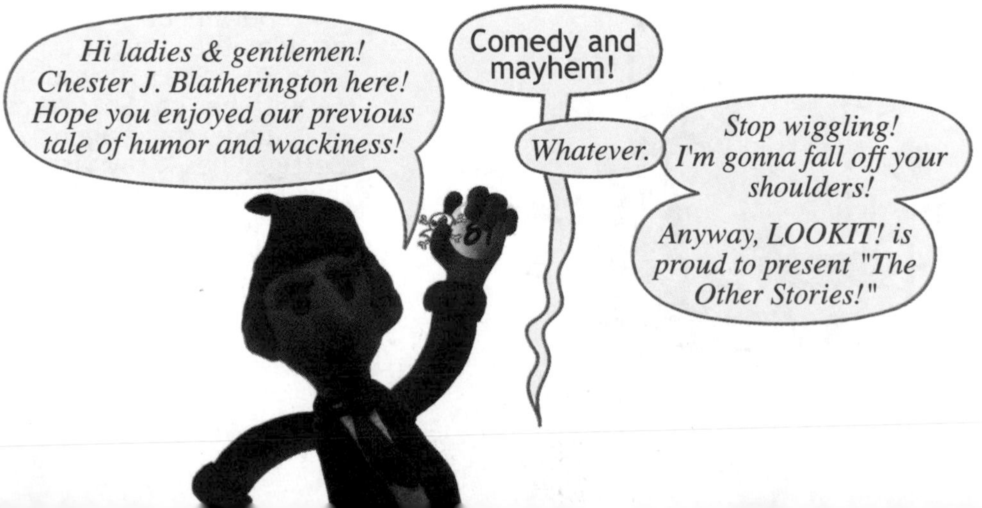
Hi ladies & gentlemen! Chester J. Blatherington here! Hope you enjoyed our previous tale of humor and wackiness!
Comedy and mayhem!
Whatever.
Stop wiggling! I'm gonna fall off your shoulders!
Anyway, LOOKIT! is proud to present "The Other Stories!"

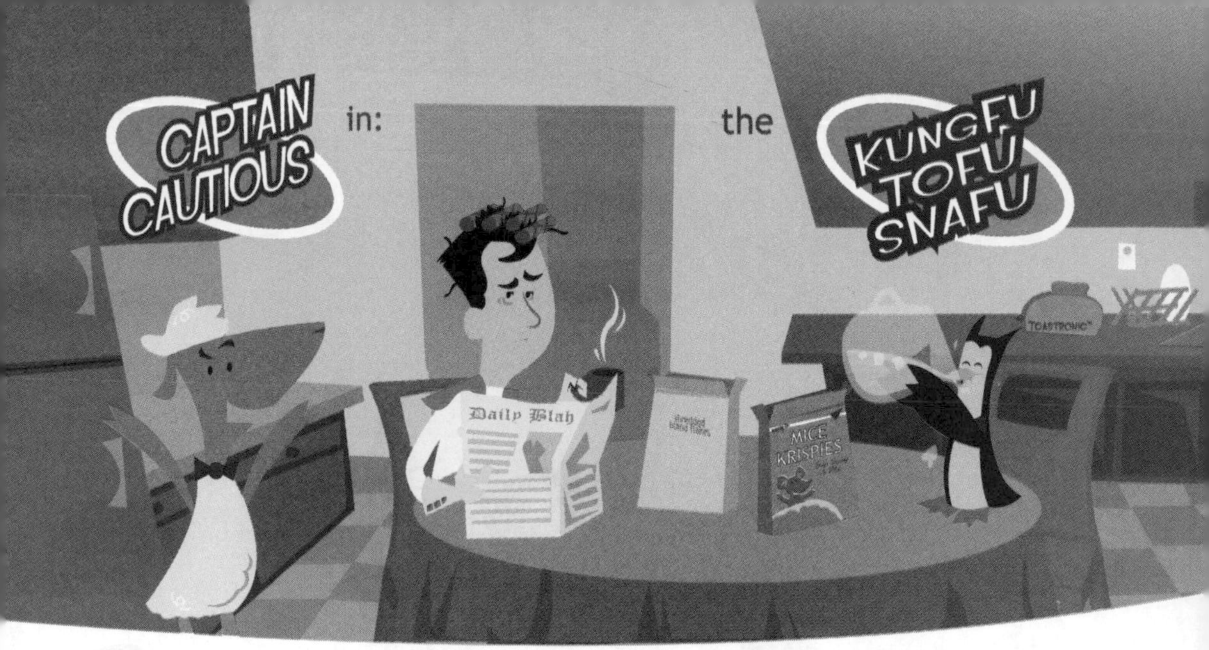
CAPTAIN CAUTIOUS
in:
the
KUNGFU TOFU SNAFU
Daily Blah
MICE KRISPIES
TOASTRONIC

So there we were, having a nice leisurely breakfast, when Mr. The Third announced he would not be shoving me down the stairs. "What?" I choked, partly because I was surprised, but also because I was drinking something. "But, I was looking forward to it!" I was upset, as you can imagine, because last night I had finally found kneepads in my favorite color, and wanted an excuse to try them out.

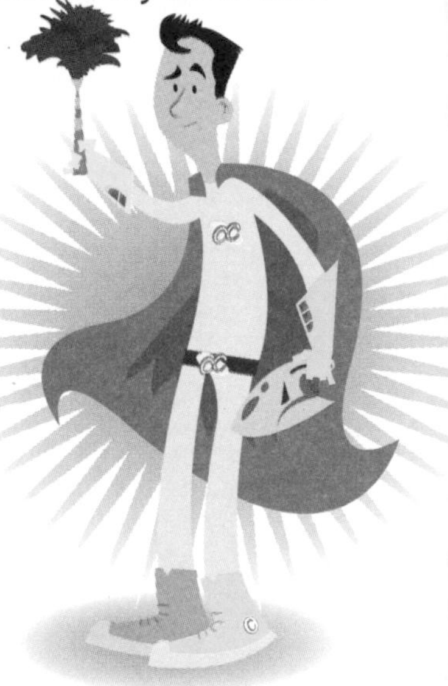

"We're gonna try something different." He got up and walked across the kitchen to a big door that I'm sure wasn't there last night. "Today, we'll put you through your paces by pitting you against the Niwatori Ninjas in unarmed combat!"

"Oh. Goody."

I suppose I should explain. I'm a super hero. Sort of.

I don't have a mild-mannered alter ego -- my regular ego is mild-mannered enough. (Also it's kind of difficult when your legal name is Captain Percival Evil-Doer-Smasher Cautious. My friends call me CC.)

And I don't fight crime. I tried to once. My cousin Jeremy The Impressive took me out heroing with him, but the first villain I ran into stole my wallet and made fun of my cape. I spent the rest of the day crying.

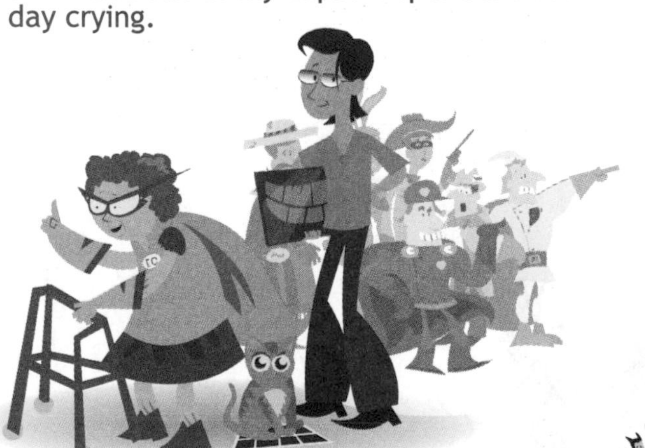

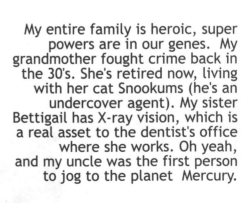

My entire family is heroic, super powers are in our genes. My grandmother fought crime back in the 30's. She's retired now, living with her cat Snookums (he's an undercover agent). My sister Bettigail has X-ray vision, which is a real asset to the dentist's office where she works. Oh yeah, and my uncle was the first person to jog to the planet Mercury.

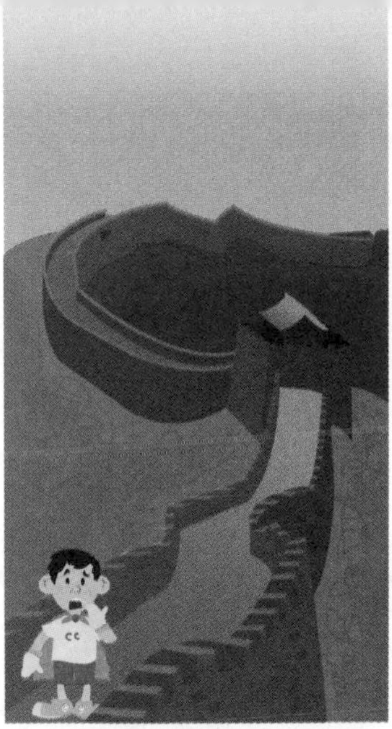

I don't really even have any super powers. Well, I do, I just don't know what they are or how to use them. I do know that I'm rather tall, have an excellent fashion sense, and of course, I went to barber college. My powers only seem to work if I don't think about them. If I try to do something, it won't happen.The power usually just sneaks out in other ways instead. Like the time when I was about four years old and I got a bad cold. When I sneezed, I rocketed backwards so far that I landed in China. Seriously. To this day I can't eat orange peel chicken, but that's mostly because I'm a vegetarian. And allergic to oranges.

When I jump, I do seem to hover a few seconds longer than usual. This probably means I can fly, but I've never tested it further, cuz I'm scared of heights

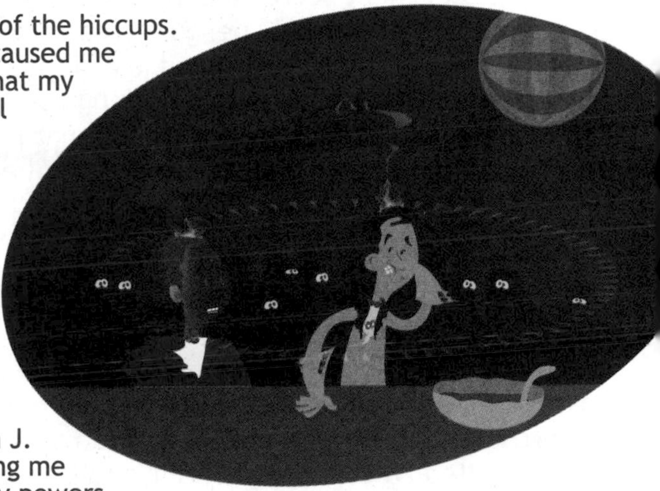

At my senior prom, I got a bad case of the hiccups. I tried holding my breath, but that caused me to hiccup harder. So hard, in fact, that my clothes blew right off, and several people nearby caught fire. That sure was embarrassing. Fortunately, most everyone was too busy yelling and screaming to notice that I was suddenly in my underwear (my boxer shorts are fireproof. Long story). I never did find that rental tux.

So, back to getting shoved down the stairs and fighting professional ninjas -- that's just my boss, William J. Woolington The Third's way of helping me continue to discover and improve my powers. At least, that's what he says it's for. I suspect it's more for his own personal amusement. He's always leaping out at me from closets, dumping buckets of water on my head and firing me out of cannons to see what super power might emerge. It's a little exhausting, but that's what he pays me for!

Of course I don't really know what my job title is. I just do pretty much whatever he tells me to, I guess. (Boy, that'll look good on my resumé: "2002 - present: did whatever a sheep told me to.") Probably most people would find it frustrating being bossed around so much (in fact he went through a dozen butlers before he met me), but I find it oddly fulfilling. (Not that I'm his butler of course. I just answer the door sometimes. And do the grocery shopping. And do his taxes and vacuuming and running errands and laying out his socks. Hmm. I'm his butler aren't I? I wonder if speaking in a British accent could be one of my super powers?) I do try to prepare a healthy lunch, which he usually ignores. He just eats fast foods. I tried giving him lectures on the importance of a healthy diet, but he just tunes me out. Literally. He gave some research scientists a huge grant to develop a remote control so he can turn the volume down on people he didn't want to listen to. It worked only too well, so when he wasn't looking I removed the batteries. He's been a billionaire his whole life, so batteries have always been changed for him. Now he just thinks the remote is broken. The scientists have asked for another grant to fix it.

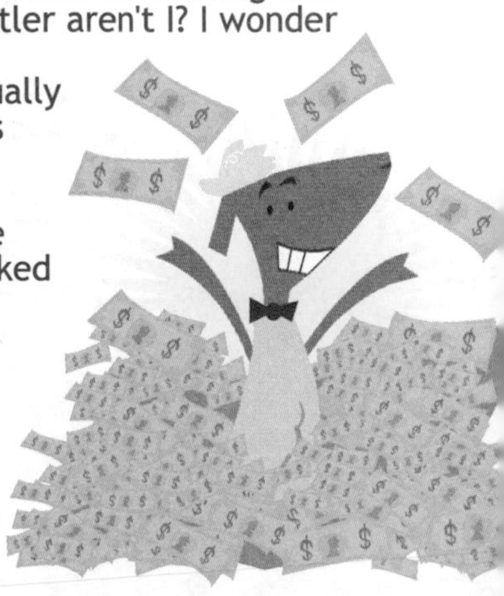

The only thing he lets me "prepare" is cereal. This house goes through a ton of cereal. Not because we're really that hungry, but because he loves the toys inside. I always remind him that he has millions of dollars at his disposal, so why not just buy the toys? But, Mr. The Third insists that would be cheating. Plus, Batguin loves ripping the box tops off.

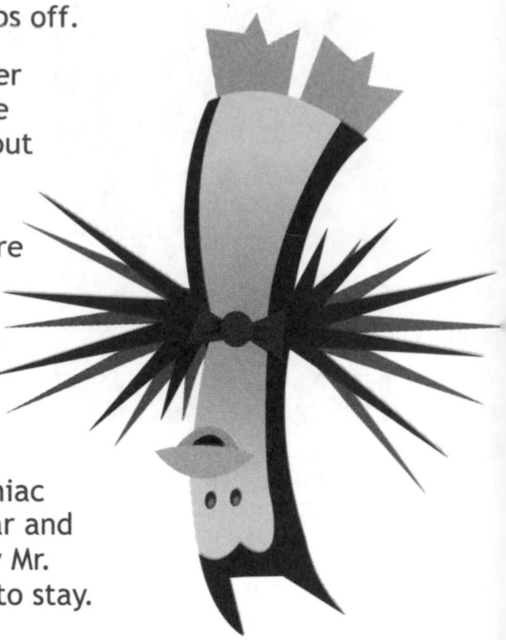

Have I mentioned Batguin? He's the third member of our happy household. He (or possibly she - we don't know what species it is, let alone gender, but we just call it "he" and that seems to be fine) came to us a few months ago, hidden in a box of Shrimpeeos cereal (now with 20% more barnacles!) Mr. The Third thinks he has some dramatic back-story -- he's an alien that was sent to earth in a meteorite, or perhaps an escapee from some secret-government-secret-genetic-experiment-secret-laboratory. He is a sorta' half-bat half-penguin creature, we think. Whatever he is, just imagine a kleptomaniac four-year old that's been eating nothing but sugar and can also fly, and you have Batguin. So, naturally Mr. The Third thinks he's my sidekick, and he's here to stay.

Anyway, when we're not eating cereal, we usually go to the nearest McLarry's Fast Food, a restaurant chain Mr. The Third owns. I don't mean we drive to get it, he has a food court IN the mansion. There's everything in his mansion -- it's huge! (The mansion, not the food court. Although, the food court's pretty big too.) For example he has an expedition planned to chart the unexplored East Wing. And the kitchen has a walk-in toaster oven. Oh, and there's a motorcycle race track on the roof. Even as we speak, he's having a secret submarine base installed (what's the difference between a secret submarine and a regular one, by the way?) He's always having new rooms installed, and stuff constructed. It's kinda exciting, actually.

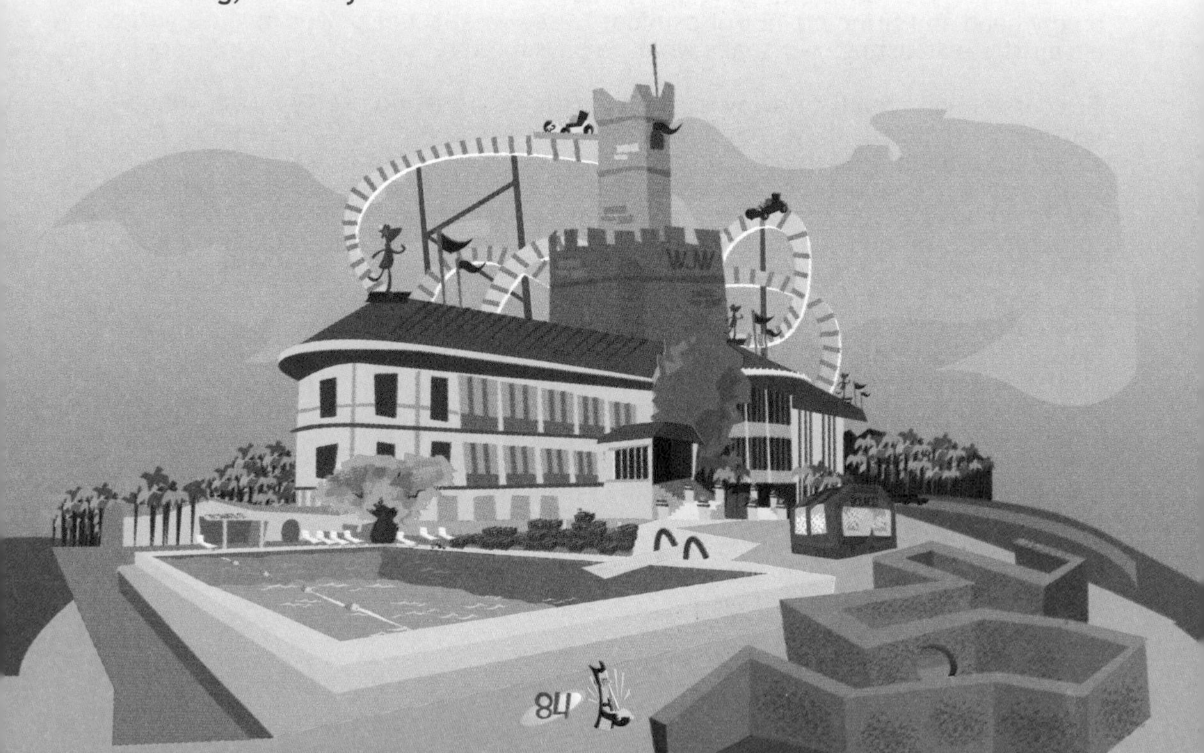

So anyway, I figured, that's how this giant room I'd never seen before came to be. I stepped through the door from the kitchen, and into a battledome. As the door locked behind me, I realized I was sealed in with the ninjas. "Okay, CC!" came Mr. The Third's voice from a loud speaker. "These guys are the best in the world, so don't hold back! I want to see what cool super-fighting powers you'll unleash! Try to make your arms shoot off like rockets, punch, then reattach! That'd be awesome! 3, 2, 1...GO!"

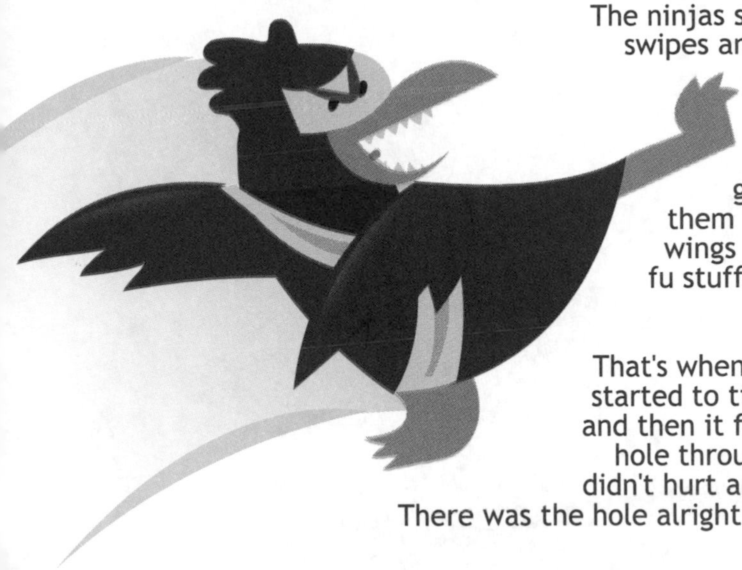

The ninjas started leaping around making swipes and kicks and other intimidating motions. I was worried. I may be invulnerable, but that doesn't mean I can't get hurt. I don't really like getting hurt. Suddenly, one of them leaped right at me, waving his wings and shouting, you know, kung-fu stuff. I closed my eyes and aimed a panicky kick at him.

That's when something happened. My foot started to tingle, like it had fallen asleep, and then it felt like my foot was bursting a hole through a wall of crackers. Oh no, I didn't hurt anyone did I? I opened my eyes. There was the hole alright, but no wall, and no crackers.

"Wow!" The ninjas looked impressed. "You just kicked a hole in the fabric of reality! That's a vortex into another dimension! Only a martial arts master of the tealish-yellow belt level can do that!" Their leader bowed to me and said, "And now, we must go. We are not worthy enough to oppose you. Also, we were paid in advance, so so long, suckers!"

Mr. The Third opened the battle doors and walked over to the vortex. "I can't believe it! My very own hole in the fabric of reality! I wonder what's on the other side?"

Something fell out from the other side of reality.

"What is it?"

"It looks like a bean. Soy I'd say, or possibly pinto. Yes, definitely a soy bean."

And then another one plooped out of the vortex. And another.
And then it just dumped soybeans.

"Ok, that's enough, CC! Turn it off!
"I don't know how!"
"Maybe if you kick it again?" suggested Mr. The Third. So I did.

"Great. Now it's twice as big!
Let's get outta here!"

We dashed from the room, and slammed the kitchen door. The alternate-reality beans gushed out of the hole. We could hear them filling the room. There was a tense moment when I could swear it seemed like the walls expanded for a moment, and then all was silent.

"I think it stopped."

KaBLAM!!!!!

"I think it didn't stop."

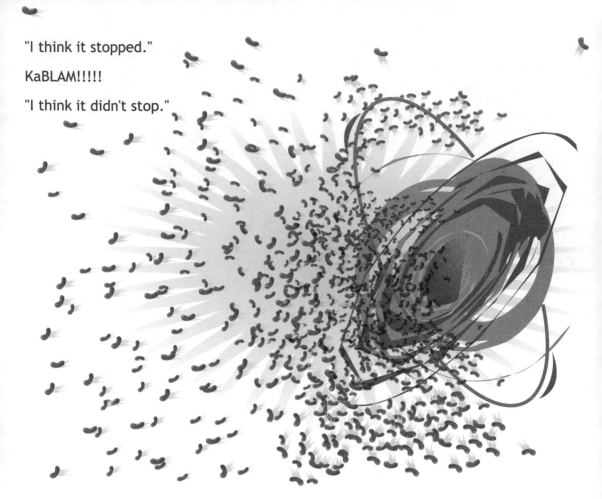

The door burst open, and the beans exploded into the kitchen. We made a break for it, slamming the door between the kitchen and the next room, and piling furniture in front of it, of course. "That's just great!" shouted Mr. The Third. "I suppose they'll just keep pouring in through the bean hole until the entire earth is overrun!" He stopped shouting and looked thoughtful for a moment. "Why is the parallel universe filled with beans, do you think?" Then the moment passed and he started shouting again. He's better at shouting. "Oh, good going CC. It's not as if you can even use soy beans for anything!"

"That's not true," I corrected him. "You can use them to make soy sauce. Or tofu. Lots of people like tofu."

"Hmmmmm, that's an idea! I could be sitting on a goldmine here! A never-ending supply of soybeans, so I could buy a tofu factory, and start manufacturing, and... waitaminute... is this tofu stuff any good?"

"Oh yes!  It's one of my absolute favorites!"
"Is it... healthy?"

"Oh my, yes!  Rats, I mean, um...." But it was too late. Mr. The Third had stuck his head out the window and was shouting to the building crew that was always somewhere on the mansion's grounds. "Hey construction guy! If I had a room with stuff leaking into it, and I didn't want it to escape, could you, like, pour cement over it and completely seal the room?"

The foreman was used to the sheep's strange requests. He replied, "Sure, if you want me to. You got a busted water pipe?"

"Something like that. Get the cement pouring right away! Cover up this whole wing!"

I couldn't believe it. I sputtered at Mr. The Third, "What did you go and do that for? Do you know how much tofu that could have made? You could have added it to the menu at your McLarry Fast Food restaurants. Started a whole new health-conscious menu, you could have changed the eating habits of the nation! You could have changed the world!"

"Hey, maybe that's another of your super powers."

"What is?"

"Optimism in the face of overwhelming evidence to the contrary. Besides, I think I had tofu once. It was like jello made out of socks. I'm doing the world a favor."

I followed him as he strolled outside and headed towards the pool. "Ok, CC, let's test something else. How long do you think you could hold your breath?"

"Oh, in the pool, you mean?" I smiled. "We've done that one before."

"Not exactly. This time I've had the pool stocked with lobsters."

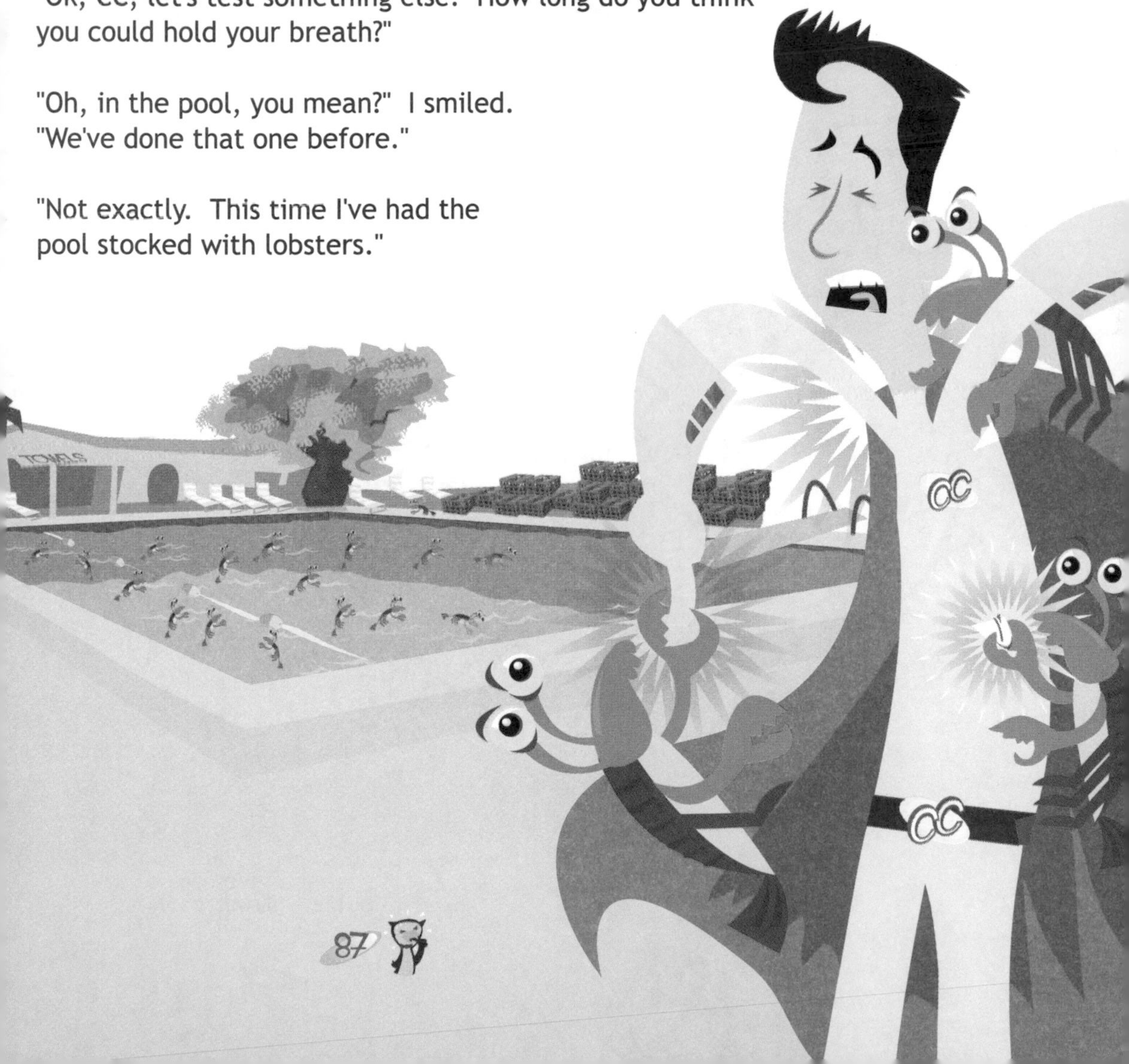
TOWELS
CC
CC

# tBYRD fearlessness

Tbyrd Fearlessness and his sidekick, Hopalong Cassowary are outlaws. At least, they think they are. Well, they wanna be. Actually, they think they wanna be. Of course, they haven't gotten around to any real criminal activities because they're easily distracted. And clueless.

But nothing can stop them from their search for fame and fortune. Except for maybe lunch.

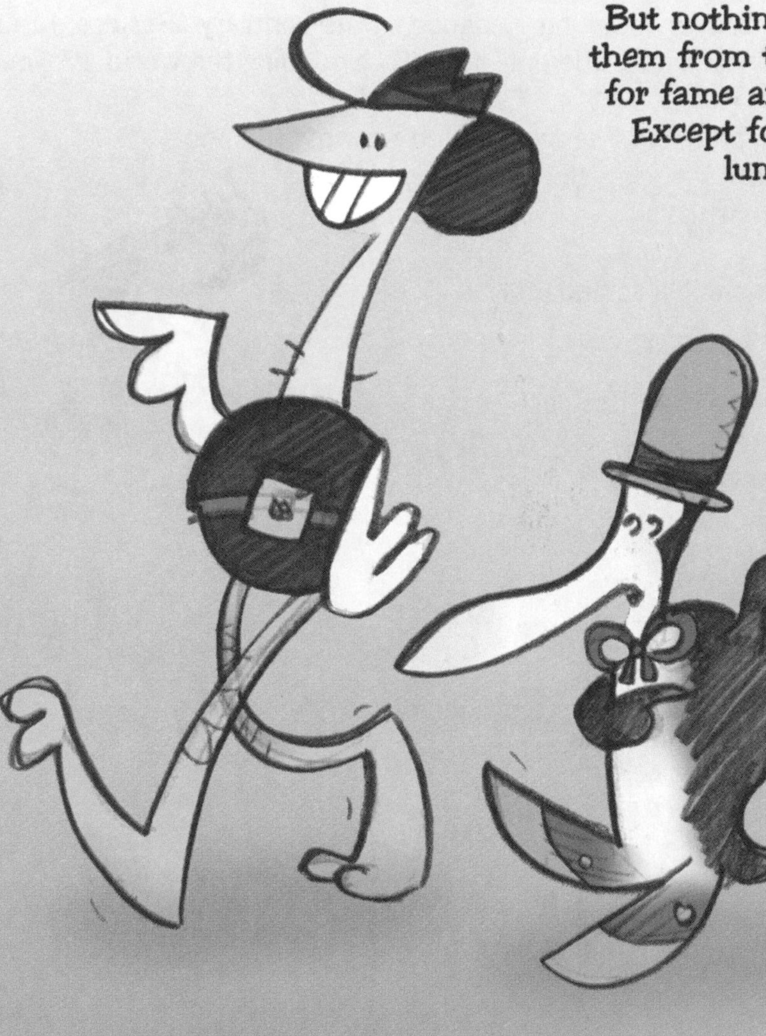

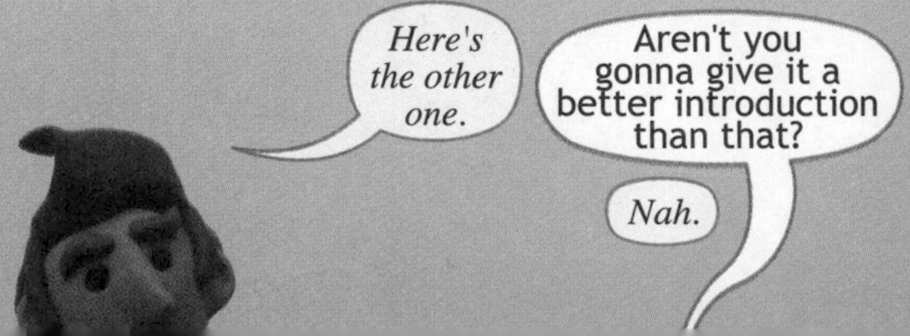
*Here's the other one.*
Aren't you gonna give it a better introduction than that?
*Nah.*

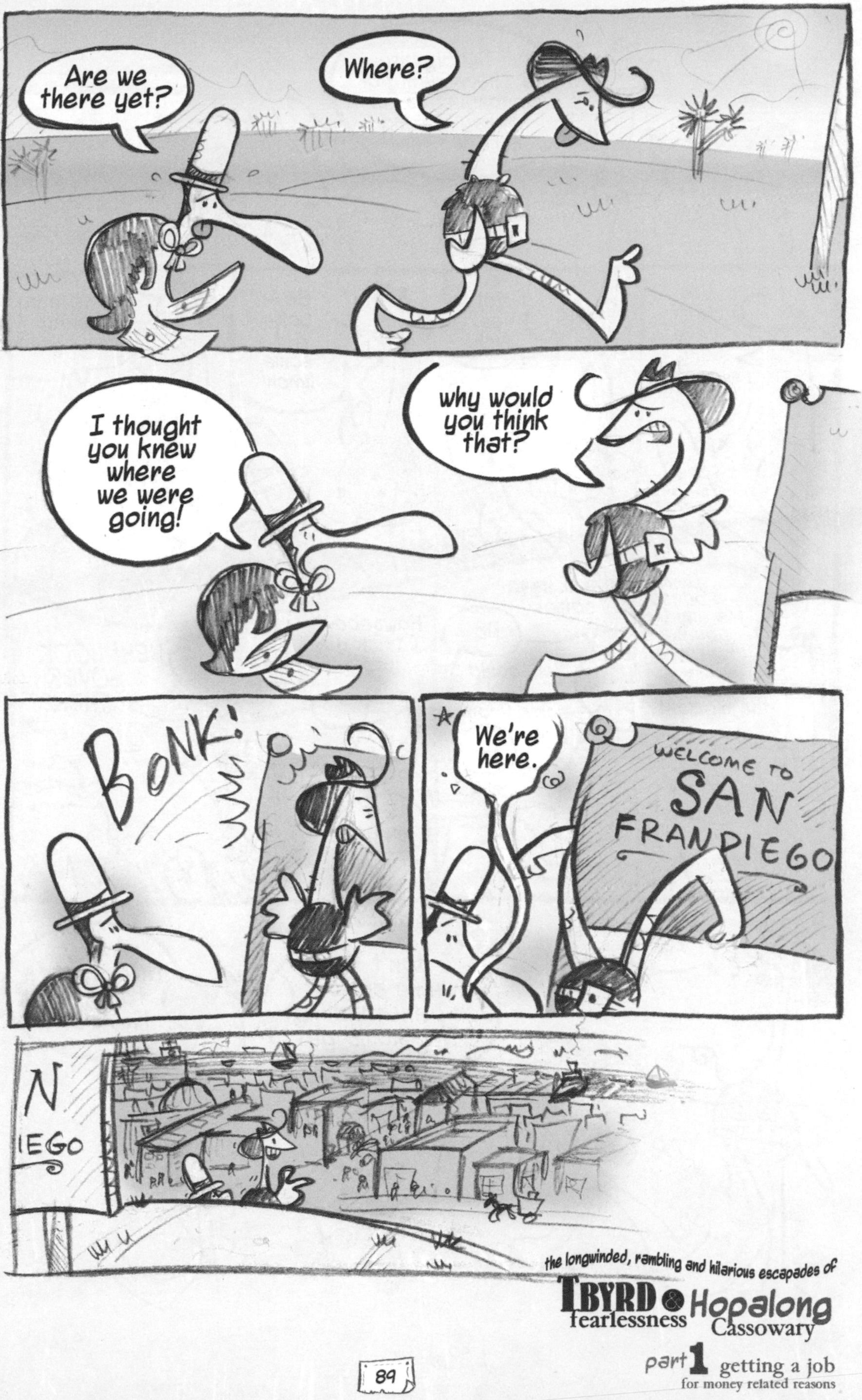
Are we there yet?
Where?
I thought you knew where we were going!
why would you think that?
BONK!
We're here.
WELCOME TO SAN FRANDIEGO
N
IEGO
the longwinded, rambling and hilarious escapades of
TBYRD fearlessness & Hopalong Cassowary
part 1 getting a job
for money related reasons

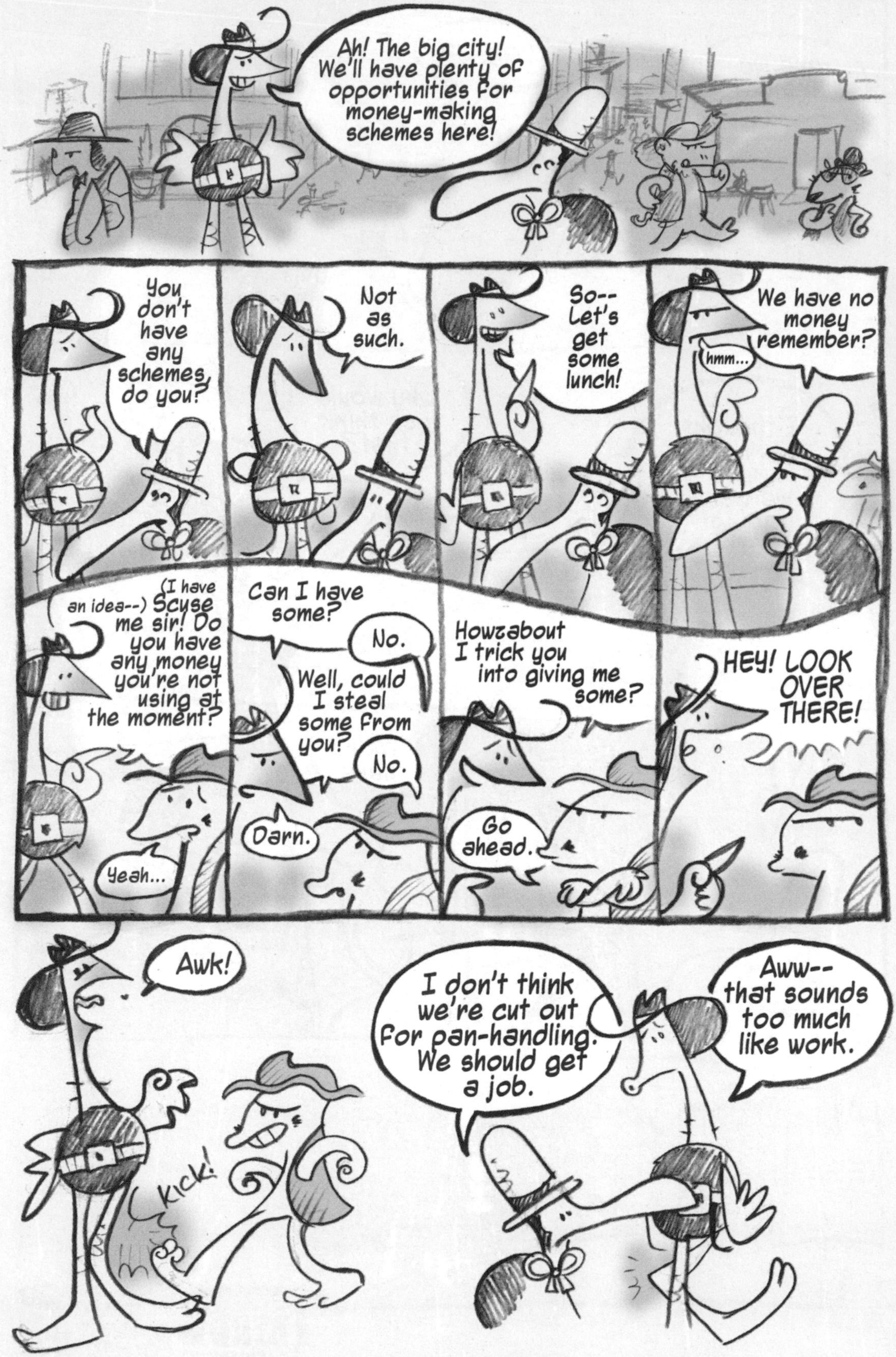
Ah! The big city! We'll have plenty of opportunities for money-making schemes here!
You don't have any schemes, do you?
Not as such.
So-- Let's get some lunch!
hmm...
We have no money remember?
(I have an idea--) Scuse me sir! Do you have any money you're not using at the moment?
Yeah...
Can I have some?
No.
Well, could I steal some from you?
No.
Darn.
Howzabout I trick you into giving me some?
Go ahead.
HEY! LOOK OVER THERE!
Awk!
KICK!
I don't think we're cut out for pan-handling. We should get a job.
Aww-- that sounds too much like work.

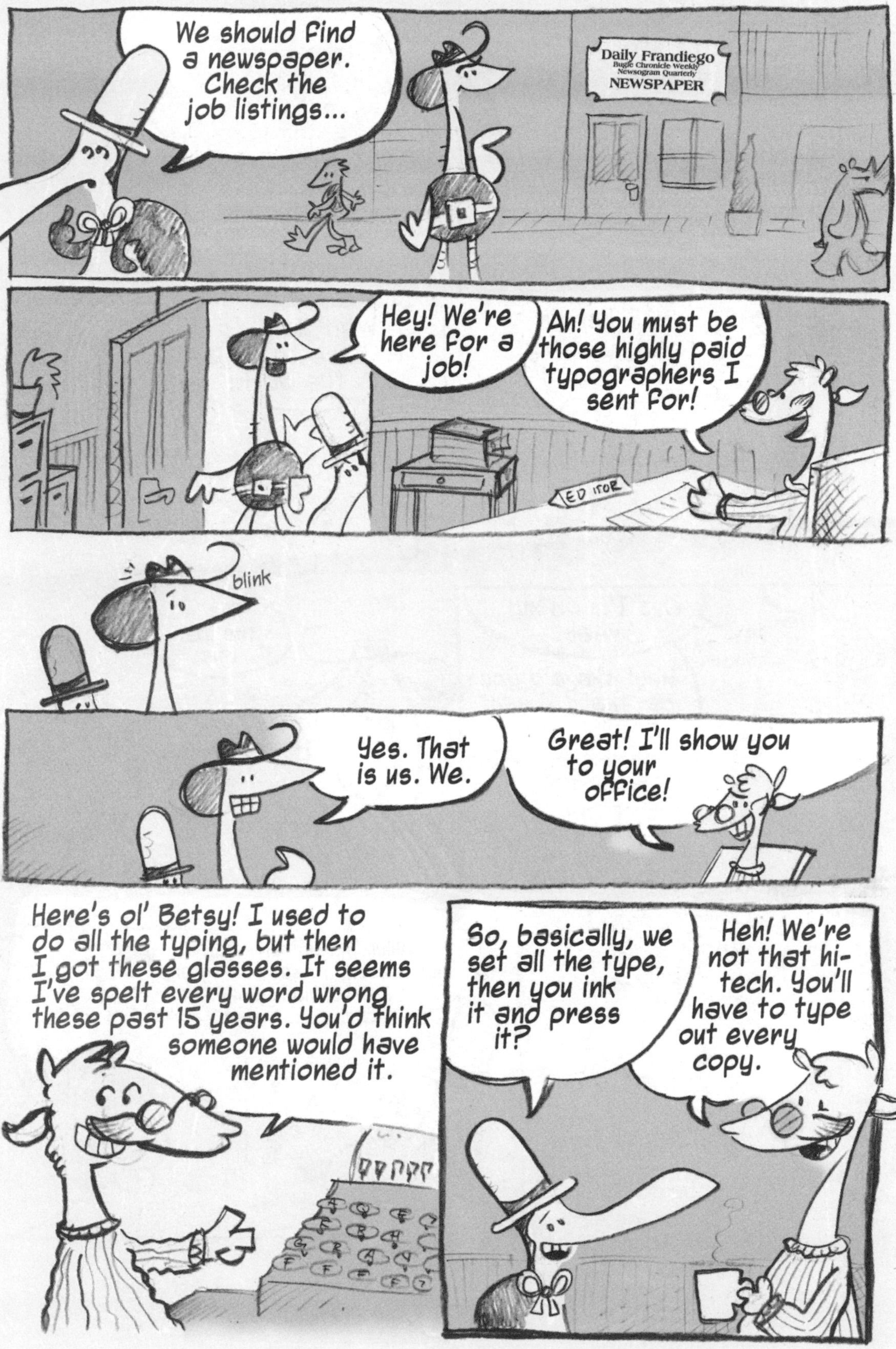
We should find a newspaper. Check the job listings...
Daily Frandiego Bugle Chronicle Weekly Newsogram Quarterly NEWSPAPER
Hey! We're here for a job!
Ah! You must be those highly paid typographers I sent for!
EDITOR
blink
Yes. That is us. We.
Great! I'll show you to your office!
Here's ol' Betsy! I used to do all the typing, but then I got these glasses. It seems I've spelt every word wrong these past 15 years. You'd think someone would have mentioned it.
So, basically, we set all the type, then you ink it and press it?
Heh! We're not that hi-tech. You'll have to type out every copy.

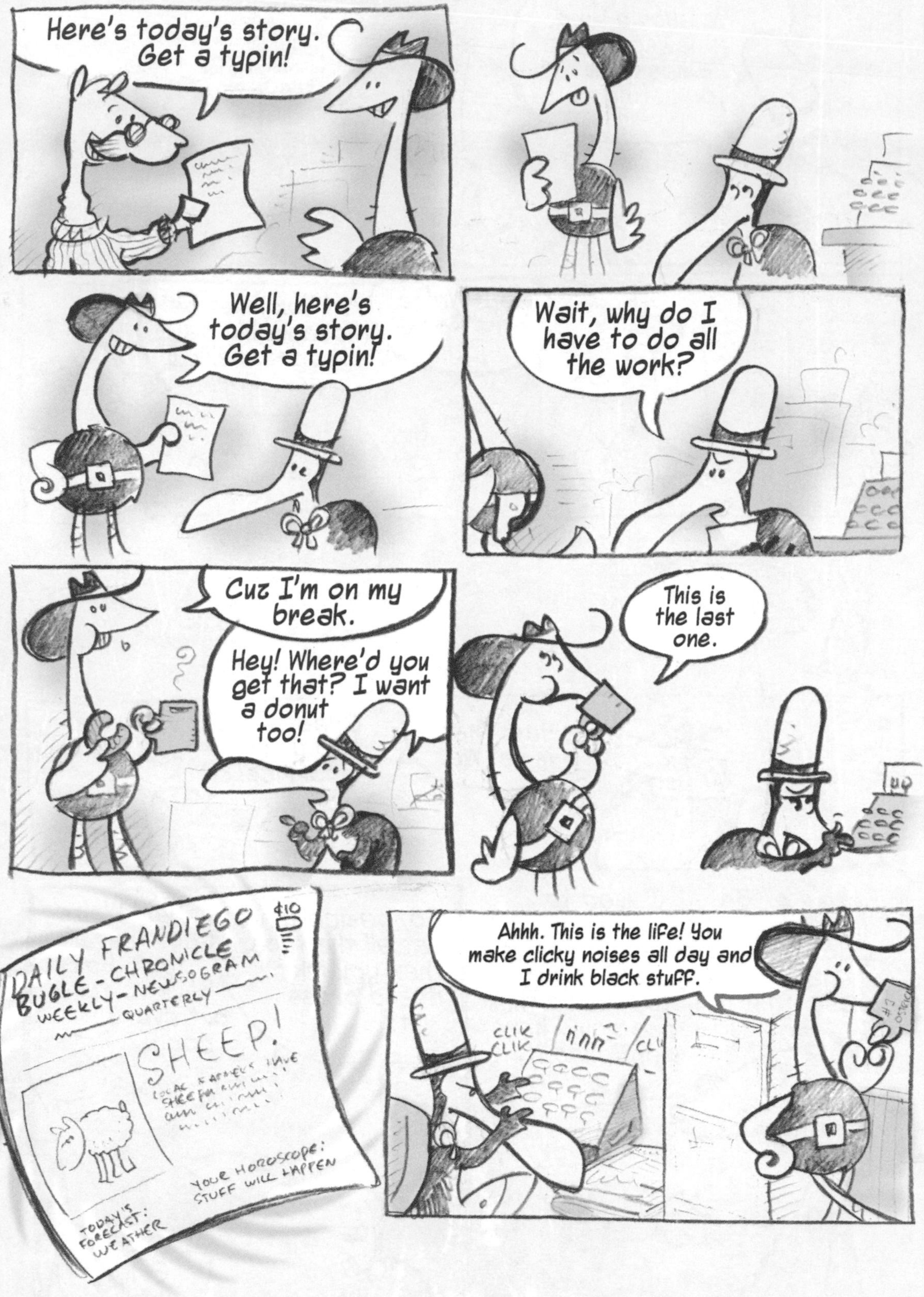
Here's today's story. Get a typin!
Well, here's today's story. Get a typin!
Wait, why do I have to do all the work?
Cuz I'm on my break.
Hey! Where'd you get that? I want a donut too!
This is the last one.
DAILY FRANDIEGO BUGLE-CHRONICLE WEEKLY-NEWSOGRAM QUARTERLY
$10
SHEEP!
YOUR HOROSCOPE: STUFF WILL HAPPEN
TODAY'S FORECAST: WEATHER
Ahhh. This is the life! You make clicky noises all day and I drink black stuff.
CLIK CLIK

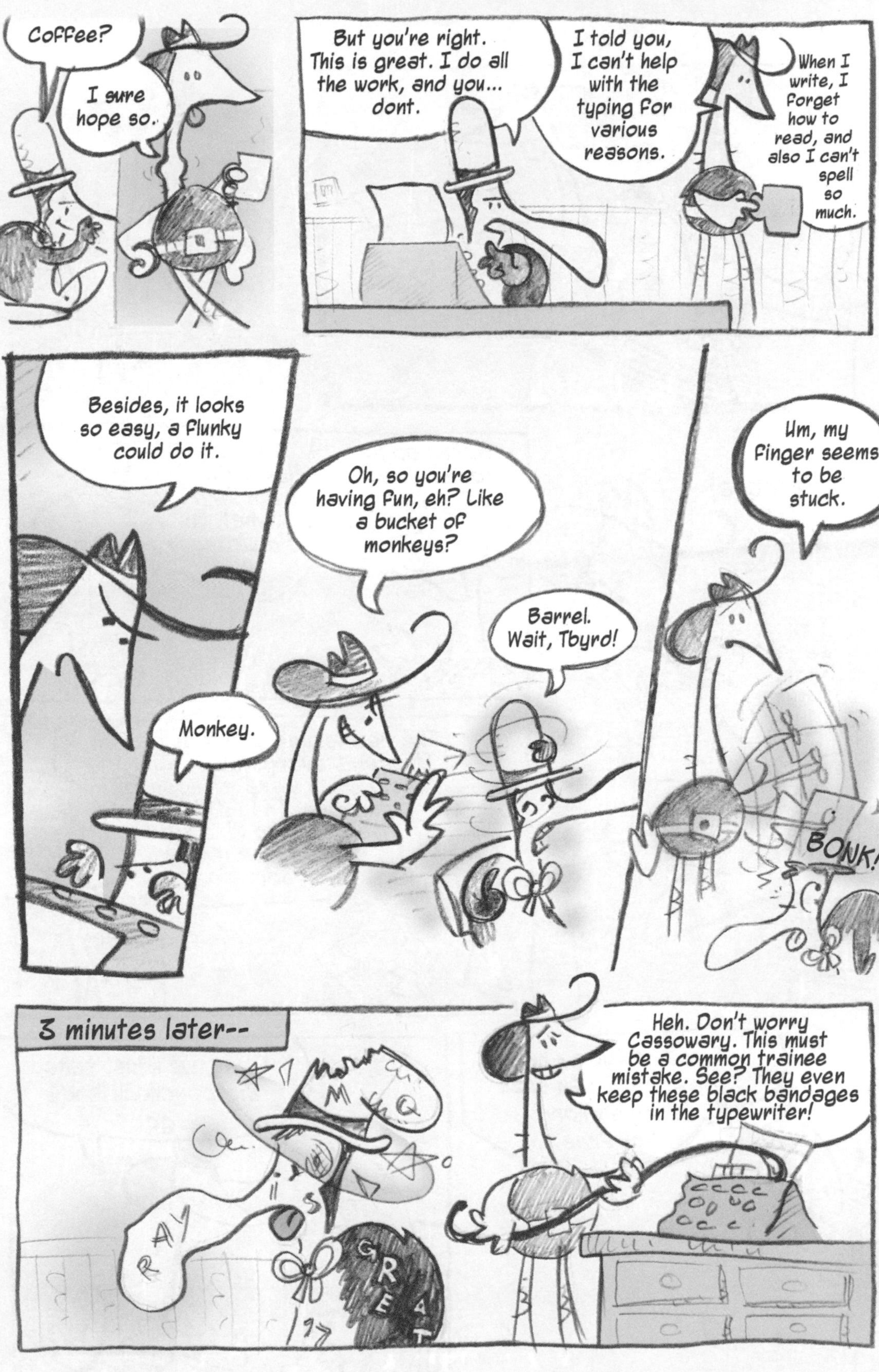
Coffee?
I sure hope so.
But you're right. This is great. I do all the work, and you... dont.
I told you, I can't help with the typing for various reasons.
When I write, I forget how to read, and also I can't spell so much.
Besides, it looks so easy, a flunky could do it.
Monkey.
Oh, so you're having fun, eh? Like a bucket of monkeys?
Barrel. Wait, Tbyrd!
Um, my finger seems to be stuck.
BONK!
3 minutes later--
Heh. Don't worry Cassowary. This must be a common trainee mistake. See? They even keep these black bandages in the typewriter!

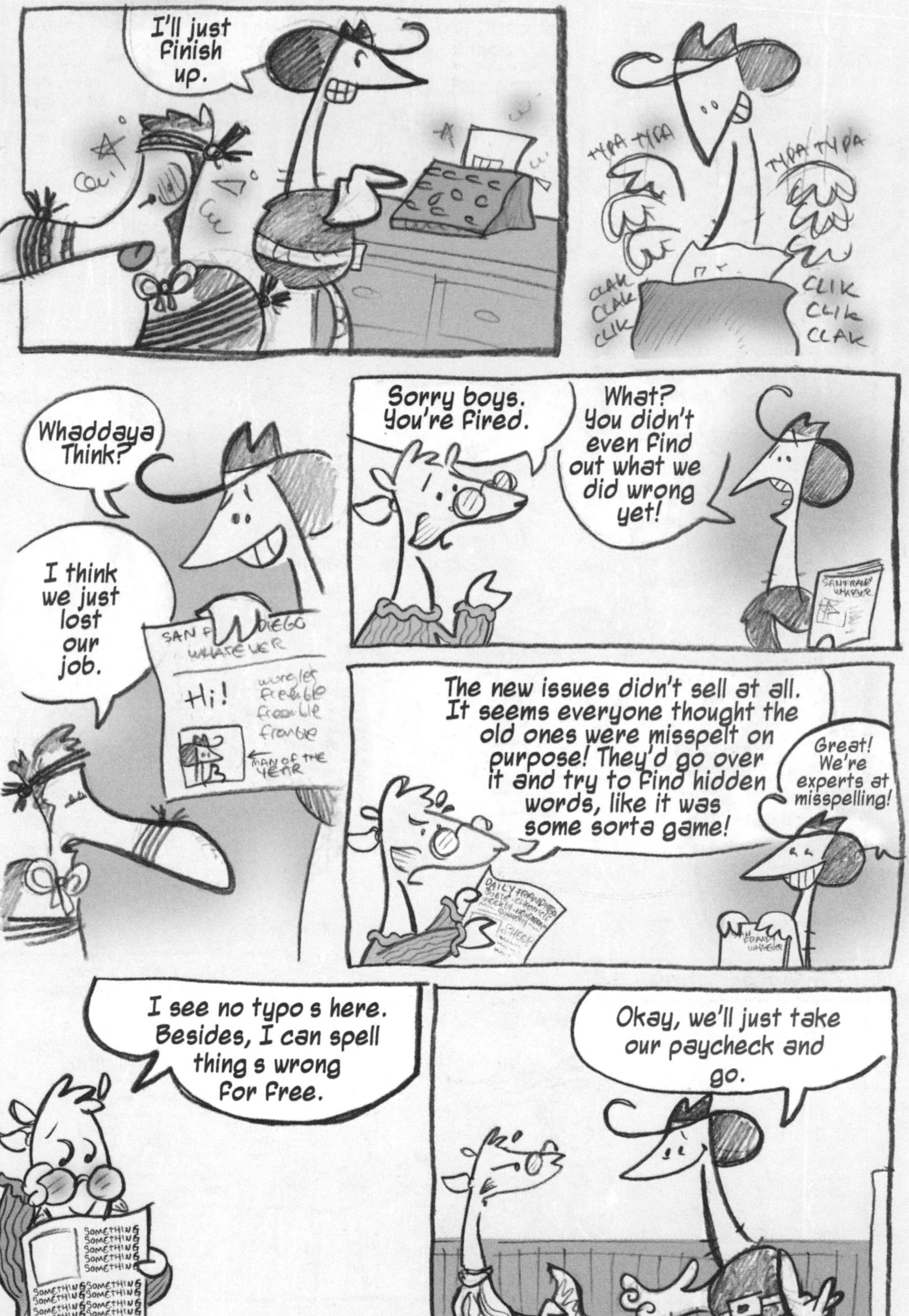

I'll just finish up.
TYPA TYPA
TYPA TYPA
CLAK CLAK CLIK
CLIK CLIK CLAK
Whaddaya Think?
I think we just lost our job.
Hi!
MAN OF THE YEAR
Sorry boys. You're fired.
What? You didn't even find out what we did wrong yet!
The new issues didn't sell at all. It seems everyone thought the old ones were misspelt on purpose! They'd go over it and try to find hidden words, like it was some sorta game!
Great! We're experts at misspelling!
I see no typo s here. Besides, I can spell thing s wrong for free.
Okay, we'll just take our paycheck and go.

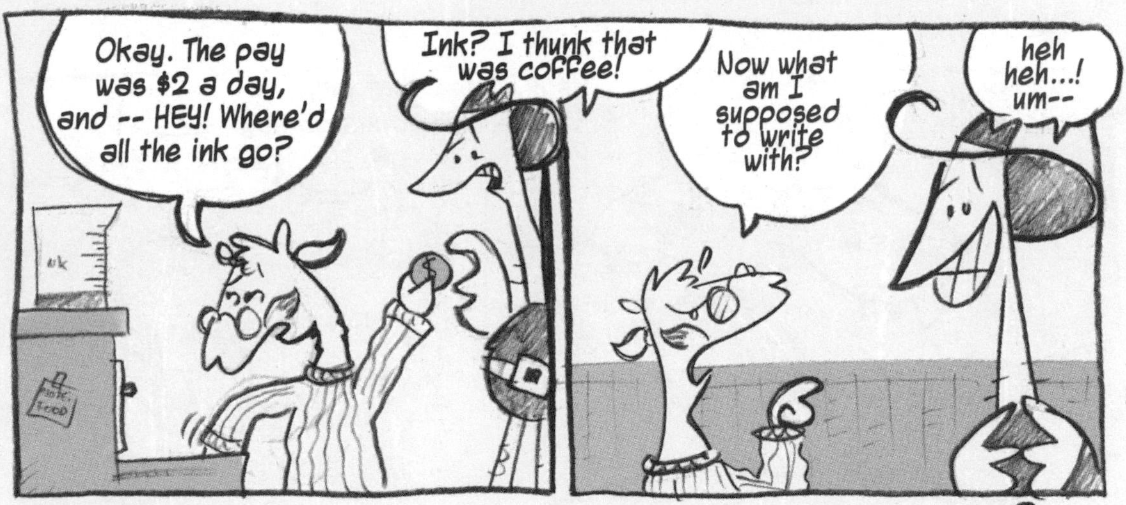
Okay. The pay was $2 a day, and -- HEY! Where'd all the ink go?
Ink? I thunk that was coffee!
Now what am I supposed to write with?
heh heh...! um--

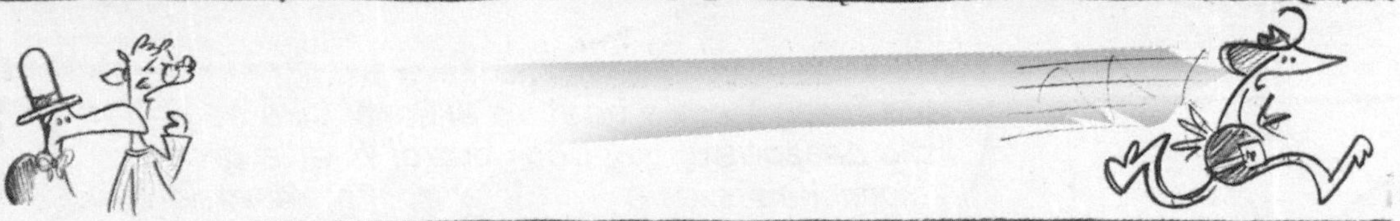

the longwinded, rambling and hilarious escapades of **TBYRD fearlessness & Hopalong Cassowary** part 2 lunch and moustaches

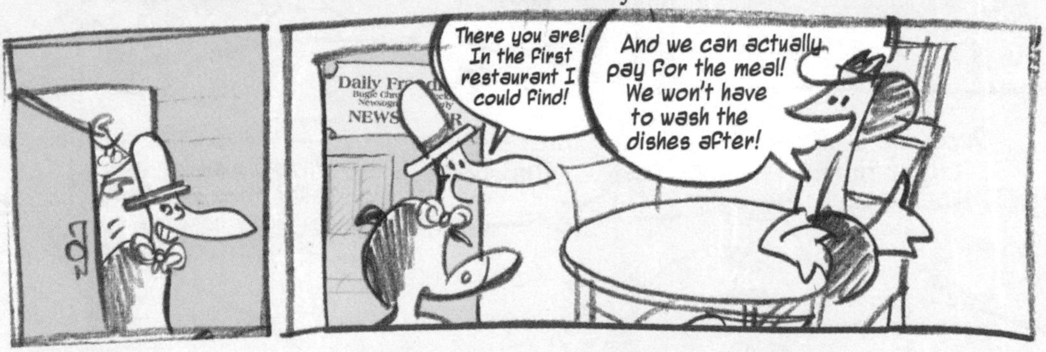
There you are! In the first restaurant I could find!
And we can actually pay for the meal! We won't have to wash the dishes after!

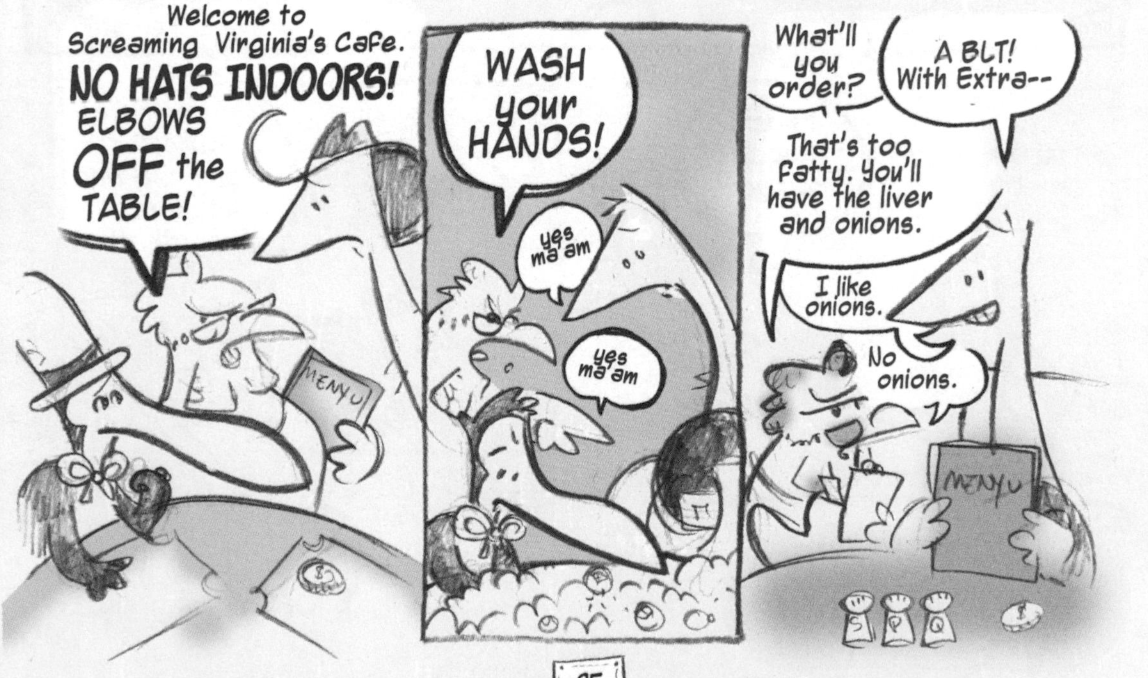
Welcome to Screaming Virginia's Cafe. NO HATS INDOORS! ELBOWS OFF the TABLE!
MENYU
WASH your HANDS!
yes ma'am
yes ma'am
What'll you order?
A BLT! With Extra--
That's too fatty. You'll have the liver and onions.
I like onions.
No onions.
MENYU

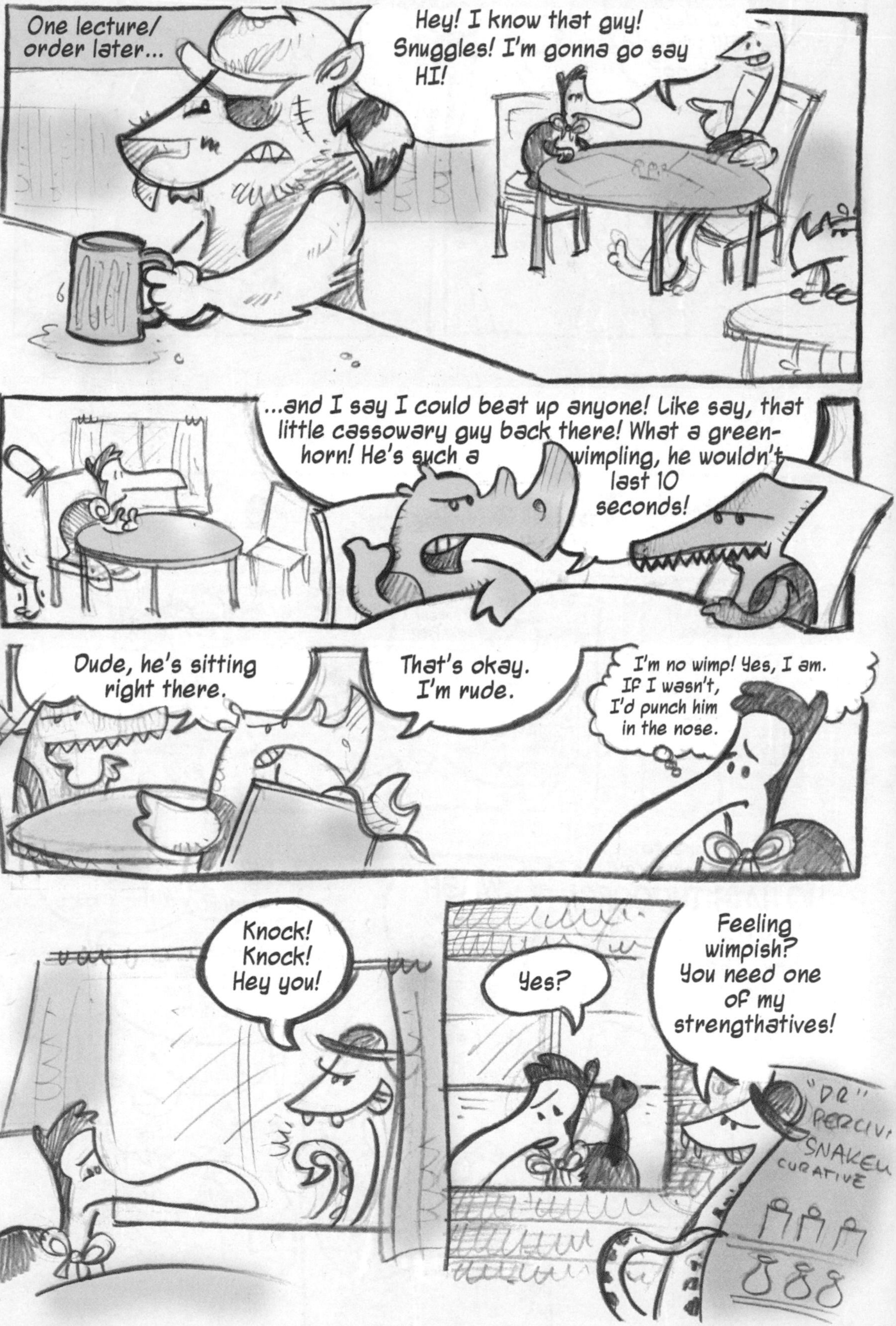
One lecture/ order later...
Hey! I know that guy! Snuggles! I'm gonna go say HI!
...and I say I could beat up anyone! Like say, that little cassowary guy back there! What a green-horn! He's such a wimpling, he wouldn't last 10 seconds!
Dude, he's sitting right there.
That's okay. I'm rude.
I'm no wimp! Yes, I am. If I wasn't, I'd punch him in the nose.
Knock! Knock! Hey you!
Yes?
Feeling wimpish? You need one of my strengthatives!
"DR"
CURATIVE

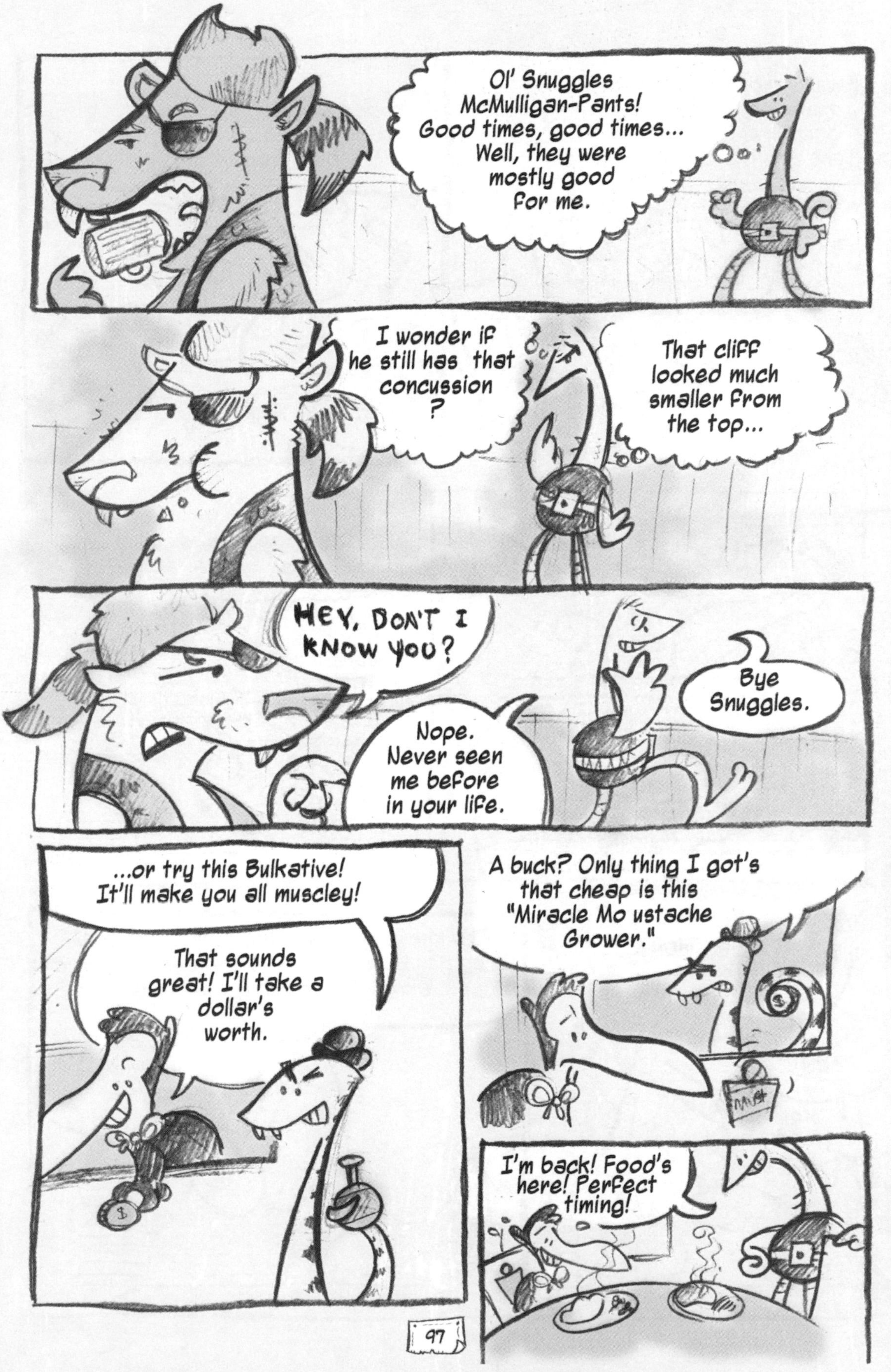
Ol' Snuggles McMulligan-Pants! Good times, good times... Well, they were mostly good for me.
I wonder if he still has that concussion ?
That cliff looked much smaller from the top...
HEY, DON'T I KNOW YOU?
Nope. Never seen me before in your life.
Bye Snuggles.
...or try this Bulkative! It'll make you all muscley!
That sounds great! I'll take a dollar's worth.
A buck? Only thing I got's that cheap is this "Miracle Mo ustache Grower."
I'm back! Food's here! Perfect timing!

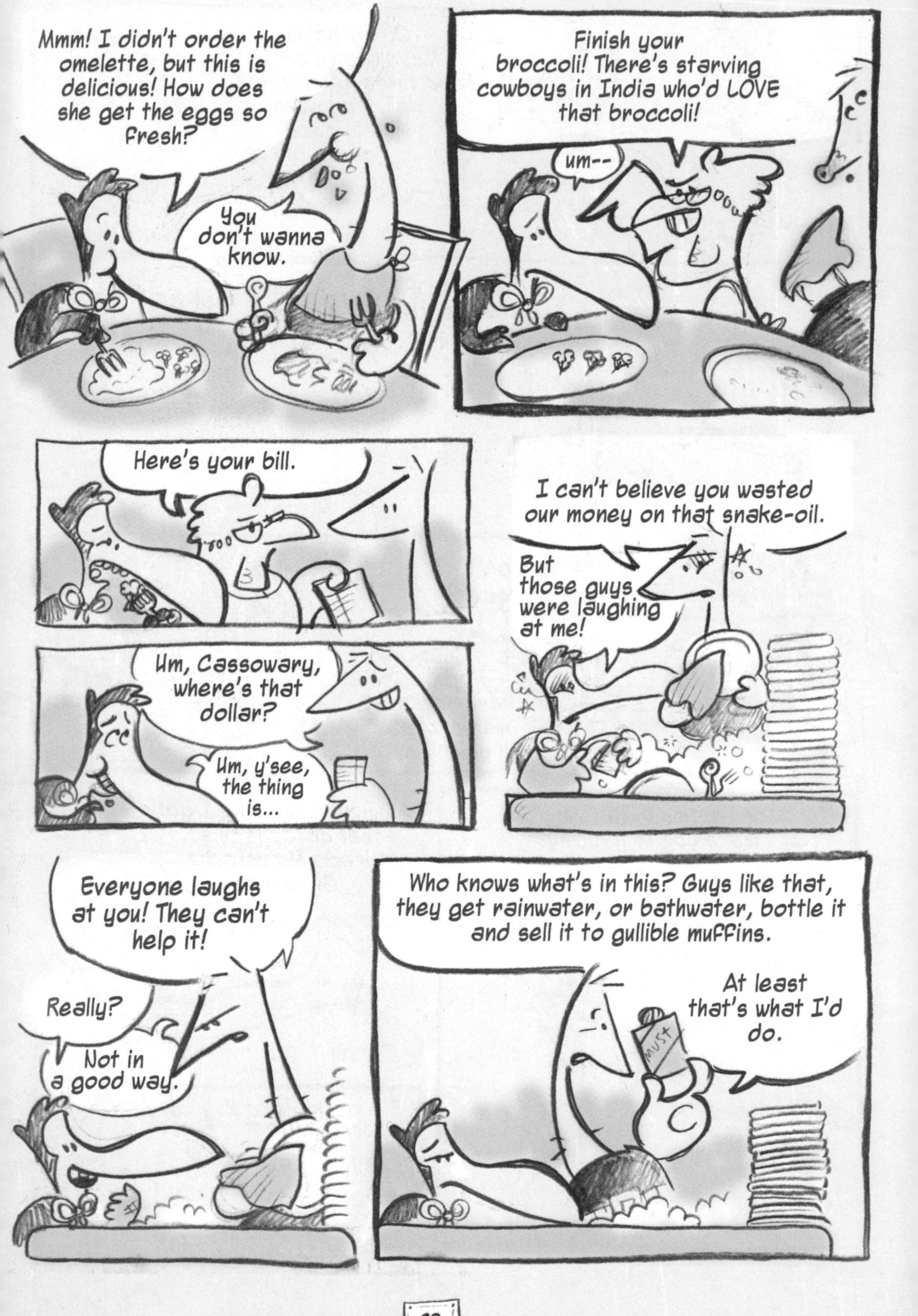
Mmm! I didn't order the omelette, but this is delicious! How does she get the eggs so fresh?
You don't wanna know.
Finish your broccoli! There's starving cowboys in India who'd LOVE that broccoli!
um--
Here's your bill.
I can't believe you wasted our money on that snake-oil.
But those guys were laughing at me!
Um, Cassowary, where's that dollar?
Um, y'see, the thing is...
Everyone laughs at you! They can't help it!
Really?
Not in a good way.
Who knows what's in this? Guys like that, they get rainwater, or bathwater, bottle it and sell it to gullible muffins.
At least that's what I'd do.
MUST

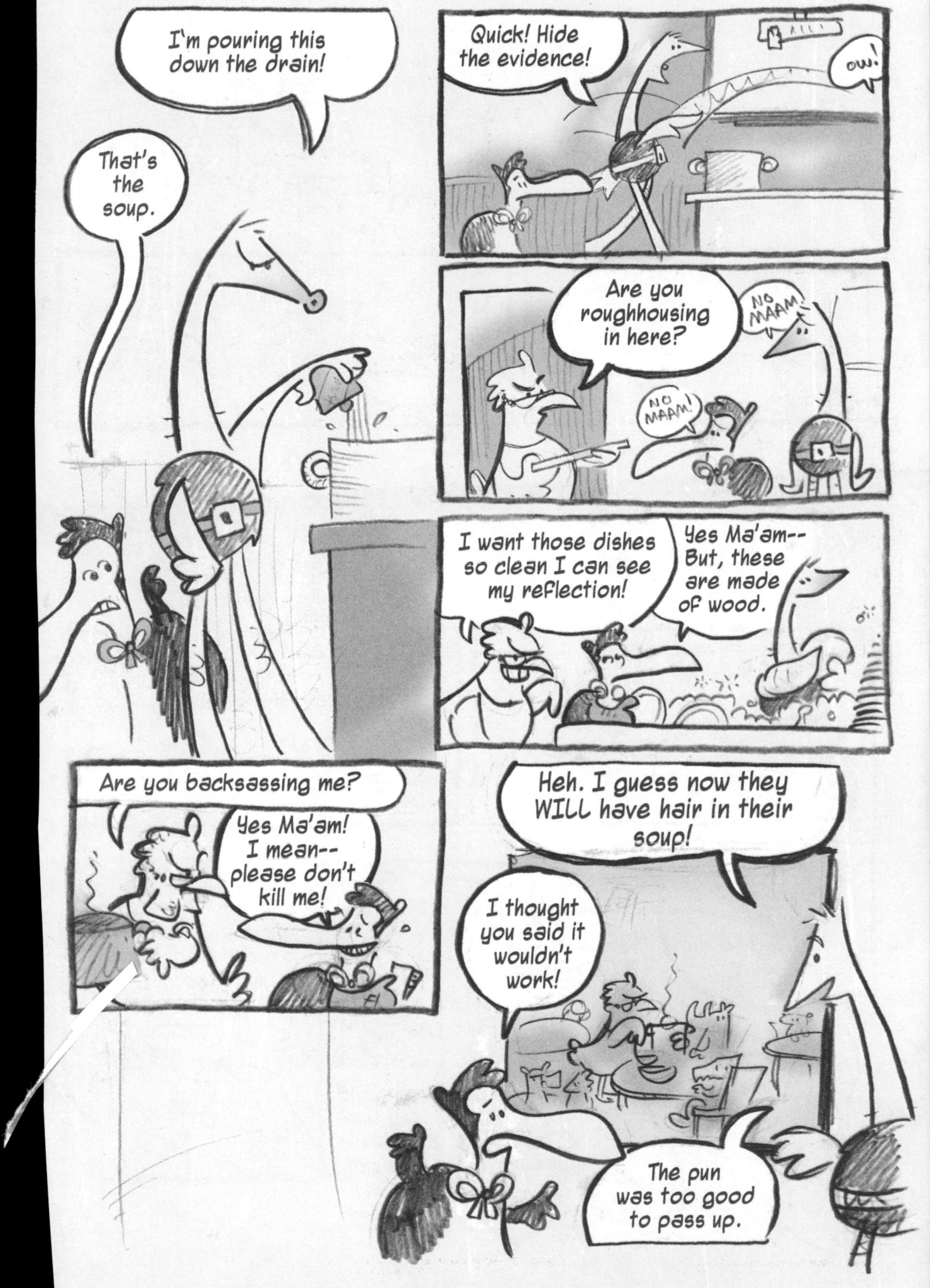
I'm pouring this down the drain!
That's the soup.
Quick! Hide the evidence!
ow!
Are you roughhousing in here?
NO MAAM!
NO MAAM!
I want those dishes so clean I can see my reflection!
Yes Ma'am-- But, these are made of wood.
Are you backsassing me?
Yes Ma'am! I mean-- please don't kill me!
Heh. I guess now they WILL have hair in their soup!
I thought you said it wouldn't work!
The pun was too good to pass up.

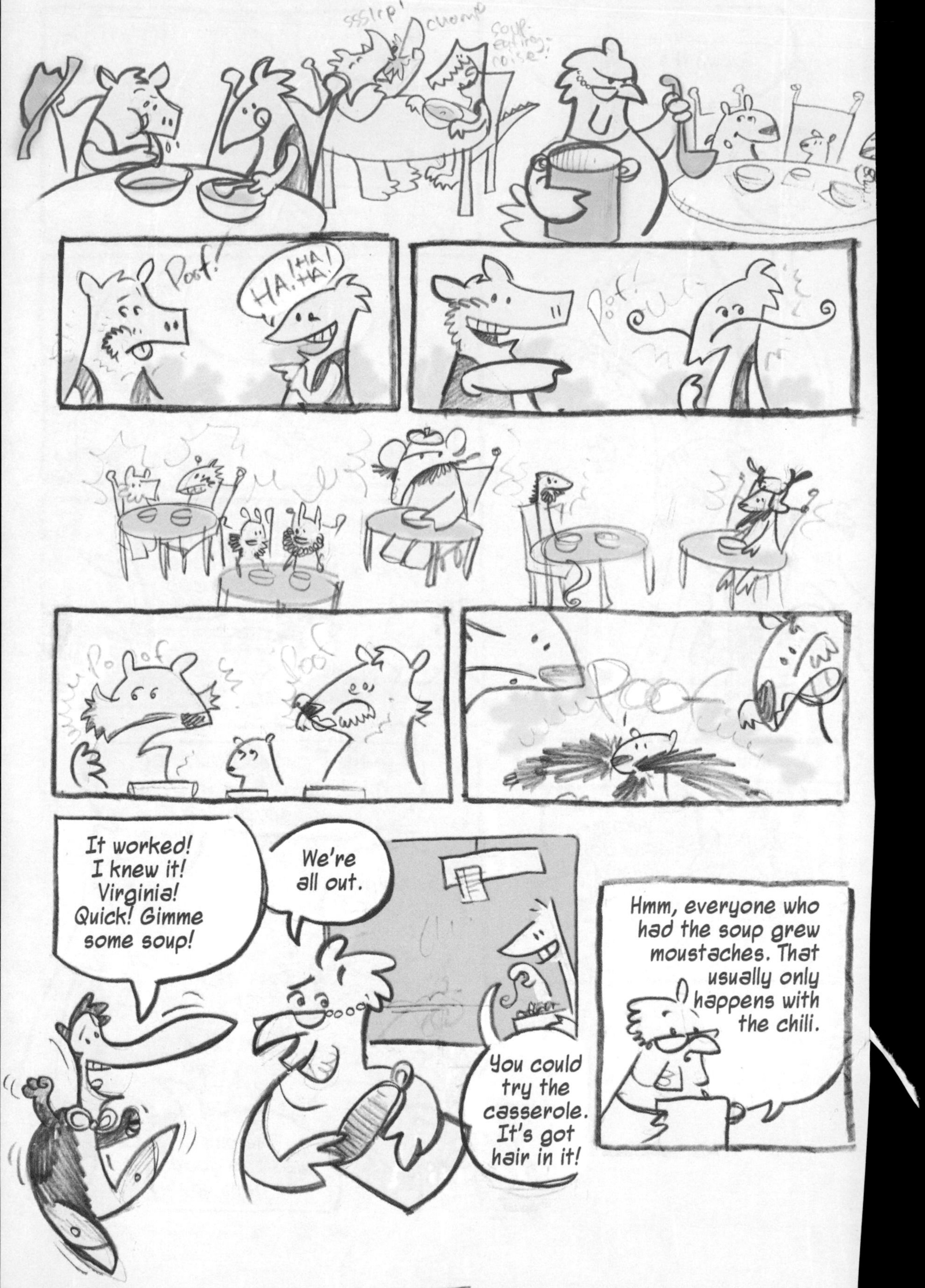

ssslrp!
chomp
Poof!
HA! HA! HA!
Poof!
Poof
Poof
POOF
It worked! I knew it! Virginia! Quick! Gimme some soup!
We're all out.
You could try the casserole. It's got hair in it!
Hmm, everyone who had the soup grew moustaches. That usually only happens with the chili.

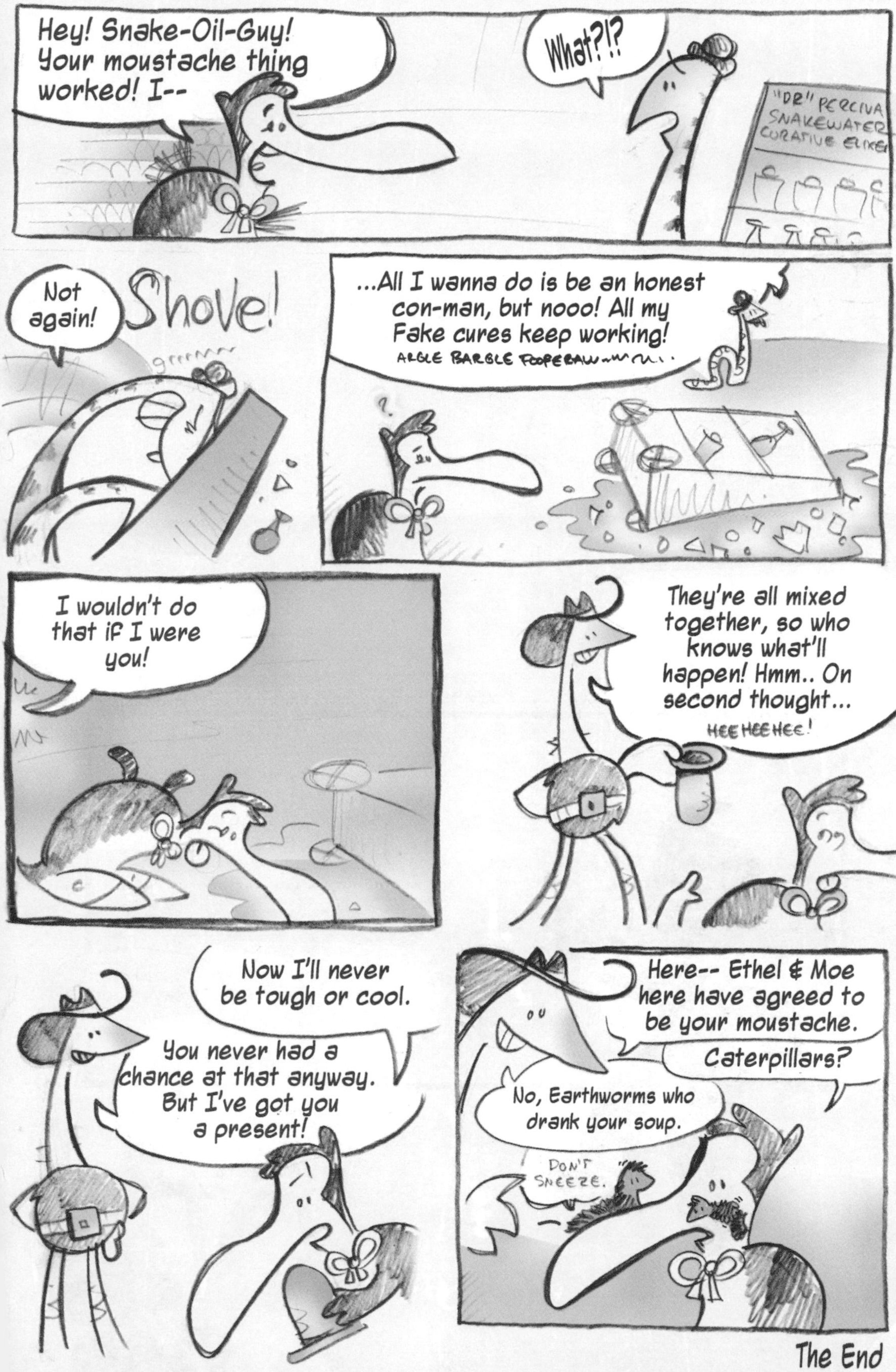
Hey! Snake-Oil-Guy! Your moustache thing worked! I--
What?!?
"DR" PERCIVA
SNAKEWATER
CURATIVE ELIXI
Not again!
Shove!
...All I wanna do is be an honest con-man, but nooo! All my Fake cures keep working!
ARGLE BARBLE FOOPERAW
I wouldn't do that if I were you!
They're all mixed together, so who knows what'll happen! Hmm.. On second thought...
HEE HEE HEE!
Now I'll never be tough or cool.
You never had a chance at that anyway. But I've got you a present!
Here-- Ethel & Moe here have agreed to be your moustache.
Caterpillars?
No, Earthworms who drank your soup.
DON'T SNEEZE.
The End

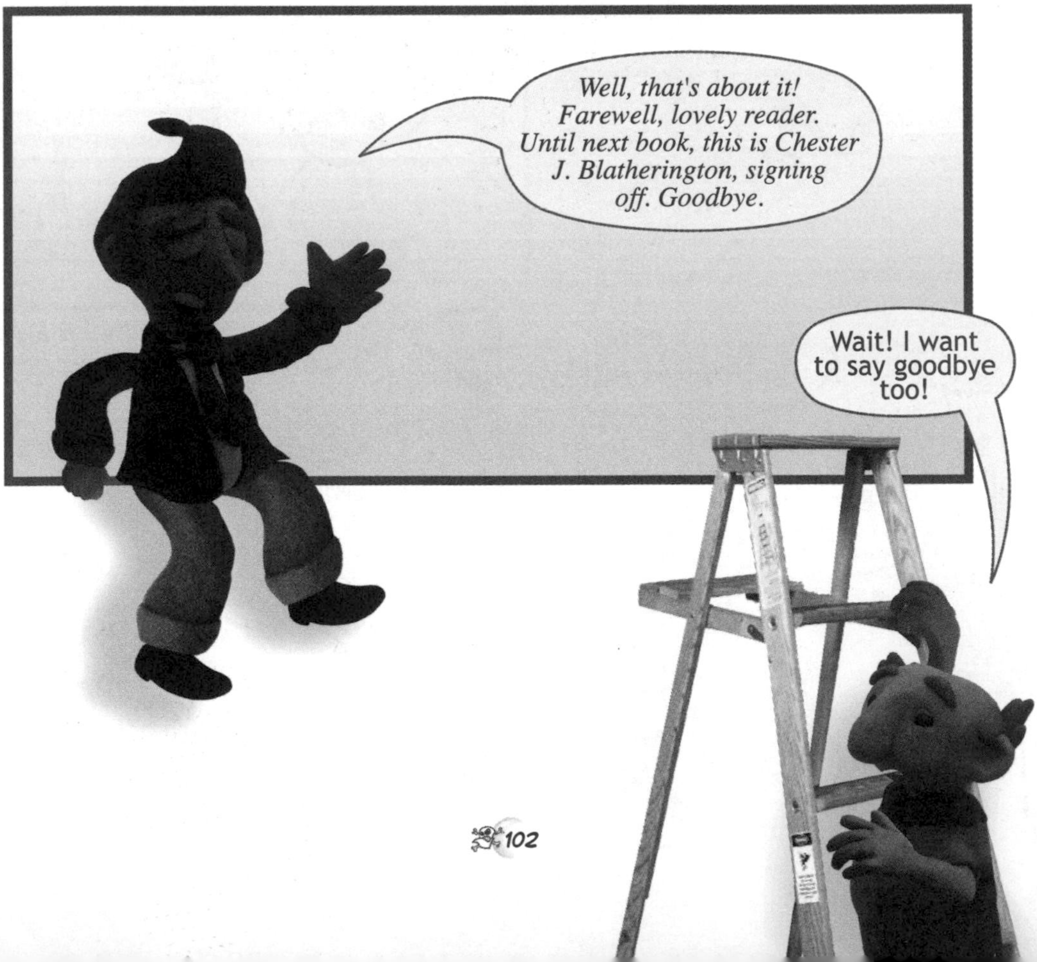
Well, that's about it! Farewell, lovely reader. Until next book, this is Chester J. Blatherington, signing off. Goodbye.
Wait! I want to say goodbye too!

DAILY FRANDIEGO BUGLE CHRONICLE WEEKLY NEWSOGRAM QUARTERLY

# CLASSIFIED ADVERTISEMENTS

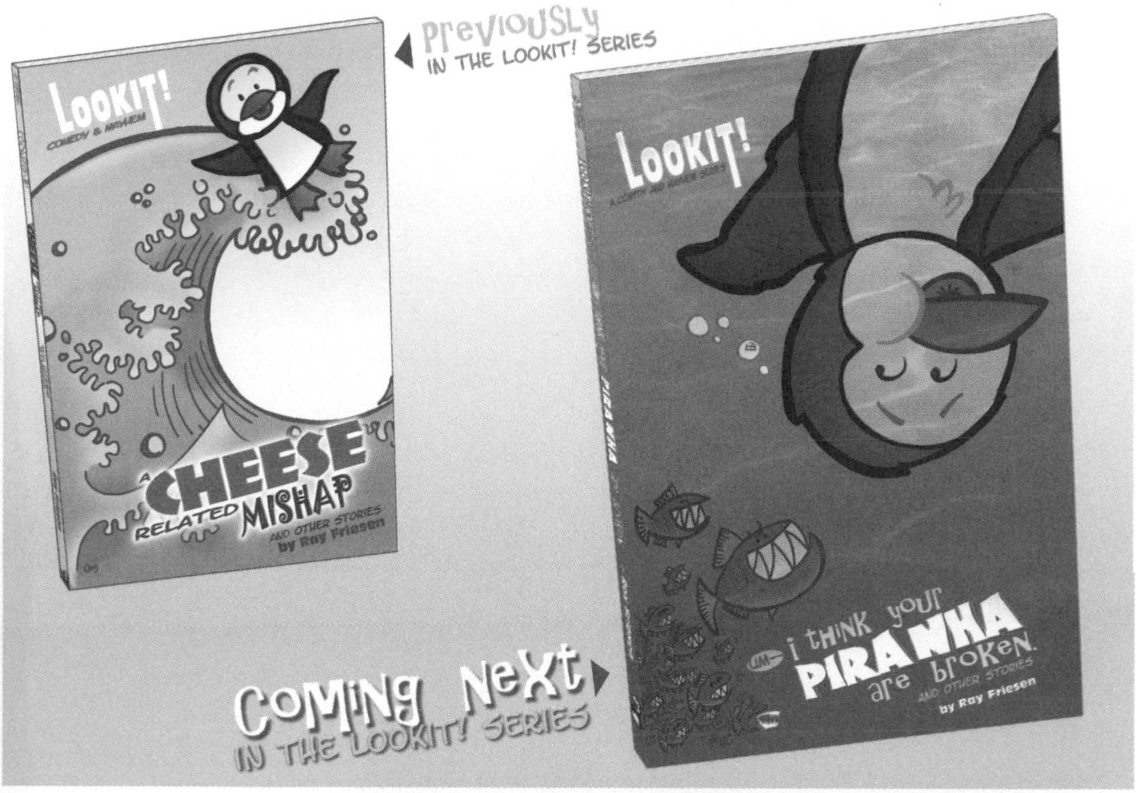

PREVIOUSLY
IN THE LOOKIT! SERIES
LOOKIT!
COMEDY & MAYHEM
A CHEESE RELATED MISHAP
AND OTHER STORIES
by Ray Friesen
LOOKIT!
I THINK YOUR PIRANHA ARE BROKEN.
AND OTHER STORIES
by Ray Friesen
COMING NEXT
IN THE LOOKIT! SERIES


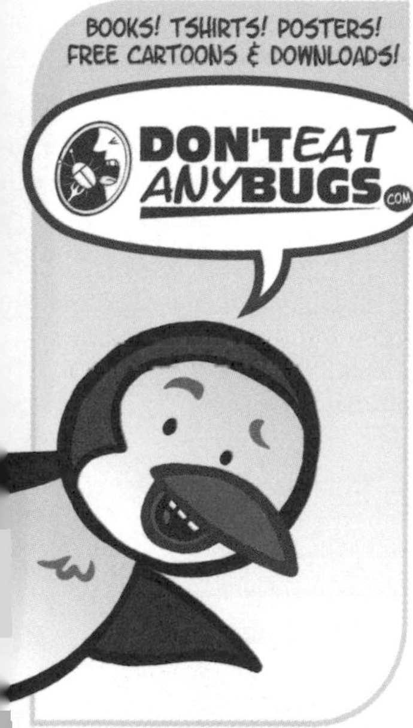

BOOKS! TSHIRTS! POSTERS!
FREE CARTOONS & DOWNLOADS!
DON'T EAT ANY BUGS .COM


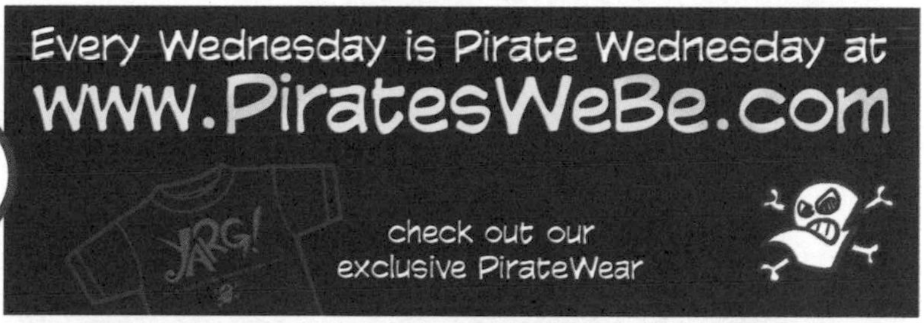

Every Wednesday is Pirate Wednesday at
www.PiratesWeBe.com
YARG!
check out our
exclusive PirateWear


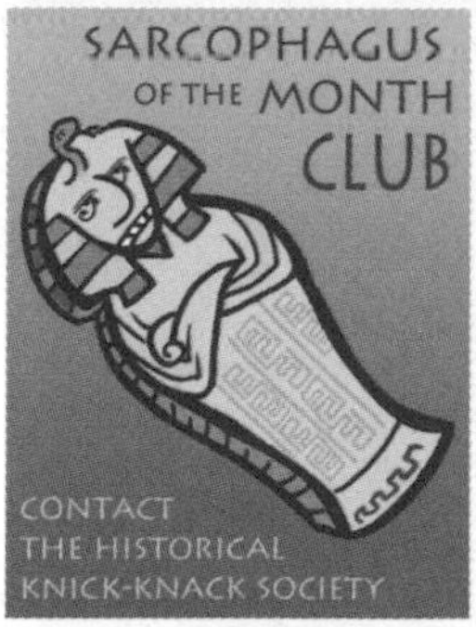

SARCOPHAGUS OF THE MONTH CLUB
CONTACT
THE HISTORICAL
KNICK-KNACK SOCIETY


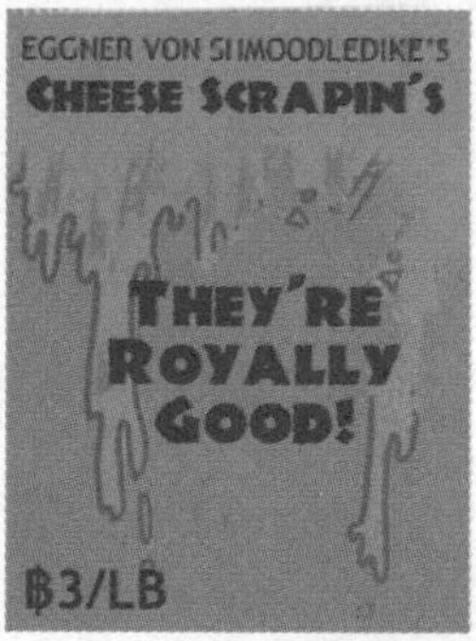

EGGNER VON SHMOODLEDIKE'S
CHEESE SCRAPIN'S
THEY'RE ROYALLY GOOD!
$3/LB


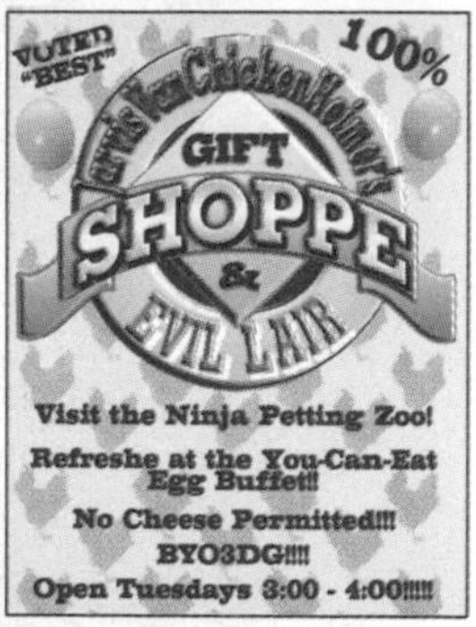

VOTED "BEST"
100%
GIFT SHOPPE & EVIL LAIR
Visit the Ninja Petting Zoo!
Refreshe at the You-Can-Eat Egg Buffet!!
No Cheese Permitted!!!
BYO3DG!!!!
Open Tuesdays 3:00 - 4:00!!!!


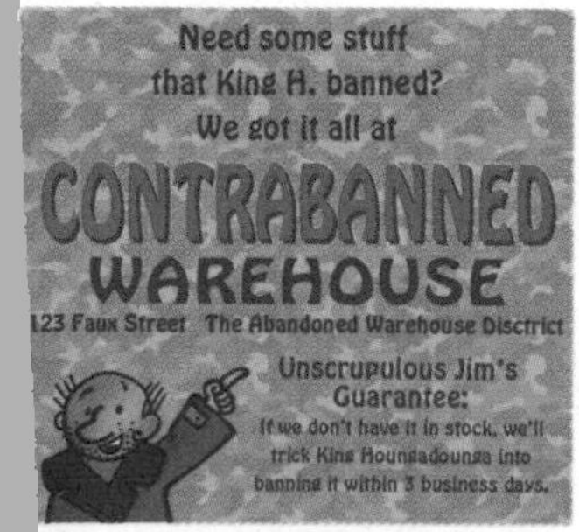

Need some stuff
that King H. banned?
We got it all at
CONTRABANNED WAREHOUSE
123 Faux Street The Abandoned Warehouse Discrict
Unscrupulous Jim's Guarantee:
If we don't have it in stock, we'll trick King Houngadounga into banning it within 3 business days.


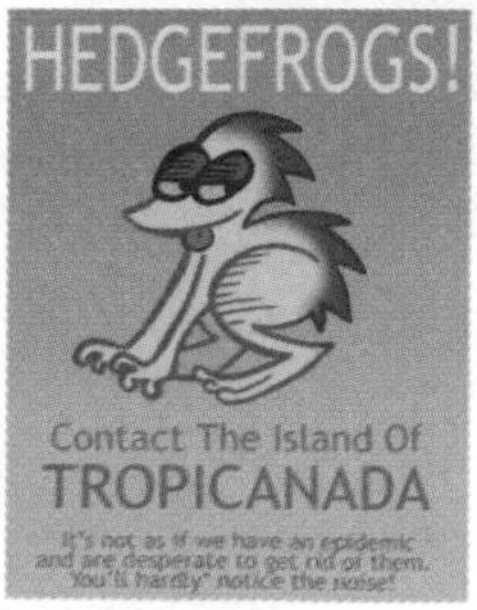

HEDGEFROGS!
Contact The Island Of
TROPICANADA
It's not as if we have an epidemic and are desperate to get rid of them. You'll hardly* notice the nose!


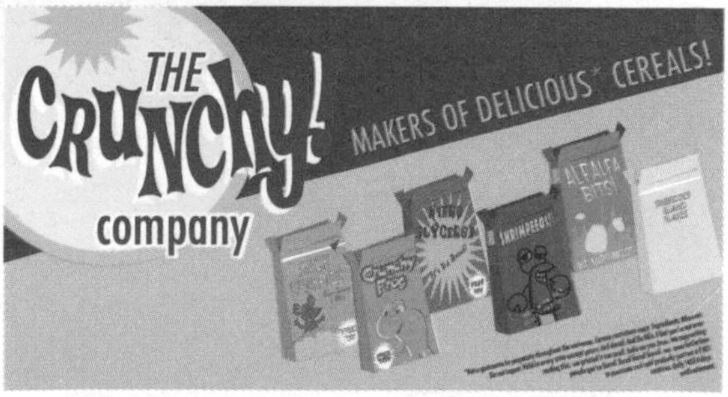

THE CRUNCHY! company
MAKERS OF DELICIOUS* CEREALS!
ALFALFA BITS


GET YOUR PELLMELLIAN PASSPORT AND TRAVEL GUIDE AT WWW.PELLMELLIA.COM

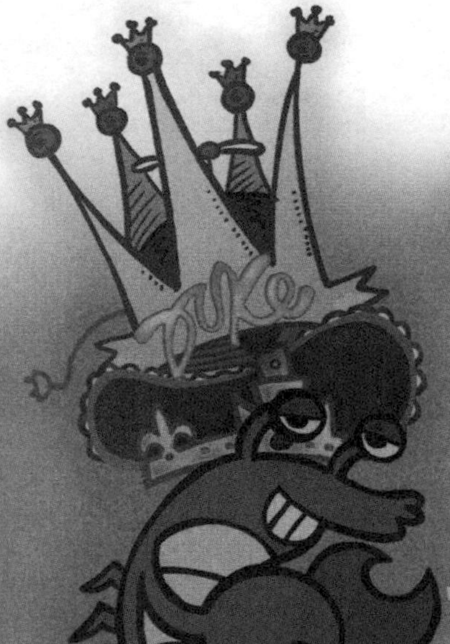
Duke

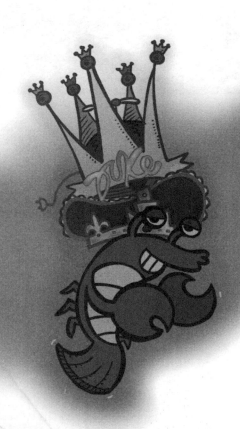